Trayvon Martin, Race, and American Justice

TEACHING RACE AND ETHNICITY

Volume 1

Trayvon Martin, Race, and American Justice

Writing Wrong

Foreword by Tyrone Howard

Edited by

Kenneth J. Fasching-Varner
Louisiana State University, Baton Rouge, USA

Rema E. Reynolds
University of Illinois at Urbana-Champaign, USA

Katrice A. Albert
University of Minnesota, Minneapolis, USA

and

Lori L. Martin
Louisiana State University, Baton Rouge, USA

SENSE PUBLISHERS
ROTTERDAM/BOSTON/TAIPEI

A C.I.P. record for this book is available from the Library of Congress.

ISBN: 978-94-6209-840-4 (paperback)
ISBN: 978-94-6209-841-1 (hardback)
ISBN: 978-94-6209-842-8 (e-book)

Published by: Sense Publishers,
P.O. Box 21858,
3001 AW Rotterdam,
The Netherlands
https://www.sensepublishers.com/

Printed on acid-free paper

ADVANCE PRAISE

Trayvon Martin, Race, and American Justice: Writing Wrong

The cold-blooded murder of Trayvon Martin cracked the world open once more, and this smart, comprehensive collection pursues every fissure and follows every fracture into the American heart of darkness. The presumption of innocence is encoded in law, but it's so much more: it's the generous assumption that we expect to find the best and not the worst in one another, and, indeed, in our students and in every proximate stranger. Black youth have an opposite experience, also encoded in law and practice and history and conjecture: they are alleged guilty until proven innocent. *Trayvon Martin, Race, and American Justice: Writing Wrong* strikes a perfect balance between rage and hope, and offers fresh perspectives on every page; its insights and lessons will be mined for years by teachers, parents, youth workers, and anyone concerned about the sorry state we're in regarding the future of young men of color, and the pathways we might pursue toward enlightenment and liberation. This text is an invitation to a rebellion—the inevitable insurgency of Black youth brewing right now across the land as the descendants of enslaved workers step up to exercise their agency, and at that moment become agents of liberty and actors in history.
– William Ayers, Retired Distinguished Professor University of Illinois – Chicago

The murder of Trayvon Martin and acquittal of George Zimmerman serves as a crucible for interrogating how race works in today's post-civil rights era. Working from diverse perspectives, the authors in *Trayvon Martin, Race, and American Justice: Writing Wrong* offer incisive and vivid examinations of the contours of white supremacy today, inviting readers into a much-needed discussion of moral questions surrounding the very foundation life in the U.S.
– Christine Sleeter, Professor Emerita, California State University Monterey

"*Trayvon Martin, Race, and American Justice: Writing Wrong* is a powerful assemblage of voices that speak to the salience of race, gender, and their intersection. Collectively, the authors provide us with poignant reminders of the multiple forces that rail against Black males in our society. Each chapter grabs our attention, ignites our activism, and encourages us to remain steadfast in the struggle toward a true democracy for all Americans – a society where Black males' lives are valued and they no longer face daily threats to their humanity."
– Yolanda Sealey-Ruiz, Assistant Professor, Teachers College, Columbia University

"While motivated by Trayvon Martin's unfortunate and tragic death, this impressive collection serves as a one-of-a-kind tribute to Martin and will help to keep his legacy alive. The contributions are evocative and accessible, and while the focus is on Martin, the contributions also call attention to mundane, severe, and systemic racial wrongdoings, biases in existing research, colorblindness and white privilege, and erasures of history and failures of memory."
– Tony E. Adams, Professor at Northeastern Illinois University and NCA book award winner

"The editors and contributors have taken a tragic topic and presented it in a way that is engaging, effective, and surprisingly optimistic. There is a style for everyone here, making it a great text for multiple audiences and classrooms. A truly superb addition to any classroom and a great read for those interested in social justice in today's world."
– U. Melissa Anyiwo, Professor and Coordinator of African American Studies, Curry College

"Trayvon Martin, Race, and American Justice: Writing Wrong is true to its title; it focuses attention—through critical writing—on the pernicious, pervasive, and persistent violence waged against black men, especially black male youth, in American society. Using the still-unpunished pre-meditated murder of Trayvon Martin as a highly emblematic example of this violence, the editors and authors use carefully crafted and sequenced poetry and prose to write truth to power about the economic, political, social, and cultural factors that produce and reproduce systemic aggression toward especially men and boys of African descent, but also toward members of other societally minoritized groups.

The breadth and depth of the contributions included in *Trayvon Martin, Race, and American Justice: Writing Wrong* makes it a particularly valuable resource for faculty and students engaged in teaching, learning, research, service, and activism related to issues of race, racism, blackness, whiteness, class, caste, classism, language, dialect, literacy, linguicism, geographic and national origin, immigration status, sex, gender, gender identity and expression, masculinity, sexual orientation, size, appearance, and, more broadly, equity, equality, and social justice.

Chapters reflect the thoughtful insight and advanced expertise of their authors, who bring increased levels of complexity to historical and contemporary dialogue, discussion, and debate about especially race and racism in the United States. The editors' selection of contributors and organization of contributions balances pain truth-telling with hope and possibility for a more just future. In sum, *Trayvon Martin, Race, and American Justice: Writing Wrong* reciprocally links theory and practice relating to issues of power, privilege, oppression, discrimination—and liberation."
– Christine Clark, Professor & Senior Scholar in Multicultural Education, and Founding Vice President for Diversity and Inclusion, University of Nevada, Las Vegas

"Chapters in this timely and probing book stare straight at a difficult incident, refuse to ignore injustice, but call on a higher purpose of great academic criticism in "writing the wrong." Here the wrong is the corrosive and sometimes lethal bias by many in power toward black males, who are too often seen as dangerous and disposable in American society. The killing of Trayvon Martin and the subsequent acquittal of his killer George Zimmerman are examined by minds informed by reflection on theory and history. We hear of conversations that black parents, particularly mothers who often felt on trial themselves, had with their teenage sons. Some of these endangered sons were outraged by the act and verdict, while some others were indifferent. Chapters are devoted to the incident, the trial and aftermath, and to the future of the struggle against racial injustice. Through what T. J. Yosso calls "resistant capital" we are urged to continue to interrogate a judicial system that prosecutes not only black males but their parents and families. There is much to learn here about the current state of social justice and the way we live with and among each other. In both prose and poetry these impassioned authors strive to write the wrong of Trayvon Martin and many others like him. I recommend this volume highly and will use it in my graduate classes."
– AG Rud, Distinguished Professor, College of Education, Washington State University

TABLE OF CONTENTS

Section 2 Deconstructing Ignorance: Reactions and Responses to Racism

**Section 3 How Much More Can We Take? The Fight for
Racial and Social Justice**

TYRONE HOWARD

FOREWORD

Next year marks the 60-year anniversary of the brutal murder of Emmett Till. The tragic nature of Till's death displayed before an entire nation and the world the horrors of racism to see how Black male bodies, and what they represent, were deemed as threats to a particular social order. In many ways, it forced the United States to confront its racist realities, and it posed many age-old questions about the value of Black life. Though many would be reluctant to admit it, Black bodies and lives have always been fundamental to the United States' moral, political, social, and economic fabric. While the nation has often been conflicted about how to deal with its citizens of African descent, especially its males, one cannot deny the invaluable role they have played in the development and maintenance of the world's most powerful nation. The United States' paradoxical relationship with males of a darker hue has been painful, confusing, dehumanizing, and at times celebratory. But what has been persistent for the better part of four centuries is that Black maleness in all of its totality has often been viewed as a menace. The lynching of hundreds of thousands of Black males during the 17th, 18th, and 19th centuries, the use of Black males as chattel slavery to build the economic foundation of the nation, Reconstruction and Jim Crow laws have had devastating social, political, and economic effects on Black communities and families. America has not always been kind to its Black male citizens.

The impressive collection of scholars in this volume poignantly remind us that race, class, and gender have always been part of the United States' DNA, and that they remain as pertinent today as ever. In a nation that promotes ideals such as egalitarianism, justice, equality and freedom, these scholars remind us that injustice, prejudice, colorblindness, white privilege, and fear are also core ideals of the United States, and they must be identified, analyzed and eradicated. As the quest for justice has unfolded, marginalized populations have made countless efforts to have their humanity affirmed in order to dismantle stereotypes that exclude and hate. This brings us to the tragedy that is the death of Martin. The tragic death of Martin, much like the death of Emmett Till over half a century earlier, raised the ugly, painful, yet always looming reality, of how race, class, and gender continue to matter in our society. At the turn of the 20th century, DuBois suggested that the problem of the 20th century would be the color line. On hundred years post DuBois' call, many thought that, the nation would have figured out its color line problem, and would be prepared to move to its first post-racial epoch. Needless to say, the Martin tragedy reminds us that we are not there. It should be noted that progress among race relations has occurred; yet our inability to look past race remains elusive. Much of what we deal with today is a more sophisticated and nuanced form of racism. No longer are we dealing with barking dogs, water hoses, the looming presence of Jim Crow, and legally segregated schools and lunch counters. Today's reality is influenced by racial profiling, police brutality, educational exclusion, and structural inequalities that create massive economic and social disparities amongst citizens, and when individuals are unable to move up the socioeconomic ladder, we blame them for their failure to 'succeed' in a meritocratic society. Moreover, this current era of racial realities remains steeped in an ideology that equates Blackness with being criminal. Much of what happened to Martin was set in motion centuries ago; the idea that Blackness has always been synonymous with crime, and that a 17 year-old Black male wearing a hoodie must be guilty of some type of criminal activity has become normalized. Racial profiling, fear of Blackness (and Brownness), and a historical legacy of race and crime created the context for Martin's death. The writers of this book address this issue head on from a multitude of angles.

In 1884, Nathaniel Southgate Shaler, a noted Harvard scientist and renowned writer on race relations of that time, stated that the United States had a major problem where race and crime were concerned, namely with Black people. About Blacks, Shaler (1884) stated, "There can be no sort of doubt that, judged by the light of all experiences, these people are a danger to America greater and more insuperable than any of those that menace the other great civilized states of the world." (p. 696) In short, thinkers and writers of the time helped to create a narrative that being Black posed a problem, and that being Black posed a threat to the sanctity and purity that was/is America. In short, messages such as Shaler's helped to create an atmosphere of fear, ignorance, and hate that remains with us today, and many would say these three ingredients contributed to Martin's untimely death.

To further emphasize the race, crime, and fear nexus consider fifteen years ago when Enis Cosby was tragically murdered on a Los Angeles highway. Cosby's mother Emille Cosby boldly stated, "America taught my son's killer to hate Blacks" (Cosby, 1998, p. 2). Elaborating on the persistent presence of racism and how it has had a long lasting influence on the health, safety, and well-being of Blacks, Cosby cited from Baldwin's (1985) "Price of the Ticket": "The will of the people, or the State, is revealed by the State's institutions. There was not, then, nor is there, now, a single American institution which is not a racist institution."(p. xvii) Martin's death resurrects the ugly reminder of how race and racism remain ever present in the United States. The scholars in this work take the task of trying to peel back the complex layers that explain the intersection of race, class, and gender in the United States. This is not a new topic, but it is one that continues to take on new shapes and forms in complicated ways.

Like Sean Bell, Jordan Davis, Amadou Diallo, Patrick Dorismond, Oscar Grant, Tim Stansbury, Ousmane Zongo, and Ramarley Graham before him, Martin should be alive today. The tragedy is that these young men are no longer with us because they represent an identity, created, and sustained within the context of U.S. life, law, and culture, that Black masculinity in all of its manifestations is to be feared, loathed, despised. Furthermore, when there is a perceived threat it is to be eliminated, while also being protected under the law. As David Stovall tells us in this text, Black youth are often deemed as disposable, and that is a reality and a narrative that must change. Nina Simone inspired us to embrace the beauty of what it means to be young, gifted, and Black. Today we must come to grips with the sobering reality of what it means to be young, male, and Black.

As we seek to identify answers as to why Black males continue to be viewed in many circles as public enemy #1, the group of scholars assembled in this work helps us to unpack the theoretical underpinnings that explain the inexplicable. They write in a bold yet unapologetic manner about the pervasiveness of whiteness, the viciousness of racism, racialized constructions of safety and space, distorted notions of justice, and the process of 'writing the wrongs.' In this book we are urged to craft a new narrative that reframes what it means to be Black and male. The authors remind us that it is time to craft a new narrative, which problematizes whiteness, and demonstrates how it manifests itself in harmful and destructive ways in the 21st century. This important volume challenges us to craft a new narrative that unpacks implicit bias, colorblind racism, and reveals the ways that it is embodied by fair, open minded citizens of this country, many of whom assume critical tasks such as educating children, authoring legislation, and enforcing the law. The writers ask us to replace the narrative of young Black males as violent predators and replace it with one that humanizes them and keeps them safe and alive. They also remind us that education scholars and practitioners play important roles in crafting this new narrative. And finally, to their credit, the editors implore us to craft a new narrative that reminds us that harsh racial realities remain enmeshed in our nation's psyche. The scholars in this work challenge us to think deeper, more critically and historically, and remind us of how far we have to go to embrace all of our citizens.

REFERENCES

Baldwin, J. (1985). *The price of the ticket: Collected nonfiction. 1948-1985*. New York, NY: Macmillan.
Cosby, C. (1998, July 7). America taught my son's killer to hate Blacks. *USA Today*, 1–4.
Shaler, N. S. (1884). The Negro problem. *Atlantic Monthly, 54*, 696–709.

ACKNOWLEDGMENTS

We would like to extend a special thank you to Melvin 'Jai' Jackson and Martha Murray for the abundance of time and skill they contributed to the book. We would also like to acknowledge and thank Benterah Morton, Berlisha Morton, Marcie Fraizer, Reagan Mitchell, Roland Mitchell, Marco Montalbetti, Valentina Fahrenrkrog, Victor Toledo, Aylin Schroeder, and B.W., for their support and assistance with during the production of this book. We are grateful to Sense Publishers as well as Peter de Liefde and Patricia Leavy, specifically, for their unwavering commitments to this book and working to support social justice for all.

The killing of Trayvon Martin profoundly changed a nation, and also ignited a spirit of activism and race consciousness among a generation far removed from the marches and sit-ins of half a century ago. The sanitization of the historic struggle for the restoration of civil rights and human dignity to all Americans was ironically given new life as news spread that Trayvon's life was tragically taken away. We honour and acknowledge the Trayvon Martins of the world, both named and unknown. We hope this volume serves as a catalyst for re-imaging and creating a society where all life is valued. May we have the courage of Sybrina Fulton and Tracy Martin to never remain silent in the face of injustice.

ANTHONY HILL

A PRAYER FOR AFRICAN BOYS

For Successful Transition to Manhood

God help us,
to be strong Black men.
Role models with our actions as well as our words.
Help us to protect, respect our women, family,
elders, community, and each other.
God, give us a vision.
If we cannot do any good, let us do no harm.
Let your will be done in us.
Help us to submit to your will.
We know that you have a special plan for our lives.
Help us to realize that it is better to build up than to tear down.
Help us to refrain from criticizing, putting down, or destroying
the character or reputation of others.
And to always remember to encourage, uplift, and support
each other in all positive endeavors.
Help us to make this world a better place than we found it.
Bless us Lord!!!
AMEN

THE 7 DEADLY AMERICAN SINS

Of the 7 deadly American sins
Being Black has become numbers 1-6

If this statement strikes you as radical, you haven't been paying attention
So let's be clear
George Zimmerman was never on trial
He murdered a child while we were more concerned with whether a boy had smoke
in his lungs, than the fact that he would never again use them to raise his chest
beneath the cloaked hoodie the Grim Reaper lends Black boys

All over the nation people claimed this wasn't a race issue
That the outcome was legally "on-par"
Accusing the left-leaning liberal Blackjack dealers of playing the race card

They asked

"What would've happened if Zimmerman were Black? Would things be different?"

Of course if Zimmerman were Black, this would have ended with a prison sentence
Ask Marissa Alexander about specifics I'm missing
Because she's sentenced to more time in prison than Trayvon spent on this planet

We live in a world where someone can be set free
After admitting to the slaying of an unarmed teen
And CBS News has the audacity to headline a piece by Zimmerman's brother
stating George would spend the rest of this life looking over his shoulder because,

"There are people that would want to take the law into their own hands"

It's funny how some things are Black and white while others taste like the rainbow
Red like the blood staining the sidewalk when he fell
After being profiled for walking too slowly
Yellow for the son of Tracy and Sybrina that shone by day
But by night had stopped glowing

Green for grass-stained pants that hung low and heightened sensitivities without knowing
Brown for an identity Zimmerman played up for the all-white
Sorry
There was one Latino so that's what we'd call a diverse jury
white for the privilege Zimmerman wore
When he was out doing his neighborhood patrolling

And Black
Black is just another name for the numbers 1-6 of America's 7 deadly sins

The 7th was believing we would find justice in the hands of a system that pioneered
Native American oppression
The enslavement of African people
Carried out forced deportations even though we know who's really illegal

But despite these conflicting things, when the verdict came in
All I heard were the words of Dr. King
Calling for us to not allow the deafening noise of injustice
To drown out the sounds of freedom's ring
So in honor of his legacy I ask you this one thing

Please join me in this final call to let freedom ring

Let freedom ring from the graves of Emmett Till, Fred Hampton, Amadou Diallo, Sean Bell, Oscar Grant, Trayvon Martin, Jordan Davis and all the brothers whose names we'll never know because even in 2013 a Black man being killed *STILL* isn't enough to make it onto the evening news

LET FREEDOM RING

Free at last
Free at last

Dear God Almighty

This isn't the freedom for which we've asked

KENNETH J. FASCHING-VARNER, LORI L. MARTIN,
KATRICE A. ALBERT & REMA E. REYNOLDS

1. INTRODUCTION

Writing Wrongs in Post-Racial American Justice

On the night of February 26, 2012, Trayvon Martin, a then seventeen-year old Black teenage male was shot to death in Sanford, Florida. We came to learn that Martin, unarmed and carrying only a bag of Skittles and an iced tea, was shot dead by George Zimmerman, a then 28-year-old, white Latino male of Peruvian heritage who served as a neighborhood watch volunteer. Martin's murder brought to the surface questions about the role of race in the United States in the allegedly post-racial 21st century. The case also presented a number of complexities about controversial stand-your-ground laws. Taken together, issues of race as applied in stand-your-ground cases generally, and in the case against Zimmerman in Martin's death specifically, created a firestorm of perspectives that at their core reveal the social problematics of race (Fasching-Varner, 2009) that trace back centuries. The months, and in fact the better part of two years, following Martin's death brought highly contested conversations, speculations, news articles, media reports, and ultimately a trial where many of the facts involved in this case were disputed. What is not in dispute was that on that rainy evening one person-emboldened by what McIntosh (1989) described as a knapsack of unearned privileges along with a loaded weapon, shot and killed an unarmed teenager (Gabbidon & Jordan, 2013).

Leading up to and throughout the course of the trial, many took to social media outlets to express their perspectives on the case. Within academic circles, particularly for academics working in the areas of social justice and race, there was a hope through all of the deliberations that justice would be served to hold Martin's killer accountable. Many of us thought that a jury would see through the rhetoric and antics. Martin, unarmed, was walking in a community where he had the right to be; he was followed, stalked, and hunted; the police instructed Zimmerman to back down and not pursue Martin; despite these circumstances Zimmerman engaged Martin in a physical confrontation, that by many accounts, and the context of his pursuit, would suggest that he, not Martin, provoked the incident. By the end of the physical altercation, Zimmerman pulled out a pistol and shot Martin dead. We thought 'the jury would have to convict Zimmerman, particularly in the allegedly colorblind post-racial society, no?' The trial itself proved to be a comedy of errors; the jury convicted Zimmerman of no crime, and appeared in post-verdict interviews

K.J. Fasching-Varner et al. (Eds.), Trayvon Martin, Race, and American Justice, 1–4.

to indict Martin for his own death, revealing the racial politics associated in our 'post-racial' moment.

Following the verdict, our internet-enabled devices figuratively blew up. Social media, text messages, and calls continuously expressed outrage over the verdict. While the jury may not have been informed with the requisite academic knowledge about how race operates within the United States, academics did possess that knowledge and took to the internet to communicate the disparity in convictions for stand-your-ground laws as applied along lines of race. In response to the verdict many academics and non-academics loudly expressed on social media that this was a case of racial profiling.

Many Americans are tired of and frustrated with the myriad of news stories about young children dying from gun violence, particularly young Black males. Given the history of race relations in the United States, where being Black has never carried the same advantages as being white, racialized homicides are especially troubling. The economic, political, and psychological costs of past cases have left the nation with a debt it certainly cannot afford to pay. Examples of racial injustice in the United States are numerous. In the early 1930s, the nine Scottsboro defendants were wrongly convicted of raping two white women. Over a decade of potential opportunities and experiences were lost while the Scottsboro nine sat incarcerated in one of the nation's most notorious penal institutions, Kilby Prison. Scores of cold cases from the 1950s and 1960s involving the homicides of Black men remain under investigation by the United States Department of Justice. In far too many instances of unsolved cases, local law enforcement officials were involved with the killings, and Black landowners and civil rights activists were permanently silenced because of fear of persecution.

During the period between 1960 and 1980, riots often stemming from unequal treatment received by Black people in the criminal justice system erupted as a result of intergroup conflicts, costing millions of dollars to local, state, and federal budgets. The riots that followed the 1986 beating death of Michael Griffith in Howard Beach, Queens, New York, is one example. Griffith, a Black male, was chased out of the predominately white middle-class community and struck by a car as he fled. Another example is the costly trial and false conviction of the Central Park Five, all young Black and Hispanic males. In its haste to convict someone for the brutal attack on a white female jogger, the City of New York allowed the Central Park Five to spend between six and thirteen years in prison for a crime they did not commit – five more lost lives. The 1990s were witness to the Crown Heights Riots in Brooklyn, New York, the brutal assault on Haitian immigrant Abner Louima, and the killing of unarmed African immigrant Amado Diallo. Both Louima and Diallo were harmed at the hands of members of the New York Police Department (NYPD).

There has been much of the same maltreatment of people of color in the justice system in the new millennium. The acquittal of NYPD officers involved in the shooting death of Sean Bell in 2006, on the eve of his wedding day, compelled many to take to the streets and demand justice for all. Similarly the conviction of involuntary manslaughter, not murder, along with the reduced two year sentence of the police shooting of Oscar Grant III, a man killed by Bay Area Regional Transit Officers on January 1, 2009, drew significant outrage, and also reminded us that it is dangerous to be Black and male in the United States in the 21st century. Zimmerman's killing of Martin drew a similar type of outrage, perhaps even more outrage than the previously mentioned cases. Prior to Martin's death, many Americans were lulled into a false sense of security that racial injustice was in our distant past.

American racial and social justice is now at a proverbial fork in the road. The nation can continue on the *wrong* racial path where private actions and public policies continue to show that the scales of justice are not balanced, and that justice is not blind. Alternatively, America can choose the *right* path and create a more equitable society where the long arm of the law reaches individuals not because of their race, gender, class position, or geographical location, but because of a universal commitment to protect and to serve *everyone*. To create a more equitable society we must first take a serious account of race, which involves recognition of the multilevel and multidimensional nature of race in our lives, not excluding our institutions.

It is with this context that this volume is born. The editors in this text represent four different institutional contexts and positions. We differ across race (three Black and one white), institutional contexts (two southern and two Midwest), positions (two assistant professors, one associate professor, and one vice president), and disciplines (education, educational leadership, sociology, and counseling respectively), but all share a common commitment to racial equity and social justice. In the wake of the verdict in the Zimmerman case we each had strong reactions and responses, as did our friends and colleagues. From those reactions and responses we initiated a conversation with Series Editor, Patricia Leavy, about the necessity of an academic volume that could explore, in earnest, not only the particulars of Martin's death at Zimmerman's hand, but larger issues of race and inequity that the murder and the subsequent trial and acquittal reveal.

With the support of Leavy and Sense Publishers we conceptualized the space of this volume as a mechanism to 'write' the 'wrong' of Martin's murder. That is, the concept of this volume was to provide, through writing, both thinking and feeling spaces to explore the various inequities and racial problematics the incident and its subsequent case reveal. This edited volume brings together a cross-section of scholars to react, respond, and analyze the state of race in light of this tragic case. Through their writing, the authors help us all to better understand how to address racial wrongs that this case, and those of many other racialized experiences, reveals.

Since the election of President Obama, many believe that we have achieved a 'post-racial' moment. We argue that if post-racial was our reality, the verdict would have looked different. Removing race from Zimmerman and Martin, if such a thing were possible, one is left with the following objective facts:

a) Zimmerman stalked and pursued Martin.
b) Zimmerman did this despite police warning not to pursue.

c) Zimmerman communicated, still alive, communicated a sole account of the incident to Martin to police, providing no corroborating evidence.
d) Zimmerman provoked, if not initiated, a physical altercation with Martin.
e) Zimmerman shot and killed Martin.
f) Martin was unarmed.
g) Martin was pursued and followed by a larger stranger.
h) Martin was on the telephone with a friend when approached by Zimmerman.
i) Martin, dead, was never able to provide an account of the events that lead to his death.

Post-racial analysis with these sets of facts would suggest that only a verdict of guilty could be reached; we know, however, that the verdict in this case revealed a different logic. This volume clarifies that not only are we not post-racial, but that race and racism are in many ways as prevalent in the 21st century as in many other times in our history.

Our contributors write about the racial wrongs and the lived experiences of people of color in the period following the tragic killing of young Martin. The is divided into five sections section focuses on a different aspect The first section brings together chapters which explore a different emphasis to provide a full range of ideas not just about the murder, but also about what this incident and case help us understand about the state of race in the United States. This volume is unique in that it is not simply a collection of academic chapters, but the work also includes unique and creative writing as well. Each section has contributions from creative writers who also write back to the racist society in which we live. The youths' contributions to this volume are not only unique, but poignant as these young men and women ask pressing and difficult questions of their society, ultimately providing us all with a more nuanced understanding of race.

Our hope is that this volume provides readers with the same sense of empowerment and liberation it provided us as editors and contributors. This historic volume provided each of us with an opportunity to reflect upon a national tragedy and allowed us to reveal that truths in the 'post-racial' are too often left unsaid. The writing has also allowed us to consider the institutional policies and personal practices that perpetuate the myth of group superiority and inferiority based upon race. It is our hope that our efforts to write these wrongs will lead to personal and institutional transformations that turn our upside-down country, where the killing of its children goes unpunished, right side up.

REFERENCES

Fasching-Varner, K. J. (2009). No! The team ain't alright! The institutional and individual problematics of race. *Social Identities, 15*(6), 811–829.
Gabbidon, S. L., & Jordan, K. L. (2013). Public opinion on the killing of Trayvon Martin: A test of the racial gradient thesis. *Journal of Crime and Justice, 36*(3), 283–298.
McIntosh, P. (1989). White privilege: Unpacking the invisible knapsack. *Peace and freedom, 49*(4), 10–12

SECTION 1

TRAYVON MARTIN: LIFE, DEATH, AND RACE IN AMERICA

BRYAN ELLIS

VICIOUSNESS

My mere existence reminds me of viciousness:
My being in America reminds me of theft;
My skin tone reminds me of rape;
My normal anxiety reminds me of past and future dreams deferred;
My everyday reality is vicious.

K.J. Fasching-Varner et al. (Eds.), Trayvon Martin, Race, and American Justice, 7.
© 2014 Sense Publishers. All rights reserved.

time there is a squad car parked at either end of my block. If, for any reason, they are not parked directly on my block, they are either in some configuration on the streets adjacent to my block, or scattered throughout the neighborhood no less than two blocks away from each other. This process is part of a larger policing strategy that has identified "hotspots" for criminal activity. Woodlawn has experienced almost 20 years of disinvestment and uneven development. In the early 1990s, a significant proportion of the housing stock was abandoned and discarded. This becomes important to the context as the University of Chicago is divided between the communities of Woodlawn and Hyde Park. Wishing to expand the campus and to make the university more attractive to donors and prospective students, the University has engaged in an expansion effort in Woodlawn. Because the University owned significant amounts of the vacant or cleared property through a land trust, the idea was to 'develop' the property and expand the University campus to the south. To 'protect' the university students from the potential 'criminal' element of Woodlawn, the University of Chicago Police in collaboration with the Chicago Police Department have engaged in a joint strategy to contain crime to specific spaces in Woodlawn.

Complicating the situation even further are competing residential interests in the neighborhood, where a segment of the new residents are also concerned with the perceived criminal element of the community. Where some are University of Chicago faculty and staff, others are professionals who have recently purchased homes in the neighborhood. Simultaneously, many long-term residents feel as if they have been infringed upon as one of the only mental health clinics on the Southside of the city closed due to city budget cuts. Additionally, a multimillion-dollar University of Chicago hospital in the northern section of the neighborhood has been built without a trauma center. This is of particular significance as there is only one trauma center for the Southside of the city that is primarily African American and Latino/a.

Often positioned as a battle between renters and homeowners, this binary is inaccurate to describe existing neighborhood tensions. Instead, similar to the Martin murder and subsequent trial, it is a complex set of relationships mired in the nexus of race, class, and gender. New residents, encapsulating a mix of African American professionals and white University of Chicago faculty, are pushing the redevelopment aspect, with property rehabilitation and land development in the center. Long-term residents seek a form of neighborhood revitalization to keep their homes, while engaging in a sustainable project of development not subjugating families that might have fewer resources and lower household incomes. With significance to the Martin decision, the conditions in my neighborhood serve as perpetual reminders of how the city has created a situation to continually remind certain residents of their disposability. For the new residents, the police state is often interpreted as a sign of protection. For families that have historical roots in the community, it is an intensified version of 'more of the same.'

SCHOOL CLOSINGS, DISPOSABILITY, AND THE CONTRADICTIONS OF 'SAFE PASSAGE'

In addition to the explicit police presence in my community, two of the forty-seven closed schools are less than two blocks away from my front door. In a neighborhood such as mine with all of the aforementioned tensions, school closings are particularly significant in reference to their relationship to uneven development/gentrification. Since the proximity of a school is the primary determinant of a family purchasing a home in the area, Woodlawn presents a particular conundrum. The majority of students attending Woodlawn schools are the children of long-term residents from families categorized as working-class/low-income. The issue, however, has become depopulation. Because of the lack of affordable housing stock, some schools have seen drastic reductions in their populations. Under austerity measures, central office (Chicago Public Schools—CPS) creates a rationale for reducing costs and makes a decision to close schools in areas that are not only depopulated, but have been historically underserved. Despite the lack of revealing their equation for school closings, the vast majority of the schools have been closed in communities that have been disinvested.

In preparation for the new gentry of residents, CPS has attempted to pacify parents through a strategy known as 'safe passage.' Created by former Marine colonel Tom Tyrell, whose primary specialization was hostage negotiation in the Kosovo conflict, CPS has teamed with the Chicago Police Department to create a series of pathways between schools and surrounding communities. Currently, hourly employees patrol the routes by one hour before school begins and one hour after dismissal, and their primary responsible is watching over students. Coupled with the hourly employees are police cruisers that are positioned along the pathways. On the first day of school in Woodlawn, there were mounted patrols and fire trucks along with the police cruisers and hourly employees patrolling the "safe passages."

Utilizing an alternative perspective, very little of this description should be considered "safe" for the young people walking along these pathways. Instead, a re-framing of the issue would consider safe passages as an extension of the police state through constant surveillance. Instead of feeling safe, like their parents, students from working-class/low-income families are reminded of the fact that there is an active plan to remove them. If there is ever a moment of perceived upheaval, the young people along those "safe" passages will be instantly reminded that they are no longer safe, but targets of the city.

MOVING FORWARD

This is a very difficult chapter to conclude. I must confess that living under these conditions can evoke the myriad of emotions and reactions. If I remain steadfast in my commitment to the project of radical healing through the process of changing my conditions, I know the process must be a collective one. If we are actively seeking to end this set of policies and implementations, we must begin with the how we have arrived at this point. We must take the bold steps of informing our communities and organizing with them in the pursuit of justice. Our roads are often hard, but we must continue to believe and know that Martin and the hundreds of thousands like him did not die in vain.

REFERENCES

Ginwright, S. (2010). *Black youth rising: Activism and radical healing in urban America.* New York, NY: Teachers College.

Yosso, T. (2006). Whose culture has capital?: A critical race theory discussion of community cultural wealth. *Race, Ethnicity and Education, 8*(1), 69–91.

LORI LATRICE MARTIN

3. BEEN THERE DONE THAT

With the Zimmerman Verdict, History Repeats Itself

Sadly, the George Zimmerman verdict was not news; rather, it was history repeating itself. I am reminded of the documentary, *Scottsboro: An American Tragedy*, which included a still image of Stanley Leibowitz, a Jewish lawyer from New York (Goodman & Goodman, 2001). The International Labor Defense (ILD), the legal arm of the Communist Party, retained Leibowitz to defend nine indigent Black males wrongfully convicted of raping two white women, Victoria Price and Ruby Bates, on a train headed for Chattanooga, Tennessee (Markovitz, 2004). Leibowitz won the right to have the defendants tried separately. The image showed a stunned Leibowitz after hearing Haywood Patterson, the first to be retried, was again found guilty and sentenced to death (Kinshasa & Norris, 1997). Leibowitz and a multiracial coalition of individuals and organizations from across the globe fought long and hard to secure the release of the Scottsboro defendants. Together they fought against a system designed to protect and serve some and to control and oppress all others (Klarman, 2009).

Despite the odds, and history being stacked against the Scottsboro defendants, supporters kept the faith. Scottsboro advocates deeply and passionately believed in the set of principles upon which this nation was founded. They believed in a set of principles and core values their ancestors fought to preserve and extend to others. The Scottsboro supporters fought within a system that had historically discriminated against the very people whose lives they were trying to protect. Far too many of the members of the multiracial coalition did not fully understand the depth of hatred, distain, and animosity the gatekeepers of the racial social order had for the defendants and the racial group to which they belonged. The Scottsboro defendants represented a group that had long been considered property (Balkin & Levison, 2012). Historically, people of African ancestry were considered subhuman and uncivilized (Hine et al., 2006). Members of the dominant racial group believed Blacks had a propensity towards violence and an insatiable thirst for white women (Williams, 2013b).

Even with the facts of the case and the evidence presented, the Scottsboro defendants were found guilty through several appeals (DeWitt, 2008). Members of the press and supporters of the defendants were stunned too. They were stunned, not because they were unaware of what they were up against, but because they believed

K.J. Fasching-Varner et al. (Eds.), Trayvon Martin, Race, and American Justice, 15–18.
© *2014 Sense Publishers. All rights reserved.*

the system, with all of its imperfections, had the structures in place to bring about a different outcome (Goodman & Goodman, 2001). More than a decade after their arrests, the last of the defendants was released but most did not receive official pardons until some eighty years later (Williams, 2013a).

The case of the Scottsboro defendants would not be the last time the justice system would shatter the hopes of a nation and remind the world of the many ways justice is not blind. Some have compared the lynching of Emmett Till with the killing of Trayvon Martin (Lewis, 2013). We must realize that there are some among us who do not understand the connection, because they know very little about Till, other than passing references to his name in musical lyrics (Sarah, 2013). Both young boys went to the store to buy candy; when their lives ended, many in the nation were turned upside down. The similarities between the killings of Till and Martin do not end there; they go much deeper.

Like the Scottsboro defendants, Till and Martin were born into a world that refused to see each young boy as a total person. The residents of Money, Mississippi, did not see Emmett "Bo" Till as a fun loving, fourteen-year-old boy with his whole life ahead of him. On the contrary, Emmett Till was criminalized and dehumanized. The torture and lynching of Till was to serve as a warning to Blacks about the consequences of violating racial etiquette and threatening the racial social order. Ultimately, the trial of Roy Bryant and J.W. Milam, the confessed killers of Till, was not about them, but it was about preserving a way of life (Campbell, 2008).

Similarly the killing of Martin and the trial that followed, was not just about prematurely taking a young man's life. It was not just about two devoted parents humbly, gracefully, and courageously seeking justice for their son. It was about race. No matter how many times people say it was not about race, race was at the core. Martin had the audacity to invade whitespace. According to Zimmerman, just as other African Americans had managed to get beyond the gates that were supposed to keep whites safe, Martin had to be stopped. Just like in days gone by, some ordinary white citizens have taken that to mean that it was their civic-even their patriotic-duty to protect their women and children from the Martins of the world (Hine, Hine, & Harrold, 2006). After all, it was the invasion of a white mother's home that led to the creation of the Neighborhood Watch program (Grace et al., 2013).

Many hoped this time would be different. Millions of Americans signed petitions calling for the arrest of Zimmerman (Stodder, 2012). The reluctance on the part of authorities to even arrest Zimmerman was a painful reminder of the unequal treatment people of color received in the criminal justice system (Alexander, 2010). The lack of an arrest was a manifestation of the white privilege afforded to Zimmerman, a white Hispanic male. In *Unpacking the Invisible Knapsack*, McIntosh (1989) addressed white privilege and outlined the unearned benefits whites received by virtue of their birth, the evidence of which whites often have difficulty seeing. McIntosh (1989) described the benefits as an invisible package containing unearned assets and provided a list with some of the daily privileges whites enjoyed. For example, whites could rent or purchase housing in a neighborhood and be welcomed or left alone. Whites could also watch television and read newspapers and see members of their race represented widely, argued McIntosh, but the same could not be said for McIntosh's friends and colleagues of color.

While Zimmerman remained freed, it was clear it was time to revisit the McIntosh's list. Zimmerman's killing of an African American male child was an unfortunate reminder of the continuing significance of race. It was a reminder that the election of the nation's first Black president, while historic and powerful, was no match for the enduring racialized social system that has been at the core of American society since the birth of this great nation. Well before the killing, many of us told anyone who would listen that race still matters. Our calls were often drowned out by louder claims of blaming the victim. Unarmed Black men who meet fatal violent force were routinely vilified. They were, so the saying goes, "in the wrong place at the wrong time" or they were "up to no good." Martin was doing what many other kids were doing on February 26, 2012. He was getting a snack and talking on his cell phone, but for Zimmerman, these very acts when draped in Blackness and clothed in a hooded sweatshirt aroused suspicion, and ultimately left a mother and father to bury their dead child. The failure to arrest George Zimmerman was an insult to fair-minded Americans, a true injustice.

The killing of young Martin but added more baggage to the invisible knapsack of white privilege. The clothing in which a white son left the house would not lead others to look upon him with suspicion. White privilege also meant that if a white child was the victim of crime, law enforcement would neither assume he was the aggressor, nor take the word of his killer as true without a thorough investigation. We could also add to McIntosh's list that if the son of white parents was killed, the parents would have time to grieve his death and not have to do themselves the investigative work commonly done by law enforcement officials. Additionally, if a white child was killed, and the killer's identity was known, the parents could be sure that at the very least the killer would be arrested. For McIntosh's friends and colleagues of color, the same could not be said.

Millions collectively proclaimed, "Justice for Martin," and declared it time to unpack the knapsack and get rid of all the racial baggage. Hundreds of thousands of individuals broke out their hoodies in a show of solidarity. The trial captured the attention of a society with a notoriously short attention span and they watched each person's testimony. Hundreds of thousands waited as word of a verdict raced across television screens and social media outlets and many were stunned; many were left without speech. Gifted writers, journalists, academicians, elected officials, mothers, fathers, sons, and daughters, suddenly, had no words.

The stunned, speechless, and angered throngs turned to action, and peaceful protests sprouted up across the nation. Editorials flowed. Much has been, and will be written, about the verdict but like too many tragedies, the furor surrounding the Zimmerman case lessened. As the collective memory fades, one thing we cannot forget is that this trial, this verdict, this episode in history, was not new; instead, it was history repeating itself.

The only way to bring about real change is to demythologize the idea that we are living in a post-racial society (Martin, 2013). We must dispel the myth that we live in a colorblind society where race no longer matters (Bonilla-Silva, 2006). Blacks and whites alike argued over the past few decades that race has declined in significance (Wilson, 1980), while others of us have argued the contrary. Oh how we wish we were wrong! The killing of Martin is just one of the many contemporary examples of the widening gap between *society as it is* and *society as it should be*.

REFERENCES

Alexander, M. (2010). *The new Jim Crow: Mass incarceration in the age of colorblindness.* New York, NY: New Press.

Balkin, J. M., & Levinson, S. (2012). Panel I: Thirteenth amendment in context. *Columbia Law Review, 112*(7), 1459–1499.

Bonilla-Silva, E. (2006). *Racism without racists.* Lanham, MD: Rowman & Littlefield Publishers.

Campbell, C. (2008). The untold story of Emmett Louis Till: A film by Keith Beauchamp. *Southern Quarterly: A Journal of the Arts in the South, 45*(4), 172–174.

DeWitt, P. (2008). Black communists speak on Scottsboro: A documentary history. *History: Reviews of New Books, 36*(3), 89–92.

Goodman, B. (Writer), & Goodman, B. (Producer). (2001). Scottsboro: An American tragedy. In D. Anker & B. Goodman (Producers), *American experience.* Boston, MA: WGBH Educational Foundation.

Grace, N., Martin, J., & Martin, C. S. (2013). *Questions raised by police video of George Zimmerman/ Interviewer: Nancy Grace (CNN).*

Hine, D., Hine, W. C., & Harrold, S. (2006). *The African-American odyssey.* Upper Saddle Hill, NJ: Pearson Prentice Hall.

Kinshasa, K., & Norris, C. (1997). *The man from Scottsboro: Clarence Norris and the infamous 1931 Alabama rape trial, in his own words.* Jefferson, NC: McFarland.

Klarman, M. J. (2009). Scottsboro. *Marquette Law Review, 93*(2), 379–432.

Lewis, W. (2013, July 18). Trayvon Martin and Emmett Till victims of same injustice. *Tulsa World (OK).*

Markovitz, J. (2004). *Anti-racist organizing and collective memory.* Conference Papers–American Sociological Association, 1.

McIntosh, P. (1989). *White privilege and male privilege.* Working Paper No. 189/Peggy McIntosh.

Sarah, W. (2013, May 4). Lil Wayne dropped by Mountain Dew over Emmett Till lyrics [Video file]. Mountain Dew. GlobalPost.

Stodder, J. (2012). Commentary: How social media has shaped the case of Trayvon Martin. *New Orleans Citybusiness (LA).*

Ward, G. (Writer), & Burns, K. (Director). (2005). *Unforgiveable blackness.* D. Schaye, P. Barnes, & K. Burns (Producers). WETA/Florentine Films.

Williams, P. (2013a). In the clear. *Jet, 122*(10), 14.

Williams, P. (2013b). The monsterization of Trayvon Martin. *Nation, 297*, 7–8.

Wilson, W. (1980). *The declining significance of race.* Chicago, IL: University of Chicago Press.

KIM L. ANDERSON

4. NO HEROES HERE

Neighborhood Watchfulness and the Role of Narcissistic Altruism in the Killing of Trayvon Martin

Every man must decide whether he will walk in the light of creative altruism or in the darkness of destructive selfishness. Martin Luther King, Jr.

Events on February 26, 2012, in Sanford, Florida, did not awaken Americans to discrepancies in how citizens are treated in the United States nor did they revitalize a justice system permeated with bias toward young Black males. The events did, however, underscore the pervasive tension between cultural groups, the frustration and fear of African American parents, and the feebleness of a nation coming to terms with its frailties. Political leaders weighed in, pundits pontificated, and mothers cried.

George Zimmerman shot and killed a collective son who dared to walk a prideful path carrying modern day ambrosia of iced tea and Skittles as he journeyed toward home. Zimmerman may well have profiled and stalked Trayvon Martin because he was a Black adolescent who audaciously and comfortably walked through a gated community. Transcripts from 911 indicate that Zimmerman was immediately suspicious if not convinced that the "Black male (in his) late teens" was up to no good (Mother Jones, 2013, p. 4), and it was his calling to make sure this interloper did no harm.

Members of the jury who acquitted Zimmerman on July 13, 2013, may have assumed that, because Martin was presumably out of place at The Retreat at Twin Lakes, Zimmerman was justified in shooting him. They were doing their civic duty by serving and they had an obligation to be diligent about the specific instructions that they were given pertaining to Florida's stand-your-ground law (Knickerbocker, 2013).

In both scenarios, the players in this tragedy thought they were doing the right thing. In both scenarios, the roles were voluntary. Zimmerman had been appointed Neighborhood Watch Coordinator because of his interest in protecting his community. His plan was to follow in his magistrate father's footsteps and become a judge after completing his education in criminal justice (Francescani, 2012). And while the American jury system is fundamentally compulsory, actual service is relatively self-determined. In most instances, juries are made up of people who are simply available and/or committed to fulfilling their responsibility as a U.S. citizen.

K.J. Fasching-Varner et al. (Eds.), Trayvon Martin, Race, and American Justice, 19–23.
© 2014 Sense Publishers. All rights reserved.

In the classic essay "White Privilege: Unpacking the Invisible Knapsack", McIntosh (1989) wrote that white privilege was "an invisible package of unearned assets" about which white people were to "remain oblivious" (p. 1). She wrote, "White privilege is like an invisible weightless knapsack of special provisions, maps, passports, codebooks, visas, clothes, tools, and blank checks" (McIntosh, 1989, p. 1).

Perhaps the killing of Martin was race based and the acquittal of Zimmerman was the result of white privilege or even the feminization of fear; yet what is certain is that those involved in the death of Martin and vindication of Zimmerman likely believed they were doing something positive, even altruistic.

We often limit our notions of the helping or altruism to passive vocations such as social work, education, nursing, or counseling, yet the desire to help and serve is seen in of occupations such as fire fighting, police work, military service, or neighborhood watch coordination. Individuals in these positions often choose their work as a way give back to their communities through support, guidance, resource procurement, or protection. Caring is a good thing; helping is a great thing, but when one's professional identity is built primarily upon these "good works" and personal identity becomes linked to them, the risk of *narcissistic altruism* is profound. Sometimes this includes a misguided belief that no one else can do a job as well: *No one else will recognize what is needed here but me . . . I have more experience with this situation . . . I can handle this challenge because I'm tough.* All of these statements may be true to some extent, but they can lead to very costly mistakes. The greatest risk of narcissistic altruism is recklessness. This kind of self-absorbed and self-propelled compulsion to help or serve has the potential to obscure our vision and muffle our hearing when we need them the most (Anderson & Davis, 2012). Remaining open and receptive is essential.

Oakley, Knafo, and McGrath (2012) asserted that instead of promoting the welfare of another, this kind of altruism has irrational and substantial negative consequences to the other or even to the self. "What we value so much, the altruistic 'good' side of human nature can also have a dark side. Altruism can be the back door to hell," (Oakley, Knafo, & McGrath, 2012, p. 4). In some circumstances, these misguided, well-meaning motivations may become the basis of fundamentally flawed concepts such as color blindness (Frankenberg, 1997; Ladson-Billings, 1994; Sleeter, 2000/2001), white guilt (Spanierman, Poteat, & Armstrong, 2006), political correctness and/or compassion fatigue (Figley, 1995; Spanierman, Poteat, & Armstrong, 2006).

In other instances, the desire to help, serve and protect become distorted reasons and/or excuses for excessive use of force propelled by unchecked impulses and blindness to consequences (Hauser, 2012). Without proper reflection, empathy opens the door to narcissism and perhaps pathology. When interpersonal dilemmas are nested within intergroup dynamics, the meaning of altruism is contingent upon perspective. Behavior intended to be helpful or altruistic within the context of the in-group may become destructive in a larger intergroup context (Krueger, 2012).

The only solution is to remain vigilant to the dangerous alliance between prejudice and self-deception (Hauser, 2012). Martin's death underscores the consequences of what happens when vigilance is replaced by vigilantism in the guise of public protection.

Prior to his acquittal, Zimmerman's community, the intergroup, gave its consent for him to serve and protect as its Neighborhood Watch Coordinator. Zimmerman was invited to spearhead this program. He legally carried a firearm. He routinely reported to police his concerns about "suspicious persons." In all instances, he described these persons as Black males. No one questioned his abilities or intentions for taking on this important voluntary position – even when he shot and killed an unarmed teenager as he walked leisurely (brazenly?) home to his family. It took a national outcry before Zimmerman was arrested and charged with a crime.

At minimum, Martin was considered "Other," first by Zimmerman who assumed he did not belong in his own neighborhood, then by the jury who ascribed to the theory that Martin was somehow a threat to Zimmerman carrying a concealed 9mm pistol. Othering is a way of defining and securing one's own positive identity through the stigmatization of an*other*. Whatever the markers of social differentiation that shape the meaning of "us" and "them," whether they are racial, geographic, ethnic, economic, or ideological, there is always the danger that they will become the basis for a self-affirmation that depends upon the denigration of the other group. A dividing line is drawn between "us" and "them" and the dividing line is imbued with negative judgments . . . (or) "othering" can be motivated by hostility . . . (sometimes) by indifference or even sympathy (Lister, 2009).At maximum, Martin was killed because he was a young Black male, an *Other*, intrinsically a threat because of his demographics; and the jury, barely peers of anyone involved in the case, decided his killing was defensible.

Rankin (as cited in Smith, 2013) wrote that George Zimmerman was protecting the neighborhood and notably, white women, from a potential criminal, a crucial aspect of the defense team's argument; Rankin noted that "Mychal Denzel Smith cogently dissected Defense Attorney Mark O'Mara's use of Zimmerman's white female neighbor, Olivia Bertalan, as a 'prop in the racist construction of Martin as a criminal threat to white women's safety'...O'Mara presented the jury with the 'perfect victim,' which Martin could never be: a white woman living in fear of Black criminals." Rankin asserted that George Zimmerman was never on trial; Black masculinity was (Smith, 2013).

One of the jurors who acquitted Zimmerman, female Juror B37, granted an interview to CNN's Anderson Cooper after the trial. Valenti (2013) wrote that Juror B37 made one of the most telling statements to Cooper during that interview. She stated that George Zimmerman's "heart was in the right place, but just got displaced by the vandalism in the neighborhoods and wanting to catch *these people* so badly that he went above and beyond what he really should have done" (Ford, 2013). The phrase "above and beyond" is interesting, given it is generally understood as a positive. To B37, Zimmerman was a protector (Valenti, 2013), perhaps a hero?

There is little doubt that racial profiling played a role in the death of Martin. The evidence shows that Zimmerman thought he was" suspicious" simply because he did not think Martin belonged in the neighborhood. Ageism also may have played a role. Martin was in his late teens, wearing the uniform of an evil do-er – a dark hoodie and jeans. Fraternalism may have played a role as the police did not arrest Zimmerman at the scene; rather he wanted to be one of them. The jury's not-guilty verdict could be viewed as a conviction of Martin rather than an acquittal of Zimmerman. The foundation of stand-your-ground law is self-defense and thus Martin was in the wrong according to the law. However, to believe that an unarmed adolescent is a threat to an adult with a firearm is communal self-deception.

Trivers (2001, 2010) argued that self-deception can run amuck, resulting in great tragedies. Deception arises when some aspect of reality, either external or internal is suppressed or manipulated – lies of omission and commission. Self-deception is a form of cognitive distortion that can become pathological if unchecked. From an in-group perspective, it is likely to go unchecked. Combined with in-group favoritism, it rapidly runs away. Self-deception would act as a powerful facilitator, creating an illusion of grandiosity for the ego and a diminution of all that is human for the Other (Hauser, 2012). Hauser (2012) referred to Haslam's (2006) identification of a dehumanization process and asserted the only solution is to remain vigilant to the dangerous alliance between prejudice and self-deception.

Sloan Wilson (2012) wrote:

> Insofar as cultural evolution is an ongoing and open-ended process, we should find tremendous diversity in the beliefs and practices that cause people to behave altruistically and selfishly, defined in behavioral terms. Our analysis of these believes and practices should be guided by a single overriding consideration: what do they cause people to do? (p. 410)

In the case of Martin, narcissistic beliefs and practices cloaked in altruism may have been among the most misguided factors that led to his death.

Campbell (2008) identified the Hero's Journey as the universal mythic adventure, which is embodied in most every story. The Hero's Journey is the quintessential story of narcissistic altruism. An ordinary individual finds himself in extraordinary circumstances. No matter how many times he rejects the sword, he takes it up *because he can, because he is called to do so*. Sadly, there are no heroes in this story. Martin never completed his journey home with his modern day elixir. Zimmerman may have been mistaken for the hero as he confronted the supreme ordeal, his greatest fear – "those people" (CNN Justice, July 2013). Campbell's (2008) description of the *Hero's Journey* explains that there is always the possibility that the challenge beats the hero because he is unprepared, has a flaw in his character, or can't surrender himself to the inevitability of the truth: Martin was not a Supreme Ordeal or a dragon to be slain. He was a young man robbed of the choice to journey forth.

REFERENCES

Anderson, K. L., & Davis, B. M. (2012). *Creating culturally considerate schools: Educating without bias.* Thousand Oaks, CA: Corwin Press.

Campbell, J. (2008). *The hero with a thousand faces* (IIIrd ed.). New York, NY: New World Library.

Figley, C. (1995). *Compassion fatigue: Coping with secondary traumatic stress disorder in those who treat the traumatized.* New York, NY: Taylor and Francis Group.

Ford, D. (2013, July 16). Juror: No doubt that George Zimmerman feared for his life. *CNN Justice.* Retrieved from http://www.cnn.com

Francescani, C. (2012, April 22). George Zimmerman: Prelude to a shooting. *Reuters.* Retrieved from http://www.reuters.com

Frankenberg, R. (1997). *Displacing whiteness.* Durham, NC: Duke University Press.

Haslam, N. (2006). Dehumination: In integrative review. *Personality and Social Psychology Review, 10*(3), 252–264.

Hauser, M. (2012). Hell's angels: A Runaway model of pathological altruism. In B. Oakley, A. Knafo, G. Madhavan, & D. S. Wilson (Eds.), *Pathological altruism* (pp. 387–394). New York, NY: Oxford University Press.

Karlamangla, S. (2013, November 2). City where Trayvon Martin was killed changes neighborhood watch rules. *Los Angeles Times.* Retrieved from http://www.articles.latimes.com

Knickerbocker, B. (2013, July 21). "Stand your ground" laws rattle US politics, society. *Christian Science Monitor.* Retrieved from http://csmonitor.com

Krueger, J. I. (2012). Altruism gone mad. In B. Oakley, A. Knafo, G. Madhavan, & D. S. Wilson (Eds.), *Pathological altruism* (pp. 395–405). New York, NY: Oxford University Press.

Ladson-Billings, G. (1994). The Dreamkeepers: Successful teachers of African American children. San Francisco, CA: Jossey-Bass.

Lister, R. (2009). *Povertyism and 'othering': Why they matter.* Conference on Challenging Povertyism, London, UK.

McIntosh, P. (1989, July/August). White privilege: Unpacking the invisible knapsack. *Peace and Freedom Magazine,* 10–12.

Oakley, B., Knafo, A., & McGrath, M. (2012). Pathological altruism—An introduction. In B. Oakley, A. Knafo, G. Madhavan, & D. S. Wilson (Eds.), *Pathological altrusim* (pp. 3–9). New York, NY: Oxford.

Policy Mic. (2013, July 27). *What juror B37's comments reveal about white womanhood.* Retrievd from http://www.policymic.com

Sleeter, C. (2000/2001, Winter). *Diversity vs. white privilege/Interviewer: Rethinking Schools.*

Wilson, D. S. (2012). Pathology, evolution, and altruism. In B. Oakley, A. Knafo, G. Madhavan, & D. S. Wilson (Eds.), *Pathological narcissism* (pp. 406–411). New York, NY: Oxford.

Transcript of George Zimmerman's call to the police. (2013, March 18). In *Mother Jones.* Retrieved from http://www.motherjones.com

Smith, M. D. (2013, July 15). Trayvon Martin: From lament to rallying cry. *The Nation.* Retrieved from http://www.thenation.com

Solomon, R. P., Portelli, J. P., Daniel, B. -J., & Campbell, A. (2005). The discourse of denial: How white teacher candidates construct race, racism and 'white privilege'. *Race, Ethnicity and Education, 8*(2), 147–169.

Spanierman, L. B., Poteat, V. P., & Armstrong, P. I. (2006). Psychosocial costs of racism to whites: Exploring patterns through cluster analysis. *Journal of Counseling Psychology, 53*(4), 434–441.

Trivers, R. (2001). Self-deception in service of deceit. In R. Trivers & R. Trivers (Eds.), *Natural selection and social theory: Selected papers* (pp. 255–293). New York, NY: Oxford University Press.

Trivers, R. (2010). Deceit and self-deception. In P. M. Kappeler & J. B. Silk (Eds.), *Mind the gap: Tracing the origins of human universals* (pp. 373–394). Berlin, DE: Springer Verlag.

Valenti, J. (2013, July 16). Fear and consequences: George Zimmerman and the protection of white womanhood. *The Nation.* Retrieved from http://www.thenation.com

KATHLEEN J. FITZGERALD

5. THE 'WHITENING' OF LATINOS

George Zimmerman and the Operation of White Privilege

Social scientists argue that race is socially constructed; in other words, racial categorization emerges out of particular times and places to meet certain social and political needs. Racial categorization is an ongoing process, thus, the racial hierarchy is always in flux, despite its static appearance. Not surprisingly, sociologists offer predictions as to what groups are likely to experience a changed racial status in the future. Some speculate that Asian Americans and Hispanics are likely to "become white" similarly to the whitening of Irish, Jewish, and Italian Americans of previous eras (Yancey, 2004). While others emphasize the emergence of a tri-racial system, where some subgroups gain a privileged status but all members of the particular racial/ethnic group do not gain access to privilege (Bonilla-Silva, 2010). In the future, some Latinos and some Asian Americans will become "honorary whites," with access to the benefits of white privilege, while many members of these groups will remain second-class citizens. Latinos who are immigrants and speak with accents, or are impoverished, or that look visibly African, are unlikely to benefit from white privilege while others will be viewed as white and will be able to take advantage of privileges associated with whiteness. In this chapter, I outline the various ways George Zimmerman benefitted from white privilege throughout the Trayvon Martin incident, investigation, and eventual criminal trial, and then I will explore what this means in terms of the "whitening" of Latinos.

White privilege refers to that collection of benefits, including abstract benefits such as credibility and trustworthiness, which are unearned and often unrecognized by whites. People perceived as white can rely on such benefits, which open doors for them and essentially make life easier. McIntosh (2008) extended the definition of white privilege by describing it as "an invisible, weightless knapsack of special provisions, maps, passports, codebooks, visas, clothes, tools and blank checks" (p. 1). White privilege, known as the "other side of racism" (Rothenberg, 2008), removes obstacles from our life, while racism places obstacles in the way of minorities.

The Martin/Zimmerman case can be understood as a key moment in the 'whitening' of some Latinos, primarily, those who are light-skinned, English speaking, and at least middle-class. Historians will look back to this case as evidence of the most recent changing racial status of some Latinos, like Zimmerman, from non-white to white. Historically, the racial status of Hispanics has shifted between white and non-white. In the 1930s, for instance, the census bureau recognized Mexicans for the first

K.J. Fasching-Varner et al. (Eds.), *Trayvon Martin, Race, and American Justice*, 25–29.

time by including a separate racial category for Mexican Americans, despite the fact that at the time, courts defined Mexicans as white (Foley, 2008). Today, the census bureau is considering adding 'Hispanic" as a racial category instead of keeping it as an ethnic category on the 2020 census. The racial status of Hispanics remains complicated: legally, Hispanics are afforded the racial status of white people, yet socially, politically, and economically, they are treated as non-whites (Foley, 2008). Latino racialization is intricately connected to skin color, language, immigrant status, and social class.

While Zimmerman no doubt benefitted from Florida's stand-your-ground laws, I argue that Zimmerman also benefited significantly from white privilege, despite the constant emphasis on his Hispanicity by the press. The emphasis on his Hispanicity seemed to imply that the killing was not racially motivated, despite the fact that Latinos tend to hold anti-Black prejudices (Bonilla-Silva, 2010). It is too easy, if not disingenuous, to repeatedly emphasize Zimmerman's Hispanic heritage. There is no doubt that he has Hispanic ancestry; his mother speaks with an accent and is clearly an immigrant. His father is white, however, George Zimmerman does not necessarily look Hispanic. A stereotypical Hispanic phenotype includes black or dark brown hair, brown eyes and a dark complexion. Zimmerman could easily pass as a brown-haired, brown-eyed, white guy with a bit of a tan. By being perceived as white, or at least as an "honorary white" as Bonilla-Silva (2010) would say, Zimmerman was able to capitalize on white privilege and ultimately be acquitted of the murder of Martin.

Zimmerman embraced his race privilege by behaving and being treated as if he was credible and trustworthy even before the shooting occurred. By acting as a volunteer neighborhood watchman, and arming himself in that capacity, Zimmerman embraced white privilege. He operated as if not only would no one question his right to be in that location, but also his right to "police" the neighborhood, to be the gatekeeper. Any actions in which he chose to engage were to be understood as beneficial to the community, despite the fact that carrying a weapon and approaching a suspect are violations of the Neighborhood Watch National Sheriff's Association guidelines, not to mention common sense (Jacobson, 2012). Throughout the media coverage of the Martin/Zimmerman case, Martin was described as "staying" in the complex rather than as a resident. Both Zimmerman and Martin's father's fiancé rented homes in the community, yet only one was perceived as belonging. While this is a somewhat accurate description of Martin's temporary residential status, it is a framing that privileges Zimmerman. Zimmerman belongs; Martin is an intruder. This fits sociologists Feagin, Vera, and Imani's (1996) notion of a radicalized space, a location where "cultural biases…help define specific areas as 'white' or as 'for all,' with the consequent feelings of not belonging or belonging" (p. 16).

Make no mistake: race mattered for all parties involved. However, race operated in very different ways for Martin than it did for Zimmerman. Martin's race resulted in his being profiled and suspect, despite his youth and that he was unarmed. Zimmerman's whiteness allowed him to be viewed as credible and innocent, despite the fact that he was armed. This extension of credibility is certainly not a minor detail as he explained himself to law enforcement personnel while standing over the dead body of an unarmed 17-year-old. Imagine if their races were reversed. Would a young Black man be given the benefit of the doubt for a killing as he stood over the dead body of an unarmed white 17-year-old?

We do not have to speculate if Zimmerman was perceived as white by responding police officers since the initial police report actually described him as a white male (Zorn, 2012). Zimmerman's perceived whiteness worked for him while Martin's Blackness worked against him. Race mattered, just not in the way it is implied when people almost reflexively point out Zimmerman's Hispanic ancestry to deflect claims Martin's killing was racially motivated.

In Zimmerman's videotaped narrative from the police precinct, he repeatedly referred to the then-dead Martin as "the suspect." We know Zimmerman viewed him as such so it is no surprise to hear those words coming out of his mouth, but the fact that the police seemed to unquestionably accept the description should startle us. Race played a very important role here: Martin's Blackness allowed police officer's to unquestionably accept Zimmerman's framing of him. But their acceptance would not have happened without the operation of Zimmerman's whiteness and the credibility it purchased for him.

After a five-hour interrogation by police, Zimmerman was not arrested because the investigators thought there was no evidence to contradict his version of the incident, which claimed that he acted in self-defense. However, there is rarely evidence to counter a claim of self-defense when the victim has been killed. Thus, the police considered more than just objective evidence in determining Zimmerman's innocence; he was understood to be credible and no doubt his perceived whiteness contributed to this. It took six weeks of nation-wide protests and negative publicity for the assignment of a special prosecutor who charged Zimmerman with second-degree murder in the killing of Martin.

Much was made of the fact that Zimmerman faced an all-female jury, most of whom were mothers. Some pundits speculated that the prosecution's closing arguments would portray Zimmerman as someone that puts their children at risk with his trigger finger. Instead of viewing Zimmerman as a mother's worst nightmare, did the six female jurors instead identify more closely with Zimmerman? Instead of identifying with Martin's anguished mother over the killing of her son, did they identify with Zimmerman's mother and her fears of his conviction? Did they instead wonder what would happen if their sons were so misunderstood, improperly maligned, and wrongfully charged? Speaking anonymously to NPR, Juror B37, the first to speak out after the verdict, confirmed the image of Zimmerman as trustworthy and as someone with whom she identified. She said she "believed Zimmerman's story, and that she'd welcome him as a neighbor to her community if…he didn't go too far… I think his heart was in the right place. It just went terribly wrong," (Allen, 2013, p. 2). The juror believed that the he most he was guilty of was not using good judgment (Allen, 2013).

The fact that prisons are full of Black and brown men, yet men of color are not more likely to be engaged in criminal activity than white men, tells us that jurors extend this kind of credibility to white defendants much more often than they do to defendants of color. In this era of mass incarceration, where over two million U.S. citizens are incarcerated and two-thirds of them are people of color, it is hard to come to any conclusion other than this is evidence of one of the ways white privilege operates in the criminal justice system (Alexander, 2010). As legal scholar Ogletree (2012) pointed out, there is "not a place in America where African Americans could receive what the law guarantees to its white citizens: a presumption of innocence" (p. 65).

Might this case provide us with an opening to challenge the racial hierarchy and white privilege? Are polls that show lack of support among Hispanics for Zimmerman and the verdict that declared him innocent evidence of a challenge to white privilege (PEW Research Centre, 2013)? While Zimmerman appears to have been granted white privilege throughout this case, such privileges are not extended to all Hispanics. Nor do all Hispanics embrace white privilege. Much like Native American resistance to forced assimilation, many Chicano activists have consistently rejected whiteness. Becoming white is not an entirely voluntary process, as the dominant group ultimately controls access to this privileged status, but not all groups and individuals that have access to it have embraced it. However, for those that do embrace whiteness, they are "complicit in maintaining boundaries around 'Blackness' in order to claim the privileges of whiteness. By embracing whiteness "… [they] reinforce the color line that has denied people of African descent full participation in American democracy" (Foley, 2008, p. 62).

The 'whitening' of Latinos is bigger than this one case, of course. This case allows us to watch the operation of privilege, to witness the policing of the boundaries of whiteness. The extension of white privilege to some groups that are currently radicalized may allow them access to privilege, however, this in no way challenges the racial hierarchy. Instead, it upholds it. While sociologists have long critiqued the claim that the election of Barack Obama made the United States "post-racial," it is important to acknowledge that in a "post-racial" society, not only would racism cease to exist, but so would racial privilege. Feagin and Vera (1995) defined white racism as "the socially organized set of attitudes, ideas, and practices that deny African Americans and other people of color the dignity, opportunities, freedoms and rewards that this nation offers white Americans" (p. 7). As the definition implies, as long as people of color are denied opportunities, white racism is at work; what goes unspoken is that the flip side of this racism is that those become opportunities for white people. In other words, these are two sides of the same coin – without white racism, there is no white privilege (Fitzgerald, 2014). Witnessing the 'whitening' of Latinos offers even more evidence that we are not a "post-racial" society. As long as white privilege remains so lucrative, individuals with access to whiteness will be lured by its benefits. Few things are as lucrative as a presumption of innocence.

REFERENCES

Allen, G. (2013, July 16). Juror B37 speaks out about Zimmerman verdict. *National Public Radio*. Retrieved from http://www.npr.org

Alexander, M. (2010). *The new Jim Crow: Mass incarceration in the age of color-blindness*. New York, NY: The New Press.

Bonilla-Silva, E. (2010). *Racism without racists: Color-blind racism and racial inequality in contemporary Americans* (IIIrd ed.). Lanham, MD: Rowman & Littlefield.

Feagin, J., Vera, H., & Imani, N. (1996). *The agony of education: Black students at white colleges and universities*. New York, NY: Routledge.

Feagin, J., & Vera, H. (1995). *White racism: The basics*. New York, NY: Routledge.

Fitzgerald, K. J. (2014). *Recognizing race and ethnicity: Power, privilege, and inequality*. Boulder, CO: Westview Press.

Foley, N. (2008). Becoming white: Mexican Americans and whiteness. In P. S. Rothenberg (Ed.), *White privilege: Essential readings on the other side of racism* (IIIrd ed.). New York, NY: Worth Publishing.

Jacobson, S. (2012, March 24). Trayvon Martin: Zimmerman was not following neighborhood watch rules. *Orlando Sentinel*. Retrieved from http://articles.orlandosentinel.com

McIntosh, P. (2008). White privilege: Unpacking the invisible knapsack. In P. Rothenberg (Ed.), *White privilege: Essential readings on the other side of racism* (IIIrd ed.). New York, NY: Worth Publishing.

Olgetree, C. (2012). *The presumption of guilt*. New York, NY: Palgrave Macmillan.

Rothenberg, P. S. (2008). *White privilege: Essential readings on the other side of racism* (IIIrd ed.). New York, NY: Worth Publishers.

Yancey, G. (2004). *Who is white? Latinos, Asians and the new Black/nonblack divide*. Boulder, CO: Lynn Reiner Press.

Zorn, E. (2012, March 27). Trayvon Martin shooting death—Initial police reports and '911' call transcript. *Chicago Tribune*. Retrieved from http://blogs.chicagotribune.com

CYNTHIA LEE

6. DENYING THE SIGNIFICANCE OF RACE

Colorblindness and the Zimmerman Trial

On February 26, 2012, at approximately 7:17 p.m., George Zimmerman spotted a young Black male in a hoodie walking in his neighborhood (Barry, 2012). Zimmerman thought the person looked suspicious, so he followed him and called 911. Within minutes of the 911 call, George Zimmerman and Trayvon Martin found themselves in a heated scuffle that ended when Zimmerman shot and killed Martin (Sanford Police Department [SPD] Offense Report, 2012). After being interviewed by police about the shooting, Zimmerman was released without arrest, causing a firestorm of protests across the nation (Wiggins, 2012a, 2012b). Eventually, Zimmerman was arrested and charged with murder in the second degree (Horwitz, 2012; Lawson, 2012).

Even though the initial failure to arrest Zimmerman focused the nation's attention on race and the criminal justice system, the trial in 2013 was nearly devoid of any mention of race. The judge ruled early on that the prosecution could use the term "profiling" but not "racial profiling" when describing Zimmerman's acts. (Roig-Franzia, 2013; Muskal, 2013; Lucas & Siemaszko, 2013). Zimmerman's attorney Mark O'Mara maintained during and after the trial that the case had nothing to do with race (Anderson, 2013). After the trial, Angela Corey, the prosecutor responsible for charging Zimmerman with second degree murder, told the press, "This case has never been about race..." (Winter, Novogrod, & Arkin, 2013, p. 3). With the judge, prosecution, and defense in agreement that race was irrelevant, it is not surprising that the jury also thought the case had nothing to do with race (Cooper, 2013).

Why were the legal decision-makers in the Zimmerman case so eager to deny the significance of race? I surmise they either sincerely believed the case had nothing to do with race or thought it improper or disadvantageous to acknowledge that race was relevant. It is likely that the judge sincerely believed the color of one's skin was irrelevant and that it would be bad to acknowledge race. The judge tried to run a colorblind trial because she thought ignoring race was the fairest way to proceed.

The prosecution and defense may have also sincerely believed race was irrelevant. It is also possible they chose to proceed as though race was not relevant for strategic reasons. The public protests over the Sanford Police Department's initial failure to arrest stemmed from a belief that the decision not to arrest was racially biased (Lee, 2013). The defense did not want the jury to focus on the possibility that Zimmerman may have thought Martin looked suspicious because he was a young Black male.

K.J. Fasching-Varner et al. (Eds.), Trayvon Martin, Race, and American Justice, 31–37.

At the same time the defense team was claiming race was irrelevant, they also tried to use race to their advantage. At trial, they called a white woman who lived in Zimmerman's neighborhood to testify about being burglarized by a Black man, perhaps hoping that her testimony combined with racial stereotypes about Blacks as criminals might lead the jury to conclude that it was not completely unreasonable for Zimmerman to have thought Martin, a Black male, looked suspicious. They also argued that their client was selected for prosecution because of his race. O'Mara told the press that Zimmerman would not have been prosecuted if he had been Black, and accused Martin's supporters of turning the case into a civil rights matter (Real Clear Politics, 2013).

The prosecution had other motivations for denying the significance of race at Zimmerman's trial. They did not want the jury to think they were "playing the race card" or impermissibly relying on race. This rhetoric is used to suggest that one claiming racial discrimination or racial bias is lying or mistaken (Ford, 2008).

In an effort to avoid being perceived as trying to gain an improper advantage by arguing race, the prosecution adopted an overtly colorblind trial strategy. At the hearing on whether the prosecution would be allowed to use the term "profiling," the State assured the judge that the word "profiling" was not a racially charged term unless one made it so, and that they had no intention of making the term a racially charged one (Roig-Franzia, 2013). The prosecution then proceeded to argue the case without any explicit references to race.

Even as it tried to present a colorblind front, it appears that the prosecution actually believed race was important. Prosecutors used six or seven of their ten peremptory challenges to strike white females from the jury, prompting the defense to raise a *Batson* objection (Smerconish, 2013a, 2013b), a claim that the opposing party is impermissibly relying on race in the exercise of their peremptory challenges (Batson v. Kentucky, 1986). The judge disallowed two of these challenges, in essence finding that the government had impermissibly discriminated on the basis of race and/or gender. Someone on the prosecution team thought race and gender mattered, or the team would not have tried so hard to keep white women off the jury.

During rebuttal closing argument, prosecutor John Guy told jurors,

> Race. This case is not about race. It's about right and wrong. . . . Ask yourselves, all things being equal, if the roles were reversed and it was 28 year old George Zimmerman walking home in the rain with a hoodie on to protect himself from the rain, walking through that neighborhood, and a 17 year old driving around in a car who called the police . . .[a]nd if it was Trayvon Martin who had shot and killed George Zimmerman, what would your verdict be? That's how you know it is not about race. (CrimeTimeVids, 2013)

Guy may have hoped his remarks would prompt jurors to think about whether racial stereotypes about African Americans had biased their perceptions in this case, but he never explicitly asked them to race-switch. He did not ask them to imagine a Black man following and confronting a White teenager in a hoodie, and then shooting the

White teenager during a fistfight. Instead, Guy prefaced and concluded his remarks by telling jurors that the case was not about race, encouraging them to believe that race did not matter and that they should continue to view the case through colorblind eyes. Ultimately, not only did the government fail to secure a guilty verdict on second-degree murder, it failed to secure a conviction on the lesser offense of manslaughter.

I suggest that the prosecution should have acknowledged, rather than denied, the significance of race. Explaining how racial stereotypes may have influenced not only Zimmerman's perception that Martin was a suspicious character, but also the jurors' own perceptions regarding the reasonableness of Zimmerman's fear, might may have encouraged the jury to think about the case more critically. The problem is that the prosecution team thought being colorblind was the proper way to proceed.

Once a tenet of liberalism, the ideology of colorblindness has become a mantra embraced by liberals and conservatives alike. Conservatives, however, use colorblindness to argue for strict scrutiny of all racial classifications, including those that seek to address past discrimination. We are encouraged not only to be colorblind; we are discouraged from acknowledging racial difference. Under the new ideology of colorblindness, anyone who pays attention to race is a racist (Cho, 2009). The good person, according to colorblind ideology, is blind to racial difference (Gotanda, 1991).

The ideology of colorblindness fails to acknowledge the reality of racial difference in today's society. While we may aspire to live in a colorblind society, we are not yet there. Research on race and social cognition has demonstrated for decades that racial stereotypes affect our perceptions, often without our awareness or intent (Lawrence, 1987; Krieger, 1995).

One of the most entrenched stereotypes is the Black-as-Criminal stereotype, which links Blacks with violence, danger, and criminality (Lee, 1996, 2003). An early study by Duncan (1976) showed how this stereotype can influence perception. In this study, participants observed two men involved in a heated verbal altercation that ended when one man shoved the other man. When the person shoving was Black and the man being shoved was White, seventy-five percent of the participants thought the shove was "violent," while only six percent characterized it as "playing around." In contrast, when the person shoving was white and the man being shoved was Black, forty-two percent of the participants described the actions of the shover as "playing around" and only seventeen percent characterized the shove as "violent."

The 'Black-as-criminal' stereotype persists today (Lee, 2013). Many social science studies have demonstrated the tendency to associate Blacks with weapons. Payne (2001, 2006) found that individuals are quicker to detect guns in the hands of armed targets when primed with a Black face than with a white face (Payne, 2001, 2006). Correll et al. (2002) found that when shown pictures of Black and white men holding either a weapon or a harmless object, individuals will fire at armed Black targets more quickly than armed white targets. Individuals will also decide not to shoot an unarmed target more quickly if the target is white than if he is Black (Correll, et al., 2002).

One might wonder how all of this research relates to the Zimmerman trial. According to police reports, at the time Zimmerman shot Martin, he was on the ground face up with Martin on top of him (SDP Investigation Report 2013; SDP Offense Report, 2013, SDP Witness Statement, 2013). Zimmerman told police that that after he tried to return to his car, Martin circled back, confronted Zimmerman, and threw the first punch (Robles & Caputo, 2012). There was no evidence corroborating Zimmerman's account that Martin threw the first punch, but the judge permitted the defense to show the jury an animated version of the defense's version of the facts, depicting Martin throwing the first punch (Sterbenz, 2013). Zimmerman also told police that when he was on his back on the ground with Martin on top of him, Martin put his hand on Zimmerman's nose and mouth and screamed, "You're going to die tonight," leading Zimmerman to believe Martin intended to kill him (Lucas & Siemaszko, 2013). Zimmerman said he shot Martin because he thought Martin was reaching for his gun. One might legitimately question whether Martin's race really mattered if the reason Zimmerman shot Martin was because he thought Martin was reaching for his gun and was about to kill him.

If individuals are more likely to view a shove as dangerous and violent when a Black male is doing the shoving, but see the same shove as playing around when done by a white man, they may also be more likely to view punches as violent and life-threatening when the person doing the punching is a Black male and the one being punched is not Black, even if they might see the same scenario as merely a fist-fight if the person doing the punching was white (Lee, 2013). If individuals are quicker to link Blacks with weapons, they may be more likely to find credible a defendant's claim that he thought a Black man was reaching for his gun than if the same claim were made against a white man (Lee, 2013).

Kelman (1981) pointed out that legal decision makers have a great deal of discretion in deciding whether to broadly or narrowly frame the issues. According to Kelman, if a court sees the defendant as culpable, it may engage in broad time framing. In contrast, if the court favors the defendant, it may engage in narrow time framing. Kelman illustrated his theory with *State v. Decina* (1956), a classic case found in many criminal law textbooks involving a man who had an epileptic seizure at the wheel, causing the deaths of four schoolchildren. Even though Decina was not acting voluntarily during his seizure, and thus arguably the prosecution could not prove that he engaged in a voluntary act that caused the social harm, the court broadened the time frame in order to find a voluntary act. The court saw Decina's act of getting into the car and turning on the ignition as the voluntary act that satisfied the actus reus requirement (Kelman, 1981 p. 140). In contrast, Kelman noted that in *Martin v. State* (1944), a different court reversed the conviction of a man charged with being drunk on a public highway. The *Martin* court said that the defendant did not voluntarily appear drunk in public because the police carried him from his home into the street. Kelman pointed out that the *Martin* court favored the defendant by focusing narrowly on what took place immediately preceding the defendant's arrest, when the court could have broadened the time-frame and considered Martin's voluntary acts that caused the police to be called in the first place.

The jury in the Zimmerman case had the discretion to focus either narrowly or broadly on the events preceding the shooting. The defense focused the jury upon the events immediately preceding the shooting, favoring Zimmerman's claim of self-defense. Alternatively, the jury could have focused on Zimmerman's culpability in starting the conflict. The law of self-defense generally prohibits an "initial aggressor" from arguing self-defense (Burke, 2013; Ross, 2014; Mannheimer, 2012). Zimmerman was the one who started the encounter by following Martin and then confronting him, asking Martin to explain his presence in the neighborhood (CNN Library, 2013). Whether Zimmerman's acts were sufficient to make him the initial aggressor is another question, but the defense precluded the jury from considering this question by convincing the judge to refuse to issue a jury instruction on the initial aggressor rule (Burke, 2013; Ross, 2014).

It is difficult to assess whether a prosecution strategy that highlighted race would have changed the outcome. Recent empirical research, however, suggests that a race conscious trial strategy might have helped. This research shows that making race salient leads jurors to treat similarly situated defendants the same, whereas not making race salient results in unequal treatment. In several experiments, Sommers and Ellsworth (2000, 2001, 2003) found that when mock jurors were merely aware of the defendant's race, but race was not otherwise highlighted, they would convict Black defendants at much higher rates than similarly situated white defendants. When the possibility of disparate treatment based on race was highlighted, the mock jurors treated similarly situated white and Black defendants the same (Sommers & Ellsworth, 2000, 2001). This research on race salience indicates that highlighting the possibility of racially disparate treatment reminds individuals of their egalitarian commitments (Lee, 2013). If the Zimmerman jury had been given such a reminder, they might have been a little less likely to see the unarmed Martin as the aggressor and Zimmerman as a man who needed to shoot in order to defend his life.

REFERENCES

Barry, D. (2012, April 2). In the eye of the firestorm: In Florida, an intersection of tragedy, race and outrage. *The New York Times*, p. A1.

Batson v. Kentucky, 476 U.S. 79 (1986).

Burke, A. (2013, July 15). What you may not know about the Zimmerman verdict: The evolution of an instruction. *HuffPost: Black Voices*. Retrieved from http://www.huffingtonpost.com

Cho, S. (2009). Post-racialism. *Iowa Law Review, 94*, 1589–1649.

CNN Library. (2013, June 5). *Trayvon Martin fast facts*. Retrieved August 29, 2013, from http://www.cnn.com

Cooper, A. (Presenter). (2013, July 15). Anderson Cooper 360: Exclusive interview with Juror B-37; defense team reacts to juror interview [Television broadcast]. New York, NY: CNN.

Correll, J., Park B., Judd, C. M., & Wittenbrink, B. (2002). The police officer's dilemma: Using ethnicity to disambiguate potentially threatening individuals. *Journal of Personality and Social Psychology, 83*, 1314–1329.

CrimeTimeVids. (July 12, 2013). Trayvon Martin: George Zimmerman trial closing arguments day 14 part 3 [Video file]. Retrieved from http://www.youtube.com

Duncan, B. L. (1976). Differential social perception and attribution of intergroup violence: Testing the lower limit of stereotyping of blacks. *Journal of Personality and Social Psychology, 4*, 590–598.

Eberhardt, J. L., Goff, P. A., Purdie, V. J., & Davies, P. G. (2004). Seeing black: Race, crime, and visual processing. *Journal of Personality and Social Psychology, 87*, 876–893.

Ford, R. T. (2008). *The race card: How bluffing about bias makes race relations worse.* New York, NY: Picador.

Gotanda, N. (1991). A critique of "Our constitution is color-blind." *Stanford Law Review, 44*, 1–69.

Horwitz, S. (2012, April 12). Charge filed in martin killing. *The Washington Post,* p. A1.

Kelman, M. (1981). Interpretive construction in the substantive criminal law. *Stanford Law Review, 33*, 591–673.

Krieger, L. H. (1995). The content of our categories: A cognitive bias approach to discrimination and equal employment opportunity. *Stanford Law Review, 47*, 1161–1248.

Lawrence, C. R. (1987). The id, the ego, and equal protection: Reckoning with unconscious racism. *Stanford Law Review, 39*, 317–388.

Lawson, T. (2012). A Fresh cut in an old wound—A critical analysis of the Trayvon Martin killing: The public outcry, the prosecutor's discretion, and the stand your ground law. *Florida Journal of Law and Public Policy, 23*, 271–310.

Lee, C. (2003). *Murder and the reasonable man: Passion and fear in the criminal courtroom.* New York, NY: New York University Press.

Lee, C. (2013). Making race salient: Trayvon martin and implicit racial bias in a not yet post-racial society. *North Carolina Law Review, 91*, 1555–1612.

Lee, C. K. Y. (1996). Race and self-defense: Toward a normative conception of reasonableness. *Minnesota Law Review, 81*, 367–500.

LSUDVM. (2013, July 14). Angela Corey: Zimmerman trial was never about race or guns [Video file]. Retrieved from http://www.youtube.com

Lucas, L., & Siemaszko, C. (2013, July 1). Trayvon Martin shooting: George Zimmerman claims teen told him 'You're going to die tonight' and jumped him in police interviews. *New York Daily News.* Retrieved from http://www.nydailynews.com

Lucas, L., & Siemaszko, C. (2013, June 21). George Zimmerman's Trayvon Martin murder trial will not open with discussion of race. *New York Daily News.* Retrieved from http://www.nydailynews.com

Mannheimer, M. J. Z. (2012, March 26). Trayvon Martin and the initial aggressor issue. *PrawfsBlawg.* Retrieved from http://www.huffingtonpost.com

Martin v. State, 17 So.2d 427 (Ala. Ct. App. 1944).

Muskal, M. (2013, June 22). Judge in Zimmerman trial limits racial references. *Los Angeles Times,* p. A12.

Payne, B. K. (2001). Prejudice and perception: The role of automatic and controlled processes in misperceiving a weapon. *Journal of Personality and Social Psychology, 81*, 181–192.

Payne, B. K. (2006). Weapon bias: Split-second decisions and unintended stereotyping. *Current Directions in Psychological Science, 15*, 287–291.

Real Clear Politics. (July 14, 2013). Mark O'Mara: "If Zimmerman was black, he never would have been charged." Retrieved from http://www.realclearpolitics.com

Robles, F. & Caputo, M. (2012, June 21). Tapes show Sanford police grew skeptical of Zimmerman's story. *Miami Herald.* Retrieved from http://www.miamiherald.com

Roig-Franzia, M. (2013, July 3). Race is playing minor part in Zimmerman prosecution. *The Washington Post,* p. A1.

Ross, J. (2014). The supreme court's invisible hand in George Zimmerman's trial for the murder of Trayvon Martin (manuscript on file with author).

Sanford Police Department. (2012, February 26). Witness Statement [Police report]. Retrieved from http://www.scribd.com

Sanford Police Department. (2012, February 27). Offense Report [Police report]. Retrieved from http://www.scribd.com

Sanford Police Department. (2012, March 13). Report of Investigation [Police report].

Smerconish, M. (2013a, August 3). Did gender, not race, decide Zimmerman verdict? *Sun-Sentinel,* p. 21A.

Smerconish, M. (2013b, August 3). Zimmerman, race and the all-female jury strategy. *The Tampa Tribune,* p. 21.

Sommers, S. R., & Ellsworth, P. C. (2000). Race in the courtroom: Perceptions of guilt and dispositional attributions. *Personality and Social Psychology Bulletin, 26*, 1367–1379.

Sommers, S. R., & Ellsworth, P. C. (2001). White juror bias: An investigation of prejudice against Black defendants in the American courtroom. *Psychology, Public Policy, and Law, 7*, 201–229.

Sommers, S. R., & Ellsworth, P. C. (2003). How much do we really know about race and juries? A review of social science theory and research. *Chicago-Kent Law Review, 78*, 997–1031.

Sommers, S. R., & Ellsworth, P. C. (2009). "Race Salience" in juror decision-making: Misconceptions, clarifications, and unanswered questions *Behavioral Sciences & the Law, 27*, 599–609.

Speakmymind02. (2013, July 16). Robert Zimmerman race profiteers [Video file]. Retrieved from http://www.youtube.com

State v. Decina, 2 N.Y.2d 133 (1956).

Sterbenz, C. (2013, July 12). Zimmerman defense shows jury controversial 'avatar'-like animation. *Business Insider*. Retrieved from http://www.businessinsider.com

Van Susteren, G. [Presenter] (2013, July 16). Zimmerman brother: Case fit the business model of the "Race Profiteers" [Video file]. New York, NY: Fox News. Retrieved from http://nation.foxnews.com

Wiggins, O. (2012a, March 25). A rallying cry for justice in teen's death. *The Washington Post*, p. A3.

Wiggins, O. (2012b, April 1). NAACP leads march on Sanford. *The Washington Post*, p. A3.

Winter, T., Novogrod, J., & Arkin, D. (2013, October 19). Zimmerman will likely get his gun back, if he requests it. *NBC News*. Retrieved from http://usnews.nbcnews.com

KAY S. VARELA & WENDY LEO MOORE

7. "HE LOOKS LIKE HE'S UP TO NO GOOD"

White Space, Constructions of Safety, and the Killing of Trayvon Martin

On February 26, 2012, in Sanford, Florida a self-proclaimed neighborhood watchman George Zimmerman called 911 after seeing a young Black man walking through a predominantly white, gated community. Zimmerman told the dispatcher, "There's a real suspicious guy here... This guy looks like he's up to no good..."Moments later, Zimmerman chased Trayvon Martin and when a struggle ensued, Zimmerman shot and killed Martin. It was clear to many commentators at the time that what made Martin appear to be "up to no good" was the fact that he was an young African American man, his Blackness all the more relevant because he was in a demographically white neighborhood.

Racialized constructions of safety and space are the dominant paradigm through which crime is viewed and the hyper-vigilant surveillance of people of color legitimized. We argue that depictions of white communities as pure, homogenous, and calm spaces permit and facilitate whites' tendency to link danger and violence to people of color, not only reinforcing existing stereotypes associating people of color with danger and constructing Black and Latino neighborhoods as unsafe, but also harking back to a history when white space was violently protected and its isolation legally sanctioned. Analyzing newspaper coverage from the Martin case, we illuminate how *racialized* constructions of safety are deployed and how they function to legitimize residential segregation as a form of white power and justify surveillance, policing, and even violence against people of color—particularly African American men and boys.

RACIALIZED NEIGHBORHOODS & CONSTRUCTIONS OF CRIME FEAR

Empirical evidence suggests that inner city residents have higher levels of fear of crime than those who live in suburbs, small towns, or rural areas (Van der Wurff & Stringer, 1988; Valentine, 1990; Pain, 1997). In explaining this spatial fear of crime, researchers have argued that the visibility of physical and social decay can explain fear of crime in inner-city neighborhoods. Generally referred to as the "broken windows" argument, researchers assert that "incivilities" are often interpreted as cues of dangerous situations, resulting in higher levels of fear of crime. Respondents often cite graffiti, teenagers on street corners, drunks, trash, noisy neighbors, loud parties, and abandoned houses and buildings as indicators that the neighborhood

K.J. Fasching-Varner et al. (Eds.), Trayvon Martin, Race, and American Justice, 39–44.

is in decline and thus unpredictable (Stinchcombe et al. 1980; Skogan & Maxfield 1981; Wilson & Kelling 1982). As a result crime becomes an ordinary component of modern life within these neighborhoods, rather than being something unusual or out of the ordinary (Brown 1995; Garland 1996; Beck 1992).

As such, it makes sense that residents of inner city communities that are predominantly Black and Brown would experience a greater *fear* of crime in their daily lives. Although scant attention has been paid in the literature to the racial dynamics of the fear of crime, several researchers suggest that because people of color are more likely to live in urban environments, they are also at greater risk of becoming victims, thus explaining greater levels of fear (Massey & Denton, 1993). This argument, however, suggests that high levels of crime and incivilities go hand-in-hand with racially segregated and poverty-stricken inner city residence (Mayhew 1989; Belyea & Zingraff, 1988). Criminologists suggest that this is not necessarily the case, but rather that it is the kinds of crimes that occur in inner-city neighborhoods that tend to be more visible than the kinds of crime that take place in predominantly white middle and upper class neighborhoods (Tonry, 2010).

Looking beyond literature on neighborhood and safety, we find additional racialized factors that help elaborate the connection between race, residential location, and feelings of safety. A large body of research indicates that particular social identifiers, including skin color and phenotype, are linked to attitudes about criminal behavior and fear of crime (Taub et al., 1984; Smith, 1986; Chiricos et al., 1997; Smith, 1984). As early as 1947, social psychological experiments revealed that images of African American men invoke a stereotypical fear of crime. This early research has developed into a vast literature highlighting the criminal-Black-man as a dominant stereotype that evokes fear among both whites and people of color. (Allport, 1947; see also Duncan, 1976; Bowes et al., 1990; Walker, 1994; Hough, 1995; Greenwald, Oaks & Hoffman 2003; Blair, Judd & Fallman, 2004; Eberhart, et. al., 2004; Dixon & Maddox, 2005). Moreover, as Pain (2000) suggested, fear, at the neighborhood level, is situated and depends on a specific set of social relations, particularly those of race, age, or class. "Situatedness of fear," she contended, impacts people's sense of community and security because "being local" and being labeled "outside" a certain community impacts individual levels of fear of crime. In this sense, fear can be understood as being focused on strangers entering a given community, often resulting in privatized, protected and defensive communities who aim to keep outsiders out (Pain, 2000; Taylor, 1995, 1996).

DEFENDING WHITE SPACE, MANUFACTURING FEAR OF THE BLACK CRIMINAL

The United States is among the most residentially racially segregated societies in the world (Massey & Denton, 1993). Before the Civil Rights Movement, this residential segregation was enforced through both legal and extra–legal means, specifically white violence targeted at African Americans. In the post-civil rights era, some people of color have experienced the upward mobility that has given them access to neighborhoods that were previously exclusively white, and the legal means of excluding African Americans from white neighborhoods has been limited. This encroachment on white space has led to a wide range of reactions from people in those communities—a racialized narrative about outsider status and fear of criminality has become a central discursive mechanism of maintaining the boundaries of white space.

The maintenance of white geographical space connects directly to the reproduction of white domination in the post-civil rights era. As Moore (2008) noted,

[r]esidential segregation enacts or enlarges many material privileges of economic opportunity, quality of life, power to influence actions and events, and convenience. At the same time, it obscures the fact of such privileges from many of their beneficiaries (p. 24).

Lipsitz (2011) likewise suggested that racially exclusive spaces create the conditions of the logic of the white spatial imaginary to be constructed, producing "hostile privatism" and "defensive localism," further allowing the continued salience of racialized space (p. 13). Behind the guise of protecting neighborhood profitability and promoting security, Lipsitz (2011) argued that the white spatial imaginary continues to create "unjust geographies of opportunity" (p. 28).

Central components of unjust geographies of opportunity connect to the ways in which safety is constructed and how racialized notions of safety are deployed to symbolically patrol the boundaries of white space. Feelings of safety, as Huey (2012) noted, require both a feeling of relative security and an absence of concern about future threats to one's physical person and one's belongings (p. 11). As such, the white imaginary constructs white neighborhoods as pure, crime-free spaces, emotionally signifying safety and security. In contrast, African Americans neighborhoods are constructed as beds of insecurity and crime, connecting these neighborhoods, as well as the *people* who live there, with the *unsafe*. Such constructions reify the trope of Black largely male criminality and potential threat to the security of white space. In this way, the construction of safety becomes a racialized privilege, which whites are willing to defend even through violent means.

WHITE SAFETY CONNECTS TO BLACK INSECURITY

By examining the discourse surrounding safety and race in the Martin case, we illustrate how safety functions as a form of white privilege. Our analysis examined 245 newspaper stories collected from newspaper outlets from all over the U.S., from March 2012, the month after Martin was murdered, to September 2013, two months following the not-guilty verdict given to Zimmerman. Expressions found in newspaper reports tend to reinforce the pathologization of communities of color and purity of white communities. Moreover, while whites construct the killing of Martin as a symbol of how the safety of white space requires defense, African Americans view his killing and Zimmerman's acquittal as indicative of their insecurity and vulnerability to white violence.

Even before Zimmerman's acquittal was handed down, Black men, and by extension Black families, expressed feelings of concern about crime in African American communities. For example, one African American man said,

> We all get upset by (the case of) Trayvon Martin, and we should…but 93% - 93%! - Of Black other Black men kill men who die of homicide. We desperately need concern over Black-on-Black crime. Many in the Black community equated Blackness with vulnerability, not only to criminal victimization but also to victimization from authority figures including police, city officials, and school authority figures. (Barnes, 2013)

As one African American man said,

> We live in a culture that far too often assumes that bad behavior is an inherent attribute of young Black youth. And that assumption plays out in the policies that encourage communities to perceive Black and brown children to as threats. (Mustafaa, 2013, p. 6)

The comments of African Americans concerning the safety of their neighborhoods, and the vulnerability of African Americans, especially boys and men, were nuanced because individuals recognized criminality in the Black community and the need to improve security in those communities. They also understood, however, the problematic constructions of criminality being equated with Blackness resulting from white stereotypes.

Following the verdict, many Black parents spoke of having to give their Black sons "the talk." Ultimately consisting of behavior modification instructions, Black parents spoke of feeling frustration in having to outline for their sons a code of conduct that could prevent them from being interpreted as "dangerous" or as a "threat" when confronted by police or others. One African American news commentator said:

> I've written about the list 'don't' my mother gave me when I was just a year younger than Trayvon. 'Don't run in public.' Lest someone think you're suspicious. 'Don't run while carrying anything in your hands.' Lest someone think you stole something. 'Don't talk back to the police.' Least you give them a reason to take you to jail or worse. Because of assumptions and suspicions, Black kids have to be 'perfect' in how they dress and how they comport themselves in public.... What this means is that Black adolescents cannot afford to be normal American teenagers. (Capehart, 2013, p. 2)

By contrast, the public narratives of whites concerning the killing of Trayvon Martin often ignored the vulnerability of African Americans, reifying the trope of the criminal-Black-man, and ultimately suggesting that the preservation of white safety legitimated the killing of Martin. For example, one white interviewee commented:

> African American young men are disproportionately criminals… It is a tragic burden that young-law abiding African American males are viewed suspiciously

because of the disproportionate bad behavior of others who resemble them. But it also was a burden for law-abiding merchants in gang-plagued neighborhoods who are forced to close their shops at night. (Landsbaum, 2013, p. 2)

The framing of safe and unsafe spaces, as such, serves a meaning-making function. It is through the construction and labeling of safe and dangerous places that racialized construction of safety as a discursive frame protects the ability of whites to portray their neighborhoods as relatively safe from violent crime, thus justifying their suspicions of Black outsiders as potential threats to their own safety. Within this context, safety is not generally understood as an element of systemic racism but is instead discursively created by incorporating racialized images of criminality. These images allow for mistaken assumptions that disconnect the white normative aspects of the safety discursive frame from the material realities from which it results.

The killing of Martin reveals that the outcome of the discursive framing of safety and the need to protect white safety from dangerous racialized outsiders is nothing less than a life-or-death issue. And as one Black woman who was interviewed at a protest after the Zimmerman verdict noted:

Every person deserves a safe walk home…. I'm here because our children can't even walk on the streets without fearing for their lives. (Barrow, 2013, p. 2)

REFERENCES

Barnes, S. (2013, July 18). Dialogue about race. *Pine Bluff Commercial Newspaper (Arkansas)*.

Barrow, B. (2013, July 21). Rallies across country press 'Justice for Trayvon'. *Sunday Gazette Mail*. Retrieved from http://www.gazettenet.com

Beck, U. (1992). *The risk society*. London, UK: Sage.

Belyea, M. J., & Zingraff, M. T. (1988). Fear of crime and residential location. *Rural Sociology, 53*(4), 473–486.

Brown, S. (1995). Crime and safety in whose 'community'?: Age, everyday life, and problems for youth policy. *Youth and Policy, 48,* 27–48.

Burt, M. R., & Katz, B. L. (1985). Rape, robbery, and burglary: Responses to actual and feared criminal victimization, with special focus on women and the elderly. *Victimology, 10*(1), 325–358.

Capehart, J. (2013, July 13). Trayvon Martin and the stolen youth of Black children. *Washington Post*. Retrieved from http://www.washingtonpost.com

Chiricos, T., Hogan, M., & Gertz, M. (1997). Racial composition of neighborhood and fear of crime. *Criminology 35*(1), 107–131.

Garland, D. (1996). The limits of the sovereign state: Strategies of crime control in contemporary society. *British Journal of Criminology, 36*(4), 445–471.

Huey, L. (2012). *Invisible victims: Homelessness and the growing security gap*. Toronto, CA: University of Toronto.

Landsbaum, M. (2013, July 27). Risk avoidance reveals prudence, not racism. *Orange County Register*. Retrieved from http://www.ocregister.com

Lipsitz, G. (2011). *How racism takes place*. Philadelphia, PA: Temple University Press.

Massey, D. S., & Denton, N. A. (1993). *American apartheid: Segregation and the making of the underclass*. Cambridge, MA: Harvard University Press.

Mayhew, P., Elliott, D., & Dowds, L. (1989). *The 1988 British crime survey*, Home Office Research Study 111. London, England: HMSO.

Moore, W. L. (2008). *Reproducing racism: White space, elite law schools and racial inequality*. Lanham, MD: Rowman & Littlefield.

Mustafaa, A. K. (2013, July 18). In the aftermath of Trayvon's murder, Zimmerman's acquittal. *The Mississippi Link*. Retrieved from http://www.themississippilink.com

O'Neil, T. (2013, July 13). Rally in St. Louis one of many protesting Zimmerman verdict. *McClatchy-Tribune Business News*. Retrieved from http://www.mcclatchy.com

Pain, R. (1997). Social geographies of women's fear of crime. *Transactions, Institute of British Geographers, 22*(2), 231–244.

Pain, R. (2000). Place, social relations and the fear of crime: A review. *Progress in Human Geography, 24*(3), 365–387.

Smith, S. J. (1986). *Crime, space and society*. Cambridge, London: Cambridge University Press.

Smith, S. J. (1987). Fear of crime: Beyond a geography of deviance. *Progress in Human Geography, 11*(1), 1–23.

Stinchcombe, L. A., Adams, R., Heimer, C. A., Scheppele, K. L., Smith, W. T., & Taylor, D. G. (1980). *Crime and punishment: Changing attitudes in America*. San Francisco, CA: Jossey-Bass.

Taub, R. P., Taylor, D. G., & Dunham, J. D. (1984). *Paths of neighborhood change*. Chicago, IL: University of Chicago Press.

Taylor, I. (1995). Private homes and public others: An analysis of talk about crime in suburban south Manchester in the mid-1990s. *British Journal of Criminology, 35*(2), 263–285.

Taylor, I. (1996). Fear of crime, urban fortunes and suburban social movements: Some reflections from Manchester. *Sociology, 30*(2), 317–337.

Transcript of George Zimmerman's call to the police. (n.d.). In *Document Cloud*. Retrieved from http://www.documentcloud.org

Valentine, G. (1990). Women's fear and the design of public space. *Built Environment, 16*(4), 288–303.

van der Wurff, A., & Stringer, P. (1988). Measuring fear of crime in residential environments. *Environmental Social Psychology, 35*, 135–148.

Wilson, J. Q., & Kelling, G. L. (1982, March). Broken windows. *Atlantic Monthly*. Retrieved from http://www.theatlantic.com

SECTION 2

DECONSTRUCTING IGNORANCE:
REACTIONS AND RESPONSES TO RACISM

RASHAAD THOMAS

"I AM NOT A DOG!"

A brown dog with Black patches scurries through an early cloudy morning while expensive cars adorned with flashy German symbols question its presence. As an eyewitness of what might occur, images of Black men's faces like Trayvon Martin and Oscar Grant III reflect of windshields. I am unable to move my legs. I am riddled with an inner compound fracture torn by Black man's guilt and self-preservation. The sound of car tires grabbing the pavement suggests that I should mind my position in society as a bystander. Even though society continues to tell me that I am a dog or less, I affirm aloud, "I am not a dog. I do not have fleas. I do not scratch or lick myself. I do not walk on all fours. You cannot simply let me loose in the street to grace yourself with the choice to run me over in broad daylight to end my struggle or bless society with one less dog." I continue to watch as my heart beats in unison with the hammering of underground-railroad spikes into the ground. I am unmoved.

I am a Black man, not a Black dog. At times I think Black men are confused with my identity. Black men bark at me, "What up dog?" and "My dog!", all while pawing five with elated salivation dribbling from the corners of their mouth signaling they're happy to see me. I paw back to play the part, but I can't help but think, "I am happy he didn't dribble urine on my shoes." For we all know how the Black man's talent to dribble rhythmic slang, basketballs and catch footballs and baseballs fascinates us. But, some Black men don't run to sign multimillion-dollar contracts for the sake of their passion, but to fulfill their fate of being a runaway slave from the ghetto. But, when a Black man understands he is no one's dog the corporate massa' puts out an APB to the ASPCA to capture his fugitive dog to throw him back into the kennel, either to die by the hands of God or the captured.

I cannot scratch at the surface any more than I have. I have scratched so hard my skin displays scars of self hate. My desire to drink and eat from bowls on the floor has evaporated. I used to dribble basketball dreams from the corners of my mouth, but I realized for change I needed to learn how to dribble words like knowledge and education so to no longer play the part. My body and spirit sit alone in the middle of the road where the sun and clouds fight for territory. I am a Black man trying to find my light in the dawn of white man's world. It's an internal struggle that forces Black men to either play the part or break free of the historical arrest of stereotypes, left roaming the streets while Black people watch, and white people choose to put me out of my misery.

K.J. Fasching-Varner et al. (Eds.), Trayvon Martin, Race, and American Justice, 47.
© 2014 Sense Publishers. All rights reserved.

8. THE ADULTIFICATION OF BLACK BOYS

What Educational Settings Can Learn from Trayvon Martin

In his groundbreaking book *The Souls of Black Folk* (1903), W.E.B. DuBois, asked a rhetorical question that seems as relevant as ever today: How does it feel to be a problem? To be sure, there is a profound difference between *having* a problem and *being* a problem. While all may have problems, Black male existence itself is a problem within a white gaze (DuBois, 1903). DuBois' ominous question captures the kind of brutal way in which American institutions view and contain Black male bodies post-enslavement. One reason that Trayvon Martin's tragic death resonates so powerfully with millions of people of color, Black and Brown men in particular, is that it embeds our social consciousness with the sober reality that America is not the post-racial, colorblind society many claim. In a rare moment, pathological thinking about Black males as perpetual problems was exposed by the slain body of a young teenager who was on the phone with a girl, yet was viewed for no logical reason as scary, out of place, on drugs, and in need of policing and confrontation.

In a number of press conferences and interviews, Sybrina Fulton reminded the public that Martin was a child -- a boy and not a man (Joseph & Somaiya, 2013). While policy definitions of persons as children or adults appear relatively uncontroversial in the public, Martin's 17-year-old body seemed an exception. Many in the courts and media who thought Martin's murder was justified also carefully ignored or summarily dismissed any construction of him as a child, reaching rather for labels like "suspect, "thug", "punk", or "asshole" [in the words of assailant George Zimmerman] (Pitts, 2013). Some pundits actually sought to debate Martin's age beyond the birth certificate's identification of him as a child in efforts to consign Martin to adulthood (Pitts, 2013). Adultification, or institutional perceptions and engagement of Black boys as adults, troubles Black male lives in society and educational settings (Ferguson, 2000; Kunjufu, 1986). The dominating and pervasive images of Black men as endangered species and criminals work to deny Black boys any access to childhood humanity. Educational settings are rich contexts to explore ways this phenomenon is institutionalized, particularly around data related to school discipline and achievement (Dancy, 2012).

It is well established in the literature that Black males remain one of the most socially and academically marginalized student groups in U.S. schools (Brown, Dancy & Davis, 2013; Dancy & Brown, 2012; Ferguson, 2003; Howard, 2013;

K.J. Fasching-Varner et al. (Eds.), Trayvon Martin, Race, and American Justice, 49–55.
© *2014 Sense Publishers. All rights reserved.*

Lewis & Erskine, 2008; Noguera, 2008; Polite & Davis; 1999). Characterizing this marginalization are differential achievement rates and school completion, curricular inequities, over-expulsions and suspensions, overrepresentations in special, general, and vocational education, and underrepresentation in rigorous or gifted and talented courses (Garibaldi, 1992; Hrabowski, Maton, & Greif, 1998; Noguera, 2003; Ross, 2012). While the plight of Black males in schools is well documented, there has been little change in policy or practice and little learning from this student group that is not associated with negative indicators (Garibaldi, 1992; Price, 2000).

Black males are disproportionately born into lives of challenge, suffering disproportionately high infant mortality rates, reared in chronic and abject poverty, and overrepresented in underfunded schools, revealing unique and harmful effects even unto adulthood (Anderson, 2008; Dancy, 2012; Howard, 2013). Black males, for instance, have chronically high unemployment, are over-incarcerated, have disparate health conditions, and ultimately lower life expectations than any of the largest racial/ethnic and gender groups in the United States (Alexander, 2012; Howard, 2013; U.S. Department of Commerce, 2007). Black males also occupy a paradox in the psyche of the United States that plays out in school and society – both admired and despised (Dancy & Brown, 2012; Davis, 1994; Davis, 2001). Pedestrian praise of Black male heroics in peer, athletic, and entertainment circles manages coexistence with labels as problems, violent, scary, and hypersexual, with modern-day police and neighborhood lynchings of unarmed Black males. Ladson-Billings (2011) observed:

> We see Black males as "problems" that our society must find ways to eradicate. We regularly determine them to be the root cause of most problems in school and society. We seem to hate their dress, their language, and their effect. We hate that they challenge authority and command so much social power. While the society apparently loves them in narrow niches and specific slots—music, basketball, football, track—we seem less comfortable with them in places like the national Honor Society, the debate team, or the computer club. (p. 9)

While awareness of the issues confronting Black males has increased, public and school failures to institutionalize supports persist. In this chapter I briefly review the troublesome perceptions of Black boys and men that infect settings in which Black males are educated. In particular, I pay attention to the ways Black American boys were scripted out of childhood humanity. Finally I close with discussion and implications for education and society.

SCRIPTED OUT OF CHILDHOOD:
PUBLIC PERCEPTIONS OF BLACK BOYS AND MEN

For decades, American social institutions have been infected with a mind-set that views Black boys and men in particular as a problem to be dealt with, managed, and controlled (Dancy, 2012). As hooks (2004) noted American culture does not love

Black males and attempts to carefully teach Black males not to love them. Major universities never can 'find' Black male students, administrators, and faculty who 'merit' admission or hire, but their ability to find Black males for major football and basketball programs fulfills tropes of Black males bodies as economic commodities (Dancy, 2010; 2012). Historically, Black men have endeavored to counter the oppressive stereotypes that proclaim them as all body and no mind, bucks and beasts, monsters and demons. However, nonviolent Black males continue to face a world that sees them as violent. Black men who are not sexual harassers or rapists confront a public that relates to them as though this is who they are underneath their skin, whether sagging their pants or wearing a suit. Morrison framed the root of this illogic in *Beloved* (1987):

> White people believed that whatever the manners, under every dark skin was a jungle. Swift, unnavigable waters, swinging screaming baboons, sleeping snakes, red gums ready for their sweet white blood…The more colored people spent their strength trying to convince [whites] how gentle they were, how clever and loving, how human, the more they used themselves up to persuade whites of something Negroes believe could not be questioned… (p. 41)

Contemporary understandings of Black bodies as inherently violent and less human play out in disparate ways for people of color vis-à-vis whites. Millions of people of color are stopped, interrogated and frisked as they are walking to school, driving to church, or heading home from the store. In 2011, the New York City police department alone stopped and frisked more than 600,000 people, the overwhelming majority Black and Brown men and innocent of any crime. Their mere existence was cause for concern, just as the sight of Martin walking leisurely through his own neighborhood was all Zimmerman needed to call the police.

Alexander (2011) showed that, in the New Jim Crow, people of color are no more likely to use or sell illegal drugs than whites, yet Black people, particularly men, have been arrested and incarcerated at grossly disproportionate rates during the 40-year-old 'war on drugs.' Another way the New Jim Crow works is to justify racially biased practices and mass incarceration with the argument that Black men commit violent crimes in Black communities and thus must be contained. Alexander argued that the problem with leaving the analysis there is that violent crime is not responsible for mass incarceration despite the media's portrayal. Violent crime rates have fluctuated over the years and bear little relationship to incarceration rates. In other words, while violent crime rates are actually at historically low levels, incarceration rates continue to climb. Meanwhile, the nation witnesses a prison-building boom unprecedented in world history.

Martin's murder illustrates how the tools society uses to manage and control Black men are visited upon Black boys. According to media reports and essays, Zimmerman's defense attorneys appeared successful in erasing any jury considerations of Martin as a child, including intuitive assumptions that childhood invokes in American culture (Ford, 2013). Juror B37's casual observations that

Martin caused his own death and was unjustified in defending himself fall outside of how America thinks about childhood, and counters the common advice public officials, educators, and parents give to children about how to react when assailed by strangers (Wikihow, 2013). The public cheers when children in movies hit, kick, and punch or otherwise mount attacks in self-defense. And the public mourns and presses for retribution even if children's actions result in their deaths or severe injuries (Ladson-Billings, 2011). However, Martin's ex-communication from this narrative of childhood responds to historical tropes about Black men.

In American culture, childhood is contrived innocence, a projection of invented pristine moments outside of the cruelties of life (Ladson-Billings, 2011). The structural classifications that persons 0-18 legally are children also respond to the modern K-12 education lifecycle as well as biological growth cycles (Aries, 1962). With the last century's proscriptions of child labor and the rise of the middle class, social understanding of childhood as "blissful innocence" has largely freed children from the public expectations of economic productivity. This classed construction, though, was not intended for the poor and certainly not people of color (Ladson-Billings, 2011). Black children in the United States historically never had a separate status from their mothers, units of an enslaver's chattel from whom wealth was extracted through the sale of bodies or abusing labor on the plantation. Black boys were fully exploitable men in little bodies (Dancy & Brown, 2013). Following the liberation of the enslaved, white supremacy fashioned a concept of both Black men and boys as menaces to society, creating a new way of knowing bodies that were no longer controllable assets (Dancy, 2012). Perhaps the most accessible example is the brutal lynching of 14-year-old Emmett Till for allegedly whistling at a white woman. Sadly, society today continues the work of organizing Black boys around this familiar circumstance with the recent death of Martin, and schools in various ways act as accomplices in preparing Black boys for containment and/or other harsh life outcomes.

WHAT DO WE TELL BLACK BOYS AND SCHOOLS?

The abovementioned realities intend deleterious life outcomes for Black males. The research and scholarship on Black boys in schools shows how it is possible for Martin, an unarmed Black male child, to be profiled, stalked, killed via shot through the heart, vilified by the criminal justice system as the victimizer, and put on trial for his own murder. Public reactions to trends and outcomes in this chapter, unfortunately, often indict Black males as creators of their own problems as opposed to the incapacities of schools (Howard, 2013; Schott Foundation 50 State Report on Public Education and Black Males, 2012). These reactions tend to reflect the narrow-minded and hidebound tenets of racism in public determination to ignore the histories of violent discrimination and uncritically construct America as post-racial. Racism refers to the global system of oppression that disempowers people based on skin-color and/or assumptions that people of particular races hold undesirable qualities (Omi & Winant, 1989). The extant research on Black male experiences and the educational pipeline requires common thought and consideration among all educational personnel—in schools, colleges, and other settings—who care about the educational experiences of Black males.

Many strategies capture the attention of school administrators, local communities, and parents as possible solutions to the problems associated with Black males in public schools. First, mentoring programs that assign professional Black men as role models for young boys, typically in elementary and middle schools, have been established in many urban and suburban school districts. Second, teachers play a critical role in reversing Black boys' academic and social behaviors that conflict with educational achievement. Teachers are leaders of the classroom experience. The messages teachers consciously or subconsciously give to Black males will manifest themselves in Black male's perceptions of schools and American society. Counselors also must refrain from stereotypical thinking about the intellectual capacity and aptitude of Black males.

This chapter encourages educational institutions to mine the sources for improving context and climate. School efforts to deconstruct oppressive environments are salient for Black male achievement, retention, and the elimination of stereotypes. Stereotypes attempting to "authentically" locate Black male identities have no place in school settings and only fuel divisiveness among its stakeholders. Black boys deserve the same and equal opportunities as any student group, to feel entitled to institutional resources deemed 'good institutional practices.' The delivery of these resources should not reflect a colonized institutional axiology of intolerance, closeness, and presumptuousness. 'What works' for general students' general educational best is in many ways incompatible with 'what works' for many Black males. It may be a burden for education workers to add to and constantly rethink how they deliver education to Black males, however, the implications in this chapter are likely relevant across student groups. A turbulent history of exclusion, a changing national populace, and a federal policy landscape demand change and accountability. While this work is required at institutional levels, we must also decide what to tell Black males in our daily interactions with them.

We must support critical consciousness among Black males and communities. They have a will to learn and we must reclaim a will to teach. We must tell Black boys that the fact that some Blacks have experienced great success in recent years does not mean that unjust race systems do not exist. No social system in the United States has ever governed all Black people; there have always been "free Blacks" and Black success stories, even during the enslavement and Jim Crow. White economic and lustful appreciation of Black male displays of masculinity and physical excellence co-exist with an understanding of the acquittal of Zimmerman as just. This is a way that the schizophrenia of racism works. Black males must face that, unless social justice works to dismantle white supremacy, nothing Black males achieve will allow them to escape the imposition of racial stereotypes.

Paying attention to critical consciousness development endeavors to bring Black boys to the reconciliation that Martin's story teaches—namely, that Black suffering is irrelevant even unto death. In the aftermath of Martin's murder, a jury of (white) mothers could not empathize with a Black boy's suffering because, as discussed earlier, Black boys are always victimizers, always a problem. Instead, the jury thought they needed to protect Zimmerman, who, though Latino, became an honorary white person through his racial profiling of a Black male body and the words of white family members and peer groups who carefully vouched for Zimmerman's whiteness. Black boys can actually use examples where white people have felt threatened and/or vulnerable to learn about Black suffering. Black boys must understand that a white supremacist America views Black bodies as disposable and, if Black boys are to feel safer and liberated from this evil, America has to undergo a paradigm shift that defines itself beyond white humanity.

The work of civil rights movements is not over and is a critical educational outcome. A citizenry's responsibility is to push people in positions of power and to resist unjust political calculus. Lovers of justice must join efforts to organize against the racist powers that threaten Black male lives in education and society. Particularly inspirational is the work of the Dream Defenders and The Million Hoodies Movement, youth movements organizing to respond to social injustice. In addition, the Rainbow Push coalition is organizing marches for jobs and justice and National Association for the Advancement of Colored People (NAACP) petitions require signatures to push social policy and practice in ways that matter. We must support these efforts or start our own; conversations, while vital, are not substitutes for legislation.

REFERENCES

Alexander, M. (2012). *The new Jim Crow: Mass incarceration in the age of colorblindness*. New York, NY: The New Press.
Anderson, J. (2008). *Against the wall: Poor, young, black, and male*. Philadelphia, PA: University of Pennsylvania Press.
Aries, P. (1962). *Centuries of childhood*. New York, NY: Vintage Books.
Brown, M. C., Dancy, T. E., & Davis, J. E. (2013). *Educating African American males: Contexts for consideration, possibilities for practice*. New York, NY: Peter Lang.
Corbin, S. K., & Pruitt, R. L. (1999). Who am I? The development of the African American male identity. In V. Polite & J. E. Davis (Eds.), *African American males in school and society: Practices and policies for effective education* (pp. 68–81). New York, NY: Teachers College Press.
Dancy, T. E. (2012). *The brother code: Manhood and masculinity among African American males in college*. Charlotte, NC: Information Age Publishing.
Dancy, T. E. (2010). *Managing diversity: (Re)visioning equity on college campuses*. New York, NY: Peter Lang.
Dancy, T. E., & Brown, M. C. (2012). *African American males and education: Researching the convergence of race and identity*. Charlotte, NC: Information Age Publishing.
Davis, J. E. (1994). College in Black and White: The academic experiences of African American males. *Journal of Negro Education, 63*(4), 620–633.
Davis, J. E. (2001). Black boys in school: Negotiating masculinities and race. In R. Majors (Ed.), *Educating our Black children: New directions and radical approaches* (pp. 169–182). New York, NY: Routledge Falmer.
DuBois, W. E. B. (1903). *The souls of Black folk*. Chicago, IL: A. C. McClurg.

Ferguson, A. A. (2003). *Bad boys: Public schools in the making of Black masculinity*. Ann Arbor, MI: University of Michigan Press.

Ford, D. (2013). George Zimmerman was "justified" in shooting Trayvon Martin, juror says. *CNN U.S.* Retrieved from http://www.cnn.com

Garibaldi, A. (1992). Educating and motivating African American males to succeed. *Journal of Negro Education, 61*(1), 4–11.

hooks, b. (2004a). *The will to change: Men, masculinity, and love*. New York, NY: Atria Books.

hooks, b. (2004b). *We real cool: Black men and masculinity*. New York, NY: Routledge.

Howard, T. C. (2013). How does it feel to be a problem? Black male students, schools, and learning in enhancing the knowledge base to disrupt deficit frameworks. *Review of Research in Education, 37,* 54–86.

Howard, T. C. (2010). *Why race and culture matters in schools: Closing the achievement gap in America's classrooms*. New York, NY: Teachers College Press.

Hrabowski, F. A., III, Maton, K. L., & Grief, G. L. (1998). *Beating the odds: Raising academically successful African American males*. New York, NY: Oxford University Press.

Joseph, C., & Somaiya, R. (2013). Demonstrations across the country commemorate Trayvon Martin. *The New York Times*. Retrieved from http://www.nytimes.com

Kunjufu, J. (1986). *Countering the conspiracy to destroy Black boys*. Chicago, IL: Afro American Publishing.

Ladson-Billings, G. (2011). Boyz to men?: Teaching to restore Black boys' childhood. *Race, Ethnicity, and Education, 14,* 7–15.

Lewis, C. W., & Erskine, K. F. (2008). *The dilemmas of being an African American male in the new millennium: Solutions for life transformation*. West Conshocken, PA: Infinity Publishing.

Morrison, T. (1987). *Beloved*. New York, NY: Vintage Books.

Noguera, P. (2003). *The trouble with black boys and other reflections on race, equity, and the future of public education*. San Francisco, CA: Wiley & Sons.

Omi, M., & Winant, H. (1989). *Racial formation in the United States: From the 1960s to the 1980s*. New York, NY: Routledge.

Pitts, L., Jr. (2013). Trayvon Martin or George Zimmerman—Who's the real thug? *Bradenton Herald*. Retrieved from http://www.bradenton.com

Polite, V. C., & Davis, J. E. (1999). *African American males in school and society: Practices and policies for effective education*. New York, NY: Teachers College Press.

Price, J. N. (2000). *Against the odds: The meaning of school and relationships in the lives of six African American men*. Greenwich, CT: Ablex.

Ross, R. E. (2012). *A counter to the proposed crisis: Exploring the experiences of successful African American males* (Doctoral dissertation, University of Colorado).

U.S. Department of Commerce, Census Bureau, American Community Survey, 2007. Bureau of Justice Statistics, Prison inmates at Midyear, Current Population Survey. 2009.

Wikihow. (2013). *How to defend yourself if attacked*. Retrieved from http://www.wikihow.com

Wright, R. (1945/2005). *Black boy*. New York, NY: HarperCollins.

DANIEL S. HARAWA

9. THE BLACK MALE

A Dangerous Double-Minority

In the summer of 1955, Emmett Till, was murdered after reportedly flirting with a white woman. In the winter of 2012, Trayvon Martin was murdered after being labeled a "punk" by a vigilante neighborhood watchman. Many, including Martin's mother, have drawn comparisons between the deaths of Emmett Till and Martin. For Black males today, their deaths reveal one important fact: Black masculinity is still often perceived as threatening and dangerous in the United States.

Although being male is often thought of as the quintessential majority status, when paired with the modifying identity Black, a unique set of detriments attaches. And the ways Black men have been pilloried has shifted from overt racist attacks to a more institutionalized, insidious, and subconscious form of racism. Although Black men may be equal on the books, reality has time and again proved this not to be the case. In recent years, the Black American struggle has been placed on the backburner by a 'post-racial movement.' But if there is something positive to glean from Martin's tragic death, it is the fact that his death made race relevant, and catalyzed discussions concerning racial inequality and the struggles faced by Black males in America.

This chapter explores how masculinity is a damning trait for the Black community. From mass incarceration, lack of education, and employment discrimination, Black men are languishing in almost every measurable achievement metric. Yet nowhere is the stark disparity between Black males and the rest more apparent than in the formation and enforcement of criminal laws. Criminal laws have been instrumental in shaping the narrative the dangerousness of Black males. Rape laws in particular have been wildly successful in casting Black masculinity in a threatening light. An important lesson for Black boys to learn, and for the U.S. to remember, is that equality in theory is much different, and often discordant, from equality in reality. Therefore, this chapter looks briefly at the history of rape laws and race, illustrating how laws impact the social construct associating Black masculinity with criminality, a construct that ultimately lead to the death of Martin.

AN ABRIDGED HISTORY OF RACE AND RAPE

The crime of rape is as old as crime itself. Rape laws, however, were originally designed for the benefit of men, not women, as women were considered property of men. Rape laws were passed and enforced as a form of insurance, giving men

K.J. Fasching-Varner et al. (Eds.), Trayvon Martin, Race, and American Justice, 57–60.

the ability to protect 'their' woman's chastity, which was intrinsically linked to the woman's 'value' (Gill, 1996). Early rape laws did not cover all women, however, as rape laws revolved around the Victorian ideal of the pure white woman. It was often the case that if a woman did not fit into this mold either she could not be raped under the law, or the rape was not important enough to warrant prosecution (Mitchell, 2010). The most immediate example of this is the history of rape laws and their failure to protect women of color, specifically Black women. At the same time white women's purity was being safeguarded by rape laws during the nineteenth century, criminal rape laws decidedly left Black slave women unprotected (Kennedy, 1998; Pokorak, 2006).

Since rape laws were used as a measure for white men to protect the chastity of white women, it is important to remember from whom the law was often protecting white women- the Black man. Historically, rape laws were disproportionately enforced against Black men who allegedly raped white women. During slavery, rape was racialized by statute; the rape of white women by Black men was legally criminalized in a way that other forms of rape were not. Laws were passed in early U.S. that stated if a Black man was found to have raped a white woman he could be castrated or given the death penalty (Caper, 2010). Post-slavery, when overtly racial rape statutes were discontinued, the focal point of rape shifted to racialized enforcement, where Black men were disproportionately arrested, prosecuted, and punished for the rape of white women. And despite the fact that interracial Black/ white rape is one of the least frequent occurring forms of rapes, the image of the Black male rapist with a white female victim is still popular and prevalent in the reporting and conceptualization of rape today.

The trope of Black male bestiality was central to the racialization of rape. The concept of the animalistic Black man was not purely a creation of slavery; "since the early days of substantive interaction between Africans and Europeans, Blacks have been perceived as only narrowly removed from the animal kingdom" (Duru, 2004, p. 1321). From the likening of Black people to animals grew the idea that Black people also had a sexually insatiable appetite that they could not control. Because of their lascivious nature, "Black men could never be trusted to not attack white women" (Pokorak, 2006, p. 9). And the enactment and enforcement of rape laws at the hands of the law and the public as a lynching phenomenon emerged and reflected the racial skewing of rape. The law directly mirrored social misperception, playing on the stereotype of the Black man's uncontrollable sexual nature and providing punishment for such.

When slavery was abolished, overtly racist slave laws gave way to new methods of punishing the rape of white women committed by Black men. Regardless of what was on the books, the way rape was prosecuted and punished post-slavery highlighted the fact that the crime of rape was still used as a means to protect white women from Black men. As reflected by the judge's statement in the *Scottsboro* case, in Jim Crow America, when the defendant was Black and the victim was white, the victim did not need to show that she "resisted to the utmost," as there was a strong presumption that a white woman did not want to sleep with a Black man (Capers, 2010, p. 1359).

As a result, it was much easier to convict a Black man for the rape of a white woman under so-called 'colorblind laws' than it was to convict a white man for the rape of a white or Black woman, or a Black man who raped a Black woman.

Black men who raped white women were not only easier to convict post-slavery, they also received disproportionately severe punishment. It is estimated that between the years of 1930 and 1967, "89 percent of all of the men officially executed for rape in the United States were Black" (Capers, 2010, p. 1351). The Supreme Court did not intervene and put a stop to the punishing of rape with death until 1977, despite the fact that up to this point the death penalty had almost been exclusively reserved for Black defendants. In *Coker v. Georgia*, the Supreme Court announced that punishing the crime of rape with the death penalty was unconstitutional under the Eighth Amendment, as the punishment was disproportionate to the crime. The death penalty was not eradicated as punishment for rape because it was largely reserved for Black defendants, however. This argument had been raised and defeated, as courts justified the death penalty by either stating that statistical racial disparities are not evidence of discrimination, or that, even if there are racial disparities, the men were still deserving of their sentence. Instead, the Supreme Court chose to minimalize the severity of rape when finding that the death penalty was disproportionate to the crime. Thus, even when laws no longer targeted the Black man as rapist, the enforcement of so-called colorblind laws both in and outside of the courts ensured that the image of the oversexed Black man as rapist remained entrenched in the socialization of the crime of rape.

Although the image of the bestial Black man finds it origins in the racist underpinnings of slavery and the Jim Crow era, the image still holds much traction today. Despite the fact that rape is largely intra-racial and committed by acquaintances, stranger rape committed by Black men against white women is often what is sensationalized in the media (Pokorak, 2006). In 2005, for example, it is estimated that the media only covered 4,700 rape cases out of the 93,934 rapes reported to law enforcement (Kosse, 2007, p. 247). Of the rapes that were covered by the media, the focus was mainly on stranger, gang, inter-racial, or celebrity rapes, evincing that racial and gender stereotypes still influence the way rape is publicized today (Kosse, 2007).

The public emphasis on the Black male rapist has a "down streaming effect," as "the potent rape meta-narrative of a stranger who is a Black man violently assaulting a white woman continues to infect prosecutorial decisions" (Pokorak, 2006, p. 1). Prosecutors rely on the motif of the bestial Black man raping the innocent white woman because the stereotypical trope has a higher rate of convictibility (Pokorak, 2006). Therefore, the history of rape as a crime that a Black man committed against the virtuous white women not only impacts the way rape is portrayed in the media, but also the way rape is prosecuted today, who is convicted of rape, and how rape is defined socially. Despite a push for reform in both how rape is defined legally and socially, a large part of how rape is currently reported, policed, and prosecuted is still predicated upon antiquated gender and racial historical stereotypes, showing how the law is shaped by stereotype and stereotypes reinforce the law.

HOW THE LAW IMPACTS PERCEPTION AND PERCEPTION IMPACTS THE LAW

This brief history of rape is crucial to understanding what happened to Martin, and what young Black men face today. Much is made of the fact that the U.S. no longer has blatantly racist laws - that the constitutional guarantee of all citizens being considered "equal under the law" is now a reality. But what often goes ignored is how stereotyping and racism intertwines with the enforcement of the law and the perception of criminality. Taking into consideration these factors reveals that equality is far from reality. Zimmerman followed and accosted Martin because he was a young Black man who he was sure did not belong. In Zimmerman's mind, Martin fit the profile of a criminal, and as a neighborhood watchman, Zimmerman believed it was his duty to protect his community from criminals. Scarily, Zimmerman believed Martin was a criminal despite having no knowledge of his person or character other than what he was able to physically observe that evening. The social script associating Black men with crime undoubtedly informed Zimmerman's misperception. But herein lies the problem - the laws can change, but if the attitudes of those enforcing the laws - the police, prosecutors, and judges, and those deciding the cases - the jury of one's peers, i.e., the community at large - the change is for nothing. As shown by the socio-legal history of the crime of rape, just because Black men are no longer the overt target of a law in writing, does not mean that they are not the metaphoric bull's-eye in practice. Until social perception shifts to conform with the "neutral" laws in place, Black children, particularly Black boys, must learn that they often will be mislabeled as dangerous based on the hue of their skin and due to no fault of their own. And this mislabeling can prove deadly, as is sadly represented by Martin's tragic death.

REFERENCES

Capers, B. (2010). The unintentional rapist. *Washington University Law Review, 87*, 1345–1396.

Duru, N. J. (2004). The Central Park Five, the Scottsboro Boys, and the myth of the bestial Black man. *Cardozo Law Review, 25*, 1315–1365.

Gill, S. (1996). Dismantling gender and race stereotypes: Using education to prevent date rape. *UCLA Women's Law Journal, 7*, 27–79.

Kennedy, R. (1997). *Race, crime, and the law*. New York, NY: Random House, Inc.

Kosse, S. (2007). Race, riches & reporters—Do race and class impact race narratives? An analysis of the Duke Lacrosse case. *Southern Illinois Law Journal, 31*, 243–279.

Mitchell, T. (2009–10). We're only fooling ourselves: A critical analysis of the biases inherent in the legal system's treatment of rape victim. *Buffalo Journal of Gender, Law & Social Policy, 18*, 73–146.

Pokorak, J. (2006). Rape as a badge of slavery: The legal history of, and remedies for, prosecutorial race-of-victim charging disparities. *Nevada Law Journal, 7*, 1–54.

PAUL M. BUCKLEY

10. TO BE OR NOT TO BE

A Problem and the Promise

Over one hundred and ten years ago, William Edward Burghardt Du Bois, a Harvard educated Black man, proclaimed the unasked question that his white counterparts pondered: How does it feel to be a problem? The persistent horrors of American racism sustain this question in our nation's racial etiquette of denial as one that is not worth asking; and sometimes mask this question with our manners of political correctness that assumes inferior cultural differences (Myers, 2005). American 'colorblindness' leads white people to ask: Why is there still a problem (with *them*)? The more 'progressive' and 'liberal' whites believe they empathize with Black souls because they believe they already know how it feels, even though their social location and experience makes it impossible for them to ever *really* know. They dare not ask the unutterable question for fear of reproducing the pain they could only imagine Blacks feel. Indeed, Black men feel a chronic psychic racial pain that is excruciating and unimaginable. This pain is sometimes numbing even to the point of death. America cannot imagine the cost of being considered 'a problem' (Smith, Allen, & Danley, 2007).

America's disdain, apprehension, and unmasked fear of Black male bodies are evidenced in its blatant assault on Black male images, the material body, and the soul. So-called fair and accurate journalism present Black men in negative and pathological ways, highlighting criminal activity, failing health, absentee fatherhood, poverty, and other ailments of society or plagues of the individual (Hutchinson, 1994; Jackson, 2006). More specifically, Black males are presented as brutes, beasts, deadbeat dads, drug dealers, gangsters, rapists, and dropouts. In sum, 'niggers.' In fact, Black men are often scapegoated to maintain white hegemony and supremacist psychology. Black male bodies are blamed and pathologized while systems of white racial oppression, terror, and inhumanity are hidden from critical view. Whatever the circumstance, Black males are perceived as the aggressors and perpetrators, not the victims, of violence and terror. Hence, the dichotomies of white/Black, good/bad, right/wrong, innocent/guilty, superior/inferior are reinforced as natural and correct reasoning when the 'bad nigger' redundancy is presented and the good, kind, great white man is coyly and quietly reproduced (Nunn, 1993). Therefore, the value of Black lives are diminished and undervalued—from constitutional measurements of Black life at three-fifths human to the greater likelihood of the death penalty for stereotypically Black looking defendants of crimes committed against white people;

K.J. Fasching-Varner et al. (Eds.), Trayvon Martin, Race, and American Justice, 61–65.
© *2014 Sense Publishers. All rights reserved.*

to the excessiveness of police responses to situations involving Black bodies; and ultimately to the ways average American citizens think about and enact justice on behalf of Black lives. This means, then, that Black bodies—in particular male bodies—are hyper-masculinized and seen as dangerous objects to be controlled, tamed, stopped or ultimately killed (Jackson & Dangerfield, 2004).

Black sons live in the midst of these tragedies. The 'open-season' on Black males does not begin nor does it end with the heinous assaults and killings of Emmett Till (1955), Rodney King (1992), Abner Louima (1997), James Byrd (1998), Amadou Diallo (1999), Ousmane Zongo (2003), Timothy Stansbury Jr. (2004), Ronald Madison and James Brissette (2005), Sean Bell (2006), Oscar Grant III (2009), James Craig Anderson (2012), Trayvon Martin (2012), and Kimani Gray (2013). The souls listed in that short sample were unarmed in each and every case. The brutal reality of the Black male experience in the United States is that on any occasion— whether walking home from a brief stop at a corner store, celebrating the last night of bachelorhood before matrimonial bliss, or enjoying quality time with family in their own homes—Black male lives can be stolen in an instant. Their lives are sometimes endangered by agents of the State who misuse their authority. Very often, Black male encounters with police officers are abusive and egregiously prejudiced (Brunson, 2007; Silton, 2002; Terrill & Reisig, 2003; Weitzer, 2002). Hence, many Black men have come to believe that "police don't like Black people" and they are not protectors or servants of the Black public (Brunson, 2007). Yet the burden of Black male death does not rest solely on police officers. Black men find themselves negotiating a history of violence against them, incarceration, and death, from the enslavement period until now (Huggins, 1990; Mellon, 1988; Alexander, 2012). This narrative of persistent violence reinforces the expendability of Black life as an answer to the framing of Black souls as a problem. Black men live in the tensions of expectant pain and death, and the hope of survival and triumph.

In November 2008, the United States of America elected its first African American president, after forty-three previous administrations since its birth two hundred and thirty two years before. It was within the historical moment of newly elected President Barack H. Obama's impending inauguration in 2009 that Oscar Grant III was killed by white Bay Area Rapid Transit (BART) officer Johannes Mehserle. Grant, a young Black man of twenty-two years was a father, partner, brother, friend, and son. He was unarmed and his neck was under the knee of another officer when Mehserle fired the shot that killed him on New Year's Day, as citizen witnesses recorded the tragic event with their cell phones (Antony & Thomas, 2010). In the shadow of hope, his body lay bleeding without justifiable cause. A Black man was lost during a national moment that seemingly signified triumph and promise.

On February 26, 2012, while walking back to the home of his father from a trip to a nearby 7-11 store, Martin was profiled as a criminal and followed by a neighborhood watch volunteer, Zimmerman. Martin's stroll home while talking on the phone with a friend seemed to Zimmerman as a guy "up to no good, or he's on drugs or something. It's raining and he's just walking around looking about" (Robles, 2012).

There's an "ecology of racial profiling" that produces increased surveillance and suspicion in whiter neighborhoods (Meehan and Ponder, 2002), where it is assumed that Blacks do not belong and white people need more protection.

It would take the outrage of citizens across the country to urge a proper investigation and charges against Zimmerman, which came six weeks after Martin's death. In the end, Zimmerman's defense attorneys prepared a case that attempted to pathologize a murdered Martin and convinced jurors to acquit George Zimmerman. The "not guilty" verdict justified Zimmerman's killing of Martin in response to *his* fear of bodily harm or death. During the trial, Martin was presented as the aggressor in the case of his own death, invoking the stereotype of savagery associated with Black people, in particular Black males (Grier & Cobbs, 1992; Nunn, 1993). Hence, Black men are blameworthy for the violence they endure and the resulting death. Martin's fate was an unconscionable death of a young man who must have been confused and terrified in his final moments before Zimmerman shot him dead, trying to defend himself against a stranger who followed him. However, America still struggles to see young Black men as innocent, needing protection, desiring protection, even being threatened, unless the perpetrator is also a Black man.

TOWARD THE PROMISE

Du Bois' discussion of being 'a problem' is situated in his larger discussion of the troubled and gifted 'Souls of Black Folk.' In his signature work, Du Bois (1903) described the double-consciousness of Black souls which has become a revelation and sphinxlike riddle for scholars interested in African American social life since then. He stated:

> It is a peculiar sensation, this double-consciousness, this sense of always looking at one's self through the eyes of others, of measuring one's soul by the tape of a world that looks on in amused contempt and pity. One ever feels his twoness—an American, a Negro; two souls, two thoughts, two un-reconciled strivings; two warring ideals in one dark body, whose dogged strength alone keeps it from being torn asunder. (p.2)

With these words, Du Bois revealed the tensions felt and negotiated by Black souls in America; and he codified the elements that coalesce and 'double' in its unity the African American identity and consciousness. This double consciousness not only captures a "negated self-consciousness" (Allen, 1992) through the eyes of oppressive others, but it also reflects a faith in and awareness of the unique gift that Blacks have to offer the world, in spite of contempt through the white lens. Hence, the double consciousness of the American Black or the Black American is a duality of sight and insight. Black men in America, then, must confront the skewed and debasing 'sight' of themselves from the white view--the sight that presents them as contemptible, a problem to be solved by violence or death. I use the term *sight* to assert the concept of looking *outside* of one's self to see one's racialized self as defined by the oppressive other. I magnify Dubois' words here: "*looking* at one's self through the eyes of others" does not make one aware of his/her racialization but simply offers a contemptible sight of self. Looking through others' eyes, through white lenses, reinforces and validates injustice, contempt, and pity. Black lives are measured, evaluated, sometimes saved, often transmogrified, or frequently exterminated. Sometimes those assassinations are public or in the media, but often ignored. Confronting this contemptible and tragic sight requires the courageous faith that informs our insight, a faith that is indeed concerned with death but also with desire. The Black man's double consciousness, his two souls and two thoughts, must wrestle with looming death through the white gaze and white desire to kill him; and with his own desire to transcend the outsider's contempt with remarkable *insight* to his life of promise.

CONCLUSION

The violent end to Martin's life and the ensuing case exposes the tacit racism that justifies Black death. Black male bodies in the United States continue to be marked as dark problems. Yet, Black male bodies also proclaim remarkable promise. Black souls in Black male bodies can be sons of promise if they are determined not to internalize white sight, but to see the panorama of contempt and death only as a test of their desire to be free. Black sons of promise must engage in the war of dualities with a desire to maintain faith in promise of triumph. They do not look for justice, love, or acceptance in white sight, nor find their faith there. Sons of promise are determined, by their faith, to live with insight and imagination. Rather than close their eyes to white sight from the American standpoint, they confront this sight with a more vivid imagination of their inner selves. This imagination produces conscientious souls, sons of promise, whose conscientiousness is greater than the sum of their double consciousness. It also keeps them grounded in the history of collective death and injustice, while promising greater insight for liberation that has not yet come, but will come, like a Black Messiah. Tell your sons (and your daughters) that violence and death underscore our collective need for liberated minds who dare to be radical, defiant, righteous, just, and triumphant in the midst of tragedy. Black sons of unimagined promise must reimagine justice and be willing to live for it.

REFERENCES

Allen, E. (1992). Ever feeling one's twoness: "Double ideals" and "double consciousness" in the souls of Black folk. *Contributions in Black Studies, 9*(5), 1–15.

Alexander, M. (2012). *The new Jim Crow: Mass incarceration in the age of colorblindness.* New York, NY: The New Press.

Antony, M. G., & Thomas, R. J. (2010). 'This is citizen journalism at its finest': YouTube and the public sphere in the Oscar Grant shooting incident. *New Media & Society, 12*(8), 1280–1296.

Brunson, R. K. (2007). "Police don't like Black people": African American young men's accumulated police experiences. *Criminology and Public Policy, 6*(1), 71–102.

Collins, P. H. (1998). *Fighting words: Black women and the search for justice*. Minneapolis, MN: University of Minnesota Press.

Du Bois, W. E. B. (1903). *The souls of Black folk*. Chicago, IL: A.C. McClurg & Co.

Grier, W. H., & Cobbs, P. M. (1992). *Black rage*. New York, NY: Basic Books.

Huggins, N. I. (1990). *Black odyssey: The African American ordeal in slavery*. New York, NY: Vintage.

Hutchinson, E. O. (1996). *The assassination of the black male image*. New York, NY: Touchstone.

Jackson, R. (2006). *Scripting the black masculine body: Identity discourse, and racial politics in popular media*. Albany, NY: State University of New York Press.

Jackson, R. L., & Dangerfield, C. L. (2004). Defining Black masculinity as cultural property: Toward an identity negotiation paradigm. In R. L. Jackson (Ed.), *African American communication and identities: Essential readings* (pp. 197–208).

Meehan, A. J., & Ponder, M. C. (2002). Race and place: The ecology of racial profiling African American motorists. *Justice Quarterly, 19*(3), 399–430.

Mellon, J. (Ed.). (1988). *Bullwhip days, the slaves remember: An oral history*. New York, NY: Avon Books.

Myers, K. (2005). *Race talk: Racism hiding in plain sight*. Lanham, MD: Rowman & Littlefield.

Nunn, K. B. (1993). Rights held hostage: Race, ideology, and the peremptory challenge. *Harvard Civil Rights-Civil Liberties Law Review, 28*(1), 63–118.

Robles, F. (2012, April 2). A look at what happened the night Trayvon Martin died. *Miami Herald*.

Silton, D. J. (2002). US prisons and racial profiling: A covertly racist nation rides a vicious cycle. *Law & Ineq., 20*, 53.

Smith, W. A., Allen, W. R., & Danley, L. L. (2007). "Assume the position... You fit the description" Psychosocial experiences and racial battle fatigue among African American male college students. *American Behavioral Scientist, 51*(4), 551–578.

Terrill, W., & Reisig, M. D. (2003). Neighborhood context and police use of force. *Journal of Research in Crime & Delinquency, 40*(3), 291–321.

Weitzer, R. (2002). Incidents of police misconduct and public opinion. *Journal of Criminal Justice, 30*(5), 397–408.

65

EBONY JOY WILKINS

11. USING AFRICAN AMERICAN CHILDREN'S LITERATURE AS A MODEL FOR 'WRITING BACK' RACIAL WRONGS

Too many Black children are forced to define themselves from a position of absence and misrepresentation. Because of the unjust and harmful messages prevalent in our society and given the discouraging trial outcome and senseless loss of life of Trayvon Martin, it is now more vital than ever to support our Black sons, by recalling textual accounts of struggle and perseverance, by consulting historic responses to racism, and by furthering all current efforts to represent truer stories of Black male life in America. Our sons have models in African American children's literature characters, stories created by Black artists that can be used to explore racial identity and to combat injustice. In this chapter I seek to uncover the ways in which these stories can effect how Black males affirm themselves in the world, and pull lessons from these stories to guide their way.

BE COURAGEOUS

One of the first depictions of a Black child in a children's story is a popular and problematic tale that has been wildly read and distributed. *Little Black Sambo* (Bannerman, 1899) is the story of a Black-skinned boy who is threatened repeatedly by a streak of tigers who aimed to destroy him. His parents outfit the boy with beautifully handmade clothes, but when Little Black Sambo meets the tigers while out on a walk and they threaten his life, he is called to sacrifice his new clothing to avoid being eaten.

Despite the danger in which he finds himself, Little Black Sambo ultimately returns home with not only all of his new clothing, but with even more than he left home. One can draw parallels to the recent tragedy and loss of life of Trayvon Martin. When considering the connections between Little Black Sambo's story and Trayvon Martin's story, readers can identify with courageous boys who meet a challenge so large that it seems possible to outrun. While both accounts tell of a Black boy trying to survive amid tremendous opposition, only one ends as we hope a story would. The other leaves readers digging for understanding and direction on what to tell our Black sons now.

K.J. Fasching-Varner et al. (Eds.), Trayvon Martin, Race, and American Justice, 67–71.

Little Black Sambo has stolen the hearts of many young readers since its creation, but first versions of this story were controversial, with portrayals of Little Black Sambo and his parents as voiceless victims, having no distinguishing characteristics and having little value. Stories with negative and demeaning Black characters were once prevalent when books for children first appeared during the 19th century. Newer versions of this story, *The Story of Little Babaji* (Marcellino, 1996) and *Sam and the Tigers* (Lester & Pinkney, 1996) have transformed the story with vivid artwork, central voices, and valued characters.

Challenges Will Come

Presently, there is a widespread attack against our Black sons, attacks including textual messages and images that cause anger, frustration and often a sense of hopelessness - messages that need re-writing. For many artists of African American children's literature this effort has been in the works since its inception as a genre in the late 1960s, when effort was made to provide Black children with books on Black history, family, and culture.

The creation of African American children's literature, books written by and about Blacks, was purposeful (Sims Bishop, 2011). These books aimed to re-write the negative images and portrayals that previously prevailed in literature designated for children. *The Brownies' Book* was created during this time to uplift Black children (Martin, 2004) for the literary exchange of Black artists and Black children, and to publish messages about Black life. Each publication of *The Brownies Book* aimed to celebrate achievements of Blacks, including writings, illustrations, photos, and artwork by African Americans. The magazine gave voice and platform to 'Children of the Sun,' and opened the door for new voices, images, and dialogues to emerge. One of the most celebrated African American writers, Langston Hughes, began submitting his work to *The Brownies' Book* as a young boy. In 1926, Hughes wrote:

> We build our temples for tomorrow, strong as we know how, and we stand on top of the mountain, free within ourselves, (p. 694)

to signify the important role of reading and writing among African Americans.

During the Harlem Renaissance in the 1920s, many writers began producing books for African American children. But before the 1960s, if Black children saw a children's book attempting to reflect their lives, the images were problematic and negative. Tensions in the U.S. were high during the desegregation of schools in 1954, the Montgomery bus boycott in 1955, and the beginning of Civil Rights Movement, which had a vast impact on children's literature and the way in which Black characters were featured. During the second half of the 20th century, there was a shift from Eurocentric to Afrocentric viewpoints with an increased number of books written and illustrated by and about African Americans. The shift resulted from Black artists celebrating Black culture and race in more accurate ways.

You Can Do It

Modern picture books also display more positive depictions and contain encouraging messages for Black children. In *Test the Ice: A True Story About Jackie Robinson* (Robinson & Nelson, 2009), the baseball great was terrified of being in the water. Although he shone and broke barriers on the baseball field, he avoided the lake near his family's home. One day when his children and their friends begged him to test the ice to make sure it is solid enough for them to skate on. Robinson hesitated because he could not swim, but he ultimately agreed to take on the challenge. He was hesitant, but that did not stop him. In fact, he decided to face his fear and stepped out on the frozen water. He reached the middle of the lake and the water began to crack underneath him. Right away he was afraid and the kids were afraid for him, but he continued his walk until he was sure the ice was thick enough for them to skate on. At another point in the story Robinson shared the story of how he became one of the first Black baseball players to step on the field of white players: "Some fans cheered me. Others shouted insults so bad I had to struggle to keep my temper from exploding."

Important lessons can be gleaned from stories like *Test the Ice: A True Story About Jackie Robinson* – like the importance of facing opposition and conquering fears. Sharing these lessons now is vital. Many of our Black sons are at a point of discord, not knowing which way to turn. In *You Can Do It* (Dungy & Bates, 2008), the protagonist Linden also finds himself at a crossroads. All of his family and friends seem to have their life purpose, their *It*, all figured out. He is a fun loving boy and enjoys making his friends laugh, but he keeps getting in trouble at school and has no idea what his *It* could be. It troubles him, so he begins to talk with his older brother and his parents hoping to find that something he is missing, but he finds nothing. His father encourages him to have faith and to pray and assures him his *It* will come. On a visit to the dentist to cure a sore tooth, Linden learns all about how to really make people smile, and decides he wants to become a dentist as well. He happily returns to school to show his friends and teacher what he has learned and to share his *It*.

In *My Name is Sangoel* (Williams, Mohammed, & Stock, 2009), Sangoel and his family are living in a refugee camp and will soon leave for America. They have to say sad goodbyes to their family in Africa, whom they may never see again. The Old Wise One in his village cannot travel with them. Instead, he names young Sangoel as the man of his family now, and reminds Sangoel to never forget his name or where he comes from in his new country. He must now care for his mother and his baby brother. They have to re-learn everything, from eating with a fork and turning on the stove in their new apartment, to learning English in his new school. Sangoel looks forward to starting school on his own, but is disappointed when the other kids can't pronounce his African name. He remembers what the Old Wise One told him and he finds a creative way to explain to the others. He draws a picture of a sun and a soccer goal on his t-shirt –Sangoel - to help his new friends learn the name the Old Wise One told him never to forget.

Historically, Black writers found their voices using their pens, discovering more about themselves in the process (Brooks & McNair, 2009). African American children's literature has continued as a vehicle to pass along culture and to share stories with more positive depictions. There is an Ashanti proverb that says when you follow in the path of your father, you learn to walk like him.

In *My Man Blue* (Grimes & Lagarrigue, 1999), Blue is a man who lost track of his own son, but he gets a second chance when he befriends a little boy named Damon and guides him, as a father would. When Damon's mother introduces Blue, Damon is hesitant because he isn't his own father and doesn't trust him. But when Blue starts spending more time with him, Damon quickly warms and begins to trust the man. Blue teaches Damon to box and play ball, he saves him from a near miss with a car in the street, and he promises to watch as he climbs a tree at the playground. The friendship bond between the two grows stronger, and to explain the hole that Blue fills in Damon's life, Grimes (1999) wrote:

> Why'd you want my friendship, Blue? I blurt out there and then. I had a son named Zeke, Blue says. These streets became his friend. He needed me but by the time I came, it was too late. He'd passed the point of trusting his old man to steer him straight. Your missing daddy also left a hole in you, says Blue. If friendship fills it, there's less chance the streets will eat at you. (p. 6)

CARVE A NEW PATH

History is passed on through story (Bishop, 2011) and historically, Black artists wrote to inform, make change within their social environment, and inspire themselves and others. As a child, I loved to read but I found it difficult to find books with African American girls telling my story. I began writing my own stories like *Sellout* (Wilkins, 2010), filled with characters that looked like me and characters to whom I could relate. Writing became my way of expressing myself and sharing my voice with others.

The Brownies' Book opened doors for Hughes and other youth at the time to share their literary insight through writing. Few mediums focusing on Black children in this manner have existed since. Today more books are available that tell stories of Black life and culture in the U.S.; some of these books are honored with a Coretta Scott King Award, which honors African American authors and illustrators whose books pay tribute to African American culture and universal human values.

In 1818, author and activist Frederick Douglass was certain that once you learn to read, you are forever free. African American youth need to read, write about, and discuss literature to help them develop cultural competence (Tatum, 2000). We should remind our Black sons of the power behind their pens, push each one to 'write back' the racial wrongs they experience and re-write present pains. Collectively, in this text we aim to write back against the wrongful death of Trayvon Martin. And now we pass on the literary torch to our Black sons.

REFERENCES

Bannerman, H. (1899). *The story of little Black Sambo* (Vol. 1). London, England: Grant Richards.

Brooks, W., & McNair, J. C. (2009). "But this story of mine is not unique": A review of research on African American children's literature. *Review of Educational Research, 79*(1), 125–162.

Dungy, T., & Bates, A. (2008). *You can do it!* New York, NY: Little Simon Inspirations.

Grimes, N. (1999). *My man Blue: Poems.* New York, NY: Dial Books for Young Readers.

Harris, V. J. (1984). The Brownies' book: Challenge to the selective tradition in children's literature.

Hughes, L., & Collier, B. (2013). *I, too, am America.* New York, NY: Simon & Schuster.

Hughes, L. (1926). The Negro artist and the racial mountain. *The Nation, 122*(23), 692–694.

Johnson-Feelings, D. (1996). *The best of the brownies' book.* New York, NY: Oxford University Press.

Lester, J. (1996). *Sam and the tigers: A new telling of Little Black Sambo.* New York, NY: Dial Books.

Marcellino, F. (1996). The story of little Babaji. New York, NY: Harper Collins.

Martin, M. H. (2004). *Brown gold: Milestones of African American children's picture books, 1845-2002.* East Sussex, England: Psychology Press.

Robinson, S. (2009). *Testing the ice: A true story about Jackie Robinson.* New York, NY: Scholastic Press.

Roethler, J. (1998). Reading in color: Children's book illustrations and identity formation for Black children in the United States. *African American Review, 32*(1), 95–105.

Sims Bishop, R. (2011). African American children's literature: Researching its development, exploring its voices. In S. Wolf, K. Coats, P. Enciso, & C. Jenkins (Eds.), *Handbook of research on children's and young adult literature* (pp. 225–237). New York, NY: Routledge.

Tatum, A. W. (2000). Breaking down barriers that disenfranchise African American adolescent readers in low-level tracks. *Journal of Adolescent & Adult Literacy, 44*(1), 52–64.

Williams, K. L., & Mohammed, K. (2009). *My name is Sangoel.* Grand Rapids, MI: Eerdmans Young Readers.

Wilkins, E. J. (2010). *Sellout.* New York, NY: Scholastic Press.

MARGARET ANN HAGERMAN & ERIC D. VIVIER

12. "I DON'T THINK HE KNOWS ABOUT IT"/"HE WAS OUTRAGED

White Parents and White Boys Talk

When Trayvon Martin was killed, I was conducting a two-year ethnographic study of how white children come to understand race, racism, and racial privilege in America (see Hagerman, 2013). Sociologists studying racial socialization—the process through which parents transmit messages about race to their children, "foster[ing] an understanding and awareness of race" (Rollins & Hunter, 2013, p. 141) and "shap[ing] children's understandings of and attitudes toward their own and other racial/ethnic groups" (Hughes, 2003, p. 15)—have historically focused on the explicit strategies parents use to help Black children navigate a hostile racial landscape (Bowman & Howard, 1985; Brega & Coleman, 1999; Hughes & Chen, 1999; Knight et al., 1993). More recent scholarship has included Latino, Asian-American, and biracial families (Knight et al., 1993; Phinney & Chavira, 1995; Rollins & Hunter, 2013), as well as the role schools play in teaching white children racial lessons (Lewis, 2001; 2003), but few scholars have considered racial socialization in white families. As sociologists have documented new forms of racism in adults, such as racial apathy and colorblind racism (Forman 2004), and have suggested that resulting racial ideologies are in part responsible for the reproduction of white racial privilege (Bonilla-Silva, 2006), I argue that it is important to understand how whites' ideas about race, racism, and racial privilege form in childhood and within the institution of the family (Hagerman, 2013). After Martin was killed, I began to incorporate questions about him in the interviews I conducted with upper-middle-class white parents and their children (ages 10-12). Their responses tended to align with their broader perspectives of race in America.

COLORBLIND FAMILIES

Many whites hold what sociologists call 'colorblind' views:

The central beliefs of color-blind racism are that (1) most people do not even notice race anymore; (2) racial parity has for the most part been achieved; (3) any persistent patterns of racial inequality are the result of individual and/or group-level shortcomings rather than structural ones; (4) most people do not care about racial differences; and (5) therefore, there is no need for institutional

K.J. Fasching-Varner et al. (Eds.), Trayvon Martin, Race, and American Justice, 73–78.

remedies (such as affirmative action) to redress persistent racialized outcomes (Forman & Lewis, 2006, pp. 177–8).

Colorblind parents not only told me that they "don't really talk about [race] because it isn't part of [their] lives," but insisted that such reticence was evidence of racial progress in America: "If you asked my daughter about Obama, she doesn't even see the big deal of it!" Cynthia exclaimed. "Race just doesn't matter to her. I think that's really wonderful." Karen similarly remarked, "It's really cool that kids don't think race is a big deal . . . we as parents try not to say much of anything about it." In terms of Martin's death, colorblind parents like Beth and Cynthia explained to me that "It hasn't come up" or "We haven't talked about that."

Despite this silence, colorblind parents convey messages about race to their children not only through racially coded language (e.g., concerns about "safety" at school) but also through the choices they make about where to live, where to send their children to school, what media to consume, what social interactions to facilitate, and so on. Indeed, my research suggests that white children in colorblind families still form ideas about race (Hagerman, 2013). Take Natalie, for example, a 12-year-old girl whose parents insist that they are colorblind, who attends a school that is 99% white, and who has virtually no friendships with children of color. When I asked her if racism still matters in America, she insisted that it did not:

Racism was a problem when all those slaves were around and that like bus thing... And Rosa Parks and how she went on the bus. And she was African American and sat on the white part... But no, racism isn't a problem today.

But Natalie clearly has noticed racial differences and has formed opinions of racial groups based, in part, on her limited interactions with the two Black girls at her school: "At the slumber party, my friends were talking about basically how [the two Black girls] are not as smart and everything, and how like…their clothes are so ugly and all." She explicitly addressed racial disparities when she told me that she did not want more Black kids in her neighborhood or school:

African American kids, those kids have a lot of problems... they could just have a cold spirit... they probably look up to older kids that are bad or take drugs and steal stuff and have guns...or their family doesn't care about them.

It is tempting to vilify Natalie for her remarks, but my research suggests that Natalie is drawing upon the limited set of tools at her disposal in order to make sense of race in America—a complex topic for a child growing up in a community in which the only messages about race are coded and contradictory.

COLOR-CONSCIOUS FAMILIES

There are also white parents who are not colorblind—who do believe that race is a salient feature of contemporary American society, who recognize their own complicity in the reproduction of racial inequality, and who attempt to challenge the racial status quo. Some of these "color-conscious" parents make active decisions to send their children to racially-integrated public schools and encourage meaningful equal-status friendships with children of color, choices that social psychologists suggest may reduce negative prejudice among whites (Allport, 1954; Pettigrew, 1998).

When I asked these parents why they make such choices, they tended to respond like Jennifer, who hoped her son would become conscious of his own privilege and of the role race continues to play in American society:

> I want [my son] to be an empathetic human being as he goes through the world, and in order to do that, you have to appreciate what someone else's experience might be vis-à-vis yours. [He] is a white male from a privileged household and he needs to be very cognizant of that so we talk about race and gender a lot.

Color-conscious parents like Jennifer's still seek to provide the best opportunities for their children, and thus implicitly participate in the very structures of privilege that they explicitly reject. But they also talk openly about race in contemporary America, providing their children with access to "propositional knowledge" about the history of race (Perry & Shotwell, 2009), model and encourage interracial friendships, send their children to integrated schools, and fight against tracking and other racialized processes within those schools.

The white children of 'color conscious' parents are generally better equipped to engage in critical conversations about race, racism, and racial privilege. As eleven-year-old Conor states:

> I think [racism] is a WAY bigger problem than people realize. It's nowhere near what it used to be... it's just different and white people don't realize it... I think it's still there. It's just not as present and people want to hide it. Because they are scared to talk about it.

Similarly, twelve-year-old Ben insisted that being white "gives you an advantage! Just like gender, you'll get an advantage just by being a white male rather than a Black female." These white children recognized the racialized nature of immigration policy, of educational inequality, and even of police enforcement:; as Sam told me bluntly, "Police are more aggressive toward Black people."

I found that most 'color-conscious' white parents in my study had talked with their children about the death of Martin. One mother said she talked to her two boys about the connections she saw between Emmett Till, who was murdered in Mississippi in 1955, and Martin. Another mother shared editorials with her son about the racialized nature of the event and about the responsibility of juries. One father provided his son with an overview of the legal system and explained the possible outcomes of the trial of Zimmerman. One family attended a 'Hoodie Rally.' The children in these families talked to each other about Martin and debated what would happen to Zimmerman. And one boy even got into a verbal fight at school after hearing what he believed to be a racist comment made by a white peer in reference to Martin. These color-conscious parents and their white children believed Martin's death was both racialized and an injustice, a tragic event that reflected the continued significance of race in America.

REACTIONS TO THE VERDICT

After the Zimmerman trial was decided, I spoke with some of the parents in my study to determine how these white families were talking about and making sense of the 'not guilty' verdict. Karen, one mother who also articulated colorblind ideology, told she had not even talked about it with her eleven-year-old son, Alex; "The kids have been busy with camps and practices and we were just on vacation. I don't think he knows about it."

In contrast, Gail, a mother with a color-conscious ideological position, told me that she and her eleven-year-old son, Darren, had discussed the verdict at length:

Darren is outraged by the verdict. Outraged…I tried to explain the distinction between a tragic event that unquestionably reflects deep and inherent race bias and a court system that is designed to identify whether a specific set of facts meets the elements of a particular crime, as charged…When it was clear he was buying none of this, I printed a few good (short) editorials for him that articulated this better than I can. I don't think he read them. He does not need my input or perspective because he is adamantly of the opinion that the verdict is an outrage and travesty of justice. To his mind, Zimmerman was flat out guilty and clearly motivated by bigotry.

These two white children are the same age, come from the same community, and share the same social, political, economic, and educational "wages of whiteness," but they had opposite reactions to an intensely racialized event: ignorance and outrage (Du Bois, 1935; Roediger, 1991). Whereas many white children, like Alex, have little awareness of how race shapes lived experiences—including their own—and effectively deny the significance of race in America, others, like Darren, possess rhetorical tools and a critical white consciousness that allow them to challenge the dominant racial ideology of a 'post-racial America'. These differences, I suggest, reflect the outcomes of their parents' divergent approaches to white racial socialization.

CONCLUSION

In the aftermath of Martin's death and Zimmerman's acquittal, what can parents possibly tell their children about injustice, race, violence, the law, oppression, and privilege in America? This is a significant challenge for parents of Black children, who already have to teach their children how to survive daily encounters with racism (Jones & Shorter-Gooden, 2003; Rollins & Hunter 2013). As my study shows, however, many parents of white children have not faced this challenge. They have the privilege to remain silent, secure in their conviction that race no longer matters. These parents participate in the production of what Forman (2004) called 'white racial apathy:' the "indifference toward societal racial and ethnic inequality and lack of engagement with race-related social issues" (p. 44). By engaging in this form of strategic avoidance, these white parents reproduce racial inequality.

The conversation about Martin's death and Zimmerman's acquittal—about race, injustice, violence, the law, oppression, and privilege in America—cannot be limited to the Black community. White parents have an ethical responsibility to talk openly about race in America with their white children, to inform their children (and themselves) about the history of race in America, and to provide their children with tools, opportunities, and information that can be used to engage with and rework rather than reproduce racial oppression and privilege in America. Of course, these parenting choices alone will not undo the persistent and pervasive structural racial inequality of American society. But systems of privilege and oppression—including those that led to Martin's death, Zimmerman's acquittal, and whites' culpable ignorance (Bartky 2002)—can only be dismantled if the ideologies that support them are understood and challenged. This work, in part, includes understanding and challenging the process of white racial socialization.

REFERENCES

Allport, G. W. (1954). *The nature of prejudice*. Reading, MA: Addison-Wesley.
Bartky, S. (2002). *Sympathy and solidarity and other essays*. Lanham, MD: Rowman & Littlefield.
Bonilla-Silva, E. (2006). *Racism without racists: Color-blind racism and the persistence of racial inequality in America* (IInd ed.). Lanham, MD: Rowman & Littlefield.
Bowman, P. J., & Howard, C. (1985). Race-related socialization, motivation, and academic achievement: A study of Black youth in three-generation families. *Journal of the American Academy of Child Psychiatry, 24*(2), 134–141.
Brega, A., & Coleman, L. (1999). Effects of religiosity and racial socialization on subjective stigmatization in African-American adolescents. *Journal of Adolescence, 22*(2), 223–242.
Du Bois, W. E. B. (1935). *Black reconstruction in America, 1860-1880*. New York, NY: Simon & Schuster.
Forman, T. A. (2004). Color-blind racism and racial indifference: The role of racial apathy in facilitating enduring inequalities. In M. Krysan & A. E. Lewis (Eds.), *The changing terrain of race and ethnicity*. New York, NY: Russell Sage.
Forman, T. A., & Lewis, A. E. (2006). Racial apathy and hurricane Katrina: The social anatomy of prejudice in the post-civil rights era. *Du Bois Review, 3*(1), 175–202.
Hughes, D., & Chen, L. (1999). When and what parents tell children about race: An examination of race-related socialization among African American families. *Applied Developmental Science, 1*(4), 200–214.
Jones C., & Shorter-Gooden, K. (2003). *Shifting: The double lives of black women in America*. New York, NY: Harper Collins.
Knight, G. P., Bernal, M. E., Garza, C. A., Cota, M. K., & Ocampo, K. A. (1993). Family socialization and the ethnic identity of Mexican-American children. *Journal of Cross-Cultural Psychology, 24*(1), 99–114.
Lewis, A. E. (2001). There is no "race" in the schoolyard: Color-blind ideology in an (almost) all-white school. *American Educational Research Association, 38*(4), 781–811.

Lewis, A. E. (2003). *Race in the schoolyard: Negotiating the color line in classrooms and communities.* New Brunswick, NJ: Rutgers University Press.

Hagerman, M. A. (2013). White families and race: Color-blind and color-conscious approaches to white racial socialization. *Ethnic and Racial Studies.* Retrieved from www.tandfonline.com

Hughes, D. (2003). Correlates of African American and Latino parents' messages to children about ethnicity and race: A comparative study of racial socialization. *American Journal of Community Psychology, 31*(1–2), 15–33.

Perry, P., & Shotwell, A. (2009). Relational understanding and white antiracist praxis. *Sociological Theory, 27*(1), 33–50.

Pettigrew, T. (1998). Intergroup contact theory. *Annual Review of Psychology, 49*, 65–85.

Phinney, J. S., & Chavira, V. (1995). Parental ethnic socialization and adolescent coping with problems related to ethnicity. *Journal of Research on Adolescence, 5*(1), 31–53.

Roediger, D. (1994) *Wages of whiteness.* London, England: Verso.

Rollins, A., & Hunter, A. G. (2013). Racial socialization of biracial youth: Maternal messages and approaches to address discrimination. *Family Relations, 62*, 140–153.

RAYGINE DIAQUOI

13. LIMITED AND LIMITLESS

Preparing Black Boys for Colorblind Racism

We are at a racial crossroads in American history, an era simultaneously marked by the election of the country's first Black president, an event which seems to beg a restructuring of what Charles Johnson (2008) calls the 'Black American narrative of victimization," and the mass-incarceration and under education of African Americans (Alexander, 2010; Johnson, 2008). This period has been prematurely labeled post-racial, a label capable of diminishing the continued impact of race and racism on the lives of people of color (Bonilla-Silva, 2002).

The dominant discourse of colorblindness or post-racialism that characterizes this post-civil rights era threatens to obscure and eventually annihilate the "experiential knowledge" (Matsuda, Lawrence, Delgado & Crenshaw, 1993, p.6) of people of color and invalidate their reality through oft-repeated master narratives, which insist that a lack of individual motivation, not structural and systemic racism, is the real limit to one's ability to succeed. This rhetoric ensures that Americans remain colorblind in the truest sense of the word—"blind to the consequences of being the wrong color in the United States today" and the way that race continues to operate in the lives of people of color (Julian Bond as cited in Wise, 2010, p. 63). The voices of people of color are the greatest hope at fully understanding race and racism because they can speak about what whites cannot understand (Degaldo & Stefanic, 2001). The 'doubleness' (Margulies, 1997, as cited in Dixson, 2006, p. 219) that people of color inherit because of their social location gives them the ability to "see contradictions of spaces and structures that appear transparent and accessible, but are not" (Dixson & Rousseau, 2006, p. 19). Additionally, the stories that people of color share about their experiences, or counterstories, are powerful tools for analyzing, challenging and dismantling dominant discourses, which uphold racial privilege.

George Zimmerman shot and killed an unarmed Trayvon Martin on February 26th, 2012, because he thought that Martin was a danger to him. In the weeks and months that followed Martin's death, the internet was flooded with posts detailing the way Black parents have been preparing their sons to navigate what Staples (1996) so aptly calls their "unwieldy inheritance" (Alcindor, 2012; Blow, 2013; Burnett III, 2012; Dell 'Antonia, 2012; Memmott, 2012). Both a single conversation and a number of conversations warned children about the way that they would be viewed by others, warned young boys about ways to interact with white authority, and reminded Black children that they must work twice as hard as anyone else in

K.J. Fasching-Varner et al. (Eds.), Trayvon Martin, Race, and American Justice, 79–84.

order to succeed, among many other themes. As individuals began to come out with their experiences of receiving and then later giving the talk, this private practice became public and, very briefly, seemed to move the experiences of people of color, particularly African Americans, from the margins to the center.

A community counterstory about a practice of survival, resistance and defiance emerged, opening a space for the telling and sharing of a 'hidden transcript' (Scott, as cited in Dawson, 2006, p. 242) among African Americans. This story shed light on the lessons in shifting, or strategies for coping with the incongruity of Blackness, that Sybrina Fulton, Tracy Martin, and many African American parents teach their children (Jones & Shorter-Gooden, 2003). This counternarrative threatened dominant claims of post-racialism and foregrounded the unique and shared ways in which many African Americans continue to navigate a society characterized by the 'mundane extreme environmental stress' of racism (Pierce as cited in Peters, 2002, p.58). Unfortunately, as the news cycle changed and Martin slowly and subtly receded from the interest of the majority, so too did burgeoning communal conversations about the talk and the chance for African Americans to share their multiple and varied tactics for navigating marginality.

This chapter draws upon data gathered as part of a larger project on racial socialization in an effort to continue the conversation about this indigenous African American practice. The project paid close attention to variations in the form and content of the talk and how the many different forms of the talk reveal the particular cultural wealth, as explained by Critical Race theorist Yosso (2002), that is leveraged by many African Americans who must teach their children to live and thrive "in the mouth of a racist, sexist, suicidal dragon" (Lorde, 1984, pp. 74–75). Using the lens of Critical Race Theory (CRT) and the method of counter-storytelling (Solorazano & Yosso, 2002), this chapter illustrates how certain elements of Yosso's (2005) theory of cultural wealth, particularly aspirational, navigational, and resistant capital, are inherent to talks that African American parents have with their sons.

RACIAL SOCIALIZATION

Chester Pierce reasoned that Black parents, unlike white parents, faced a unique task as they raised their children (Peters, 2002, p.58). They had to teach their children to be healthy "in a society in which being Black has negative connotations" (Peters, 2002, p. 59). Ward (2000) wrote, "a primary job of Black parents is to prepare our children for the realities they must face in America, including racial and economic discrimination" (p. 8). This becomes important for adolescents who will encounter increased discrimination, as they get older (Fisher, Wallace, & Fenton, 2000; Romero & Roberts, 1998; Stevenson, Davis, & Abdul Kabir, 2001). For many African American families, the preparation of adolescents for encounters with racial discrimination, termed racial socialization, has been and continues to be, a normal part of their growth and development.

The literature on the 'the talk,' or racial socialization, as it is called by psychologists, mirrors many of the personal stories that have been shared in the media about 'the talk.' Racial socialization has been defined as the process by which African American parents teach their children, particularly males, strategies for navigating an American racial hierarchy (Yosso, Smith, & Solórzano, 2009). Within the field of psychology, the discussion of racial socialization practices has been dominated by four themes: cultural socialization, preparation for bias, promotion of mistrust, and egalitarianism (Hughes et. al., 2008). Conspicuously absent from the literature on racial socialization is a CRT analysis of the practice.

CRITICAL RACE THEORY

CRT counters dominant discourse by elucidating the experiences of communities of color and focusing on their encounters with race and racism with the aim of destroying the foundation upon which our racialized social system rests. Among the key tenets of CRT is the idea that the experiences of people of color remain underutilized as a tool for dismantling racism and the dominant narratives that perpetuate it (Dixson & Rousseau, 2006, p. 5). Key to the disruption and dismantling of dominant narratives about racism is the "experiential knowledge of people of color" (Matsuda, Lawrence, Delgado, & Crenshaw, 1993, p. 6). CRT shares the narratives or counter-stories of marginalized groups to counter commonly accepted beliefs, like color blindness and post racialism. I share the counter-stories of two parents, alongside sentiments shared by Martin's parents, to illustrate elements of the "array of knowledge...possessed and utilized by Communities of Color to survive and resist macro and micro-form of oppression" (Yosso, 2005, p. 77), or what Yosso (2005) calls community cultural wealth.

ASPIRATIONAL CAPITAL

Aspirational capital, pedagogy of hope, is demonstrated by the ability to dream and plan a different future, despite knowledge of structural and systemic constraints. Leanza, a Trinidadian mother of two sons, illustrated an example of aspirational capital when she described her expectations for her son Shane:

> I wanted the best for him. I grew up with parents that loved me and spoiled me. They spoiled me for sure, so I wanted him to have everything, to excel at everything. I didn't want there to be anything that was impossible or out of reach for him...he would...be all that he could and should be.

In Leanza's aspirations for her son she created an alternate reality for him, distinct and separate from the racializ☺ed reality that pervades the United States. She expects her son to do well, to become successful. Tracy Martin envisioned the same for his sons, sharing that he tried, "to prepare them to become teenagers, to become upstanding citizens and [teach them] how to conduct themselves in public" ("Sybrina Fulton," 2013.) Both parents maintain rather reasonable aspirations for their sons, choosing not to engage dominant discourse about Black males. However, for Martin's parents, this carefully crafted alternate reality was shattered when their son was killed. Tracy Martin wonders when " an unarmed teen gets shot in the heart for doing absolutely nothing...you have to say to yourself 'what is it that I can tell my child now?" In the face of the grim realities of a racialized society, African American parents do not tell their children to stop dreaming; they figure out ways to help to continue to believe that everything is possible.

NAVIGATIONAL CAPITAL

Navigational capital includes those skills necessary for knowing how to navigate spaces that are hostile to and dismissive of the experiences of Communities of Color. When discussing her son Nicholas, who started his freshman year in college, Bernadette, a Jamaican mother of two girls and one boy, described the tools that she hopes Nicholas will remember to use while he is away:

He's away from me...I'm hoping that he is able to use whatever he learned here, while he was growing up. He was taught early to remove himself from certain situations because he is a Black boy...If he is out in a mall and he is with kids of other races and they are doing things that they are not supposed to do he will be considered the ring leader because he is a Black boy...maybe he will be the first one to be questioned. He has to learn to be really careful, know his surroundings, be careful of his surroundings and who is hanging with.

Later, Bernadette shared the various talks that she had with Nicholas about the way that he should behave in public. She reminded him that he is not safe, to be cautious and ever vigilant. Her talks echo Sybrina Fulton's fears for her eldest son Jahvaris in the wake of his brother Martin's death. She shared, "I'm very afraid right now, because I have no clue what to tell him. I have no clue if I should tell him to run or walk, if I should tell him to defend himself or just lay there. I have no clue what to tell him" (Fulton, 2013). Both mothers are fully aware of their sons' hyper visibility and the ironic reality that people will never truly see them. "When they approach [a Black boy] they only see [his] surroundings, themselves, or figments of their imagination – indeed, everything and anything except [a boy]" (Ellison, 1952, p.3). African American parents must prepare their children to walk through such treacherous terrain.

RESISTANT CAPITAL

At the end of their interviews both Leanza and Bernadette revealed what they believe was the most important form of capital for Black boys. Bernadette shared that she often tells Nicholas, "you have to be proud to be Black, although there is a lot of negative press, just negative stuff out there when it comes to the Black race, he has to understand that this is who you are…you just have to love yourself." Leanza stated:

I think it's important that there is a sense of pride that is instilled in them. I think its important to talk to them about and just even hear from them their thoughts… about what it means to be a successful Black man and you know hear from them, in terms of the race piece. How that has impacted them? I think it's important to use all of those stories as the way to teach them to affirm them and teach them to question.

In their discussion of the value of having pride, Leanza and Bernadette revealed a competency that they have shared with their sons so that they can challenge their marginalization. Yosso (2005) classified this practice as resistant capital. Both mothers teach pride to their sons so that they can resist and challenge dominant discourses and identify the rhetoric and structure of racism. They imbue their sons with pride and self-love in a system that denies Black humanity, enabling them to remain healthy in the mouth of what Lorde (1984) aptly named a "dragon." In a system that literally refused to see Martin, it is important that families impart their sons with resistant capital so that Black boys can truly see themselves.

The greatest danger posed by the myth of post-raciality is that it creates a false sense of progress. "Racism is a permanent component of American life" (Bell, 1992, p. 13). As Leanza and Bernadette illustrate, we must remember to tell our sons about and prepare them for this truth. Our silence about this truth will not serve them.

Dedicated to Tracy Martin, Sybrina Fulton, and all Black boys.

REFERENCES

Alexander, M. (2010). *The New Jim Crow: Mass incarceration in the age of colorblindness.* New York, NY: The New Press, Inc.

Alcindor, Y. (2012, April 19). Trayvon Martin's father says he warned son about stereotypes. *USA Today.* Retrieved from http://usatoday.com

Bell, D. A. (1992). *Faces at the bottom of the well: The permanence of racism.* New York, NY: Basic Books.

Bonilla-Silva, E. (2002). The linguistic of color blind racism. How to talk nasty about blacks without sounding "racist". *Critical Sociology, 28*(1–2), 41–64.

Blow, C. M. (2013). The whole system failed Trayvon Martin. *The New York Times.* Retrieved from http://www.nytimes.com

Burnett, J., III. (2012, April 7). After Trayvon Martin, it's time for 'the talk'. *Boston.Com.* Retrieved from http://www.boston.com

Dawson, M. C. (2006). After the deluge: Publics and publicity in Katrina's wake. *Du Bois Review, 3*(1), 239–249.

Delgado, R. D., & Stefanic, J. (2001). *Critical race theory: An introduction.* New York, NY: New York University Press.

Dell'Antonia, K. J. (2012, March 26). Trayvon Martin and 'the Talk' Black parents have with their teenage sons. *The New York Times.* Retrieved from http://www.newyorktimes.com

Dixson, A. D. (2006). The fire this time: Jazz, research and critical race theory. In A. D. Dixson & C. K. Rousseau (Eds.), *Critical race theory in education: All God's children got a song.* New York, NY: Routledge.

Dixson, A. D., & Rousseau, C. K. (Eds.). (2006). And we are still not saved: Critical race theory ten years later. In *Critical Race Theory in Education: All God's Children Got a Song.* New York, NY: Routledge.

Ellison, R. (1952). *Invisible man.* New York, NY: Random House.

Fisher, C. B., Wallace, S. A., & Fenton, R. E. (2000). Discrimination distress during adolescence. *Journal of Youth and Adolescence, 29*(6), 679–695.

Johnson, C. (2008). The end of the Black American narrative. *American Scholar, 77*(3), 32–42.

Jones, C., & Shorter-Gooden, K. (2003). *Shifting: The double lives of Black women in America.* New York, NY: Harper Collins.

Lorde, A. (1984). *Sister, outsider: Essays and speeches.* New York, NY: Crossing Press.

Matsuda, M. J., Lawrence C. R., III, Delgado, R., & Crenshaw, W. K. (1993). *Words that wound: Critical race theory, assaultive speech, and the first amendment (new perspectives on law, culture, & society).* Boulder, CO: Westview Press.

Memmott, M. (2012, March 22). After Trayvon Martin's death, we're all having 'The Talk'. *National Public Radio.* Retrieved from http://www.npr.org

Peters, M. F. (2002). Racial socialization of Black children. In H. P. McAdoo & J. L. McAdoo (Eds.), *Black children: Social, educational, and parental environments* (pp. 57–72). Newbury Park, CA: Sage.

Romero, A. J., & Roberts, R. E. (1998). Perception of discrimination and ethnocultural variables in a diverse group of adolescents. *Journal of Adolescence, 21*, 641–656.

Stevenson, H. C., Davis, G., & Abdul-Kabir, S. (2001). *Stickin' to, watchin' over, and gettin' with: An African American parent's guide to discipline.* San Francisco, CA: Jossey-Bass.

Solorzano, D. G., & Yosso, T. J. (2002). Critical race methodology: Counter-story-telling as an analytical framework for educational research. *Qualitative Inquiry, 8*(1), 23–44.

Sybrina Fulton and Tracy Martin talk to Anderson Cooper about Zimmerman trial. (2013, July 18). *Huffington Post.* Retrieved from http://www.huffingtonpost.com

Wise, T. (2010). *Colorblind: The rise of post-racial politics and the retreat from racial equality.* San Franciso, CA: City Lights Books.

Ward, J. V. (2000). *The skin we're in: Teaching our children to be emotionally strong, socially smart and spiritually connected.* New York, NY: The Free Press.

Yosso, T. J. (2005). Whose culture has capital? A critical race theory discussion of community cultural wealth. *Race, Ethnicity and Education, 8*(1), 69–91.

LAURA S. ABRAMS

14. TALKING TO MY WHITE SONS ABOUT TRAYVON MARTIN

The Privilege of Protection

I have put off this writing project for some time. As much as I like to believe that I am comfortable talking about white privilege I feel a strong sense of reluctance in writing about it. So now I sit down and face my fears.

I am a white, married, upper-middle class, Jewish mother of two young sons, who are also white and Jewish. I am also an academic, a criminal justice researcher, and a professor who teaches graduate social work students about such topics as racism, oppression, and social justice. In my research, I study the lives of young people, mostly African American and Latino/a, who have interfaced with the juvenile and criminal justice systems. I see myself as someone who is committed to addressing the racial disparities that permeate America's criminal justice system. I am deeply troubled by the murder of Trayvon Martin and what this injustice means for African American men in the United States. But this chapter is not about my academic credentials or analysis, which is a fall-back comfort zone for me. Rather, it is about my personal story.

The night that George Zimmerman was declared "not guilty" of the murder of Martin on July 13, 2013, I was at Dodger Stadium with my family for a baseball game and movie night, where they were showing "42- The Jackie Robinson Story." I was excited to share this movie with my boys, as I thought that it would be a perfect way to teach my sons about racism in American history through baseball, subject matter to which they would relate. Since Jackie Robinson was a Dodger, it seemed particularly special to watch the movie at the stadium. When the baseball game ended, my husband Owen decided to head home with my ten year old son Noah who felt sick. My older son, Eli (then 10) and I decided to stay to watch the movie and we were excited to find our way home on public transportation- a trip we considered an 'adventure' in Los Angeles since we almost always travelled by car. The Dodger Stadium staff informed us that we could take a free bus to downtown Los Angeles and from there, grab a series of two trains to get home. We looked forward to the journey together.

About halfway through the movie, I checked Facebook and found out that the jury had delivered a not guilty verdict for Zimmerman. I was aware that the verdict might come in over the weekend, but did not expect it on a Saturday night. At the same time

K.J. Fasching-Varner et al. (Eds.), Trayvon Martin, Race, and American Justice, 85–88.

that I became aware of the verdict, Eli was sobbing on my shoulder during a scene in the movie when the Phillies manager was shouting brutal racial epithets at Jackie while he was up to bat. Until this point in the movie, Jackie had quietly internalized the racism he experienced, but at this point, he finally revealed the extent of his rage and frustration by screaming and breaking his bat against a wall. My son, who has grown up in a world with an African American president and in which most of his sports and music idols are African American, was horrified by the blatant racism depicted in the movie. I did not know that he even truly understood the content of the film, but I knew he was upset. Instinctively, I reached out to comfort him in the midst of my own sense of confusion about the Zimmerman verdict. The juxtaposition of these experiences felt entirely surreal.

In the midst of comforting my son and fielding my own text messages about the verdict, I paused momentarily to remember that Eli and I were taking public transportation home. Somehow our big adventure now seemed like a plan gone awry. My mind left Jackie Robinson and Martin and turned to our safety. I thought to myself: if there is a riot in downtown Los Angeles, will Eli and I be safe taking public transportation home? Will we be targeted in a wave of random violence because we are white? My mind filled with images of the Los Angeles riots post Rodney King, and I texted my husband and asked him to turn on the news and to monitor the situation. He assured me that nothing is happening and I did not need to worry. I Googled 'Los Angeles riot' and saw nothing. I checked the news every few minutes. Inside, I felt the weight of these strange paradoxes. My maternal instinct reigned: I will do anything to protect my son. Yet, I questioned myself, of what am I afraid? Of course if I have to be honest with myself; I must be afraid of an angry mob of people of color, but I so hated admitting this to myself that I cringe even as I write this today.

While my mind anxiously pondered our situation, Eli watched the movie, visibly upset and with tears, and I sought to comfort him with hugs, promises of popcorn, and my words. I assured him that eventually some of his teammates come through for Jackie and show their goodness and humanity. I half-heartedly assured him that people of color are not treated 'that way', that the world is a better place than it was 60 years ago, but with the events of the night, this did not sit well. For at the same time I was telling Eli that the racism he saw in the movie was a memento of the past, I could not quite reconcile the words I was speaking with the events of that evening. I couldn't explain why Martin was murdered just for being an African American young man buying candy, and why Zimmerman walked free under the guise of the supposedly race-neutral law. I realized I was simply not ready to explain this to him, because perhaps I did not understand this myself. I deliberately chose not to tell Eli about the ruling, or put any fear into his mind about the ride home. He did not know about Martin yet, and this was not the time to tell him.

Riding the bus and our two trains back home, I looked around at the people sharing this ride, thinking about who they were, and about the fabric of our society. The buses and trains were full of diverse Los Angeles: Young Latino couples, Asian families, and die-hard Dodger fans of all ages, sizes, and colors. People seemed animated and happy. I wondered if they know about the verdict and what they were thinking. Were they also afraid? Were they outraged? Were they ready to join a riot? There was no sign of violence or unrest in downtown Los Angeles, but I remained on guard and aware of my surroundings. As we rode the light rail to the very last stop, the train emptied. An older African American man sporting a Dodger cap talked to my son about Jackie Robinson, about his memories, about the Dodgers of decades ago, and about the new baseball sensation from Cuba, Yasiel Puig. The man was so kind to my son. Things felt peaceful, even normal. But I knew deep down inside, that the verdict rendered that evening meant that I could not be complacent with a 'normal' where innocent young Black men die and their killers are set free.

We arrived home safely, and I put Eli to bed knowing that my sons, and their safety, are my first priority; that I will do anything to protect them. I kissed my sleeping son Noah goodnight and whispered that I loved him. I experienced for a moment a connection to all mothers who love their children, and thought to myself how fortunate that I was that my children are, for the most part, safe from violence because of our race and class privileges. At the same time, I felt a wave of guilt that while I was able to tuck my sons in and watch them sleep safely, many mothers of color have lost their own sons, or must fear losing them to senseless violence. This is injustice: plain and simple. There is no other way to rationalize these differences.

I headed to my living room to watch the news. I saw one white person after another denying that race was an issue, wanting to frame the verdict a 'human' issue rather than a 'race' issue. I knew better than this and I was infuriated. I understand from my academic work and critical analysis that colorblindness is not the reality in our society and that this myth serves to perpetuate, rather than solve racism and racial disparities (Bonilla-Silva, 2006). In the comfort of my home, my anger at the verdict was fueled. I vowed, like other well-meaning white people, to do more, to use my privilege to work toward racial justice. But how long will these feeling last? Will this anger fade in a matter of weeks or months, as my daily routines and the concerns of work and motherhood and life take over?

It is now four months later, almost to the day. I know that this experience has changed me, but I am still sorting out exactly how I have changed. In all honesty, I still cannot quite figure out how to explain to my sons that the days of legal segregation and Jackie Robinson may be over, but that we still live in a society where a young African American man's life is not valued as much as their own; that the privilege of their skin color and social class will never have to render them a threat while walking down the street. I hate (but have) to admit that I still have not talked to them about Martin. My justification for this decision is that I tend to shield my sons from information that seems beyond their maturity or comfort zone. They are sensitive. It is like school shootings- I opt to not tell them about current events that will make them scared or upset. I must admit that it is part of my package of white privileges that I can protect my sons from having to understand the realities of modern day racism at such a young age. As a white mother, I exercise this 'privilege of protection' to do what I think is best for my children, but not without some conflict with the anti-racist educator components of my identity. I know that my African American friends do not have this privilege; and like other unearned privileges, I end up feeling guilt, which is, as I often teach and write about, an unproductive and immobilizing state in which to get stuck (Abrams & Gibson, 2007).

So I move forward. Little by little, I educate my sons about racism, using examples from the news, our own experiences and observations, and from the books they read. Their progressive school and Jewish education reinforce my own values around acknowledging, rather than ignoring, racism. We are not raising them to be colorblind. For this, as well as the safety and protections that I offer my children through my own set of privileges, I am grateful. In an ideal world, all mothers would enjoy the privilege of protection, but I cannot even try to fool myself into thinking that we are anywhere near this goal. While we may no longer be living in a time when people of color are not allowed to play major league sports, we must admit that enduring racism deeply shapes the experiences of nurturing and raising our sons.

REFERENCES

Abrams, L. S., & Gibson, P. (2007). Reframing multicultural education: Teaching white privilege in the social work curriculum. *Journal of Social Work Education, 43*(1), 147–160.

Bonilla-Silva, E. (2006). *Racism without racists: Color-blind racism and the persistence of racial inequality in the United States.* Lanham, MD: Rowman & Littlefield.

SECTION 3

HOW MUCH MORE CAN WE TAKE? THE FIGHT FOR RACIAL AND SOCIAL JUSTICE

TORIN JACOBS

REVOLUTIONARY IN UNIFORM

In your time they held picket signs
Wore Black pants tucked in Black boots with Black berets as cherries on top.
In my time with hoods over our heads
We sag our pants to protest.
Cryptic, quaint, silent, nonviolent.
Yet everywhere, thunderstorms over earthquakes, screaming in your subconscious
Something is terribly wrong with society.

The perfect weapon.
Lost tribes of youth wide legged; John Wayne walking.
Hidden faces, hijabed hoodlums
Ashamed of the landfill we were born in.
Flying pants at half-mast for the brave souls
Dead and dying to live America's dreams.

Born from prison culture
Lest we forget we live in a prison culture.
The forgotten (Leonard Peltier), the wrongfully accused (Anthony Graves), the electrified (George Stinney Jr., Bennie Foster, Lynda Lyon Block), the injected (Stanley Williams) and the belt noosed self-inflicted (Matthew Brockman).
On the outside
Walking around beltless
They accuse us of promoting homosexual prison behavior.
I say let us walk.
Lest we forget the countless victims of sexual abused sodomy.
Extinguishing ignorance with ignoble denim bumper stickers.
The low fashion labels reading:
"Support Our Inmates."

Lost tribes of youth
Telling America to lip lock their backsides

For refusing to pull up
A sagging economy, sagging schools, sagging neighborhoods.
A multitasking battle.

K.J. Fasching-Varner et al. (Eds.), Trayvon Martin, Race, and American Justice, 91–92.

Fighting uptight waist strangled persons with aluminum foiled badges designated
Authority: Obey me.
Or those vigilantes who would love to don white hoods once again, that are always
trying to kill me if I ever walk by in a hoodie.

Even those who wear their belts and lose the hoods are still stopped, frisked a
questioned the color of their skin
We sag for them.

The perfect protest.
So successful
Louisiana, Georgia, Chicago fine and impose prison culture to pacify beltless
freedom fighters.
America you have clipped and outright crippled the arms and legs of men with your
flashy limousine of consumer Conformity license plated AMCNDRM.
Reminded we are not the chosen passengers
We are run down with the guarantee of a better life made easy, in the throes of
helpless wheel chairs.

Refusing to sit
Forever pushed by bulky cinder block hands
We stand to sag proudly
Against a society who will not pull us up with love
Making sure we are securely snug around your waist
So we do not waste
As bodies sagging in back alleys or behind baskets of barbed wire.

America head, held so high, John Wayne walking.
Look down and notice
We are slipping off
Eventually left to fall, wrapped around your ankles
Tripping over your own selfishness into destruction.

Hooded sweatshirt with backside bulging out
I am a revolutionary in uniform.

KIRSTEN T. EDWARDS

15. IS IT "MARISSA" OR "MICHELLE?"

Black Women as Accessory to Black Manhood

During the question and answer period of a campus program addressing the tragic death of Trayvon Martin, and the equally tragic acquittal of his murderer, one young Black woman asked the panel of speakers, "So I've been hearing about this woman—is it Marissa or Michelle Alexander—Michelle Alexander, who also tried to stand-her-ground in Florida. What do you think about that?" I cringed as the words escaped her mouth. I immediately felt the need to clarify the details of *Marissa* Alexander's (as distinct from the noted author Michelle Alexander) case, and encourage her to research the important factors that led to Marissa's egregious 20-year sentencing. Unfortunately, I was simply the moderator for this event, and as such, held my tongue in hopes that the panelists would provide clarification. Clarification never came. The young woman and her question were briefly addressed and quickly dismissed.

Similar incidents have juxtaposed the profiling and shooting death of Martin and have offered several revelations. Throughout this chapter, I will discuss three distinct yet interlocking avenues by which Black women's lives function as accessories or instruments for the hyper-visibility of Black manhood. This service to Black male hyper-visibility exists parallel to the hyper-invisibility of Black femininity (McKittrick, 2006).

I identify three Black women accessories to the Martin tragedy: Marissa Alexander, Rachel Jeantel, and Sybrina Fulton. By juxtaposing rhetoric in the media concerning these women with historical and contemporary stereotypes associated with Black womanhood—Mammy, Jezebel, Sapphire, Cassandra, Welfare Queen, and Matriarch (Yarbrough & Bennett, 2000)—first, I detail the phenomenon of Black women as accessories. Second, I identify ways in which the tragedy of Black manhood becomes mechanism for the re-inscription of these markers onto Black women's bodies. Third, I discuss Black women's unreciprocated commitment to Black men as an example of silenced tragedy. Finally, I argue that Black male tragedy illuminates not only the silencing of Black women in Black spaces, but also the lack of solace available for them in white feminist spaces (Hull, Bell-Scott, & Smith, 1982).

K.J. Fasching-Varner et al. (Eds.), Trayvon Martin, Race, and American Justice, 93–99.

ACCESSORIZE: A TALE OF MARISSA ALEXANDER

From spray-painted T-shirts and canvas banners, square Black stickers and solemn portraits, Trayvon Martin's face stared out at a Leimert Park rally... hours after [Martin's murderer] was found not guilty... But on pamphlets distributed at the edge of the crowd, a different image stirred protesters. It was the face, they said, of another Black victim of unequal justice: Marissa Alexander. (Mueller, 2013, para. 1-2)

Similar to the scene at Leimert Park, Marissa Alexander resides at the edge of the public conscience, living solely within the confines of the tragedy of Martin. Curious readers will be hard-pressed to locate an article that provides an independent analysis of the injustice Alexander has suffered within the Floridian judicial system. Almost exclusively, publications covering Alexander's case also make requisite reference to Martin. These two cases have been inextricably linked merely because of their relation to the unjust deployment of the stand-your -ground law in Florida. This connection, however, does not take into account Alexander's experience as a Black battered woman. It does not interrogate the ways racism and sexism dangerously intersects in the lives and judicial experiences of Black women.

By a sad twist of fate, individuals who care about the existence of Black women are grateful on one level that the tragic shooting death of Martin and his murderer's subsequent acquittal has had one silver lining: attention being paid to Alexander's plight. On another level, this troubling coincidence becomes a reminder of the ways Black women's lives are often ignored, silenced, and subsequently forgotten (Austin, 1995; Crenshaw, 1991; Hill-Collins, 1986; Hull et. al., 1982). How quickly did the nation forget the shooting death of Miriam Carey, a new mother suffering from postpartum depression? Consider the case of Renisha McBride, a young Black woman seeking help after a car accident. Does the public remember Glenda Moore, the petite Black woman who watched her two young sons drown in a flood during Hurricane Sandy *after* being refused help by a nearby white resident? Absent ofro,a direct connection to Black male tragedy, these women's lives and deaths have been erased. Similarly, apart from the tragedy of Martin, Alexander was dismissed in much the same way.

Alexander is an accessory of Black male tragedy. She only exists as a complement or decoration to the killing of Martin, as evidence to support the claims of Black male persecution. The particularities of her case have gone largely unaccounted. The lack of attention paid by the judicial system to domestic violence endured by Black women, or the ways Black women are seen as not only beat-able but also rape-able, suggesting that their bodies cannot be violated or violenced, are rarely discussed (Crenshaw, 1991). The material results of this national and judicial apathy are glaring. Black women are victims of domestic violence and domestic fatalities at decidedly higher rates than any other racial group in the U.S. (Rennison & Welchans, 2002). Cases involving Black women victims are treated more leniently and defendants in these cases are least likely to be prosecuted (Kutateladze, Lynn, & Liang, 2012). These realities are reflected in the ways Alexander's story is told and embraced in public discourse. Simply the similarities and dissimilarities between her situation and Martin's are addressed. As protestors celebrate the retrial and possible release of Alexander, they do that with a political focus on racial profiling and injustice, and not injustices that arise at the intersections of race, gender, and class. Alexander's story is used to illustrate the ways racism, primarily against Black men, manipulates the justice system, resulting in differentiated outcomes. Alternatively, no recounting of Martin's story illuminates for us the ways Black women are violenced, silenced, and forgotten, or how their abusers are absolved.

WHAT DID YOU CALL ME?

This disparity compels me to reflect on the ways Black women manifest in our national lexicon. In their article "Cassandra and the 'sistahs': The peculiar treatment of African American women in the myth of women as liars," Yarbrough and Bennett (2000) offered readers an analysis of the ways Black femininity has been mythicized in the public consciousness. Complicating the three most recognizable historical tropes—Mammy, Sapphire, and Jezebel—the authors offered three additional related stereotypes that emerge in recent history:

1. Cassandra–The perpetually assumed liar. Regardless of the accuracy of her testimony, she is never believed.
2. Matriarch–The overly aggressive antithesis to Mammy. She emasculates the men in her life, and rears her children in an unhealthy, dysfunctional home.
3. Welfare Queen–The lazy breeder, producing undisciplined offspring who threaten economic solvency (p. 636).

A Welfare Queen Named Cassandra: A Tale of Rachel Jeantel

"[T]he most common criticisms about [Rachel Jeantel] was that she looked like Precious" (Beusman, 2013, para. 3)

After Rachel Jeantel's testimony, several news outlets and bloggers weighed in, with overwhelmingly negative commentary. Regardless of political affiliation, most legal analyses focused less on the substance of her testimony, and more on the substance of her image, and by extension the credibility of her testimony. It became profoundly clear in the weeks following her testimony that "who" Jeantel was and not the value of "what" she knew, was most important.

[Rachel Jeantel's] is a body that holds no value in this society so she is perceived as a person who is not valuable or credible. So for some people anything that came out of her mouth, even in the most perfect English grammar and diction, would be meaningless. (Beusman, 2013, para. 3)

Additionally, the nature of her relationship with Martin is constantly in question. "There is no middle-of-the-road opinion on Rachel…the *'friend, not-girlfriend'* of … Martin" (Johnson, 2013, para. 1, emphasis added). Why is this distinction important to make? It is important because Jeantel is a Black girl/woman, an individual not afforded innocence or friendship. Instead, Jeantel diminishes the value of Martin's life by bringing into question the character of a (adultified) Black boy (Dancy, 2012) that would potentially participate in a romantic relationship with a disreputable Black woman.

Most disheartening about Jeantel's treatment during the course of the trial and in its aftermath is the ways Black feminized mythical imagery resurfaced in such virulent ways, often unchallenged and sometimes accusatorially. In certain respects, Jeantel is blamed for Martin's lack of vindication. Although these stereotypes are written onto her body absent of her own voice, she remains partially culpable for the acquittal of Martin's murderer. While the Black community and allies mourn Martin, they are just as suspicious and skeptical of Jeantel as the conservative white community, giving her the proverbial "side-eye." There is no en masse recognition of the victimization Jeantel also experienced(s). By sheer epistemological ignorance, the public is unable to recognize that the system of injustice that could let the murderer of a Black child walk free is also the same system that reduced to lies the testimony of a young woman who looks and sounds like Jeantel. Before our very eyes, Jeantel was made a second-class citizen, a sub-human. Without possessing the accouterment of white, middle-class sensibilities, Jeantel became subject to 19th century Black Code—her Black, three-fifths human body was not allowed to testify against Martin's white murderer. She does not bare the markers of whiteness, and therefore was excused from the benefits of a white judicial system. What's more, she has been blamed for her own injustice.

Black Motherhood as Cultural Dysfunction: A Tale of Sybrina Martin

> Kinthenorthwest: What really irked me was to find out that she barely even had custody of Trayvon, and when she finally took over his care Trayvon went downhill into drugs, fights, burglary, skipping school and who knows (sic) what else.

> Steve: The psychology of the parents is so overwhelming here to their guilt. Their battles are self-fulfilling prophecies because they are in denial about their horrible parenting. (Rothman, 2013)

The above exchange is taken from the comments section of an article written about Sybrina Fulton on *Mediate.com*. In this exchange there is no discussion of the particulars of the case, but instead a critique of the assumed particulars of Martin's home life. In relation to the stereotype of the harsh, absent Matriarch, the commenters question Fulton's presence in the home, her failure as a mother, and her rearing of a delinquent Black menace to society. The commenters do not empathize with Fulton's loss. They do not recognize the tragedy of Black motherhood. Instead, Fulton becomes part and parcel of the on-going social drama of Black male fear and violence. Simultaneously, she becomes rationale for the punishment of Black men and boys. Martin is not murdered. Instead, on February 26, 2012, he received the punishment and discipline he needed, which was absent in the home of his Black Matriarch.

Additionally, Fulton, like Jeantel, is an accessory to Martin's character. The son of a Black Matriarch in the U.S. imaginary somehow invites his own murder. His life is meaningless, and worse a public threat, precisely because it is a product of Fulton's womb (Jones & Shorter-Gooden, 2003). The challenges of single-parenthood for Black women are not discussed. The lack of social and public support for Black mothers is ignored (Jones & Shorter-Gooden, 2003). The high incidents of poverty and low wealth attainment for Black women as a result of a "white supremacist capitalist patriarchy" (hooks, 1999) are not considered. Fulton did not do her job. Being a Black woman makes her incapable of doing the work of a loving mother.

Martin's murder also reveals the ways Black mothers' tragedy is available for public consumption (Jones & Shorter-Gooden, 2003). Everyone is allowed an opinion and assessment of the son of a Black mother. Unlike his white middle-class peers, who are afforded protection and discretion through "special help" and private clinics when tragedy touches their lives, Martin is prosecuted before his murderer. Under this public white gaze (Yancy, 2008), Black mothers are also on trial. They are unable to protect the innocence of their children from their own defamation (Jones & Shorter-Gooden, 2003).

WHERE ARE MY BLACK BROTHAS (AND WHITE SISTAHS)?

These myths (i.e., Mammy, Jezebel, Sapphire, Cassandra, Welfare Queen, and Matriarch) of Black womanhood are understandably commonplace. Living at the intersections of multiple systems of injustice makes Black women particularly vulnerable to political disenfranchisement, personal violence, and persistent disregard. Sadly, tragedy and pain are in many ways cornerstones to theorizing the lives of Black women. This reality becomes particularly problematic when hurtful lies manifest in Black and feminist spaces (Austin, 1995; Barnes, 2006; Baszile, 2008; hooks, 1981).

Within the Martin tragedy, the stereotyping of Black womanhood is particularly telling. Repeatedly, in the midst of efforts to affirm the sanctity of Black male life, the value of Black women's lives is undermined (Hull et. al., 1982; Perkins, 1983). While it would seem the recognition of patriarchy and sexism, although locally enacted, would incite solidarity; white feminists are largely silent, unwilling to bear witness. They appear more enamored with the "slut-shaming" of the privileged Miley Cyrus than the reproduction of oppressive tropes on the bodies of Marissa Alexander, Rachel Jeantel, and Sybrina Fulton. In regards to both Trayvon Martin and Miley Cyrus, there is "no room left in the inn" for Black women. Not only are the lives of Black women not supported, the perpetuation of their struggles becomes *support for* the platform of Black men and white women. Black women become accessories to the on-going drama of their lives. Whomever we need to be to support their political and social aims is justifiable, whether or not that being-ness heals or destroys us. This is the ultimate Objective position.

At this juncture, requisite solutions elude this essay. Quite frankly, this project has afforded the space to seriously consider the ways Black women (do not) exist epistemically within multiple movements. The work has been spiritually draining. Albeit dangerous, one suggestion does emerge. Is it time for Black women to abandon the need for community with those who have proven not to love them? Have Black women arrived at that periodic moment, as Alice Walker (1983) suggested separating for their own health and spiritual renewal? Can Black woman's need for survival now be allowed to supersede her commitment to a non-separatists agenda, particularly for those of her body who are committed to a non-separatist agenda? The answers are unclear. What is clear is that the stakes are high, the politics are obvious, and survival is not promised.

REFERENCES

Austin, R. (1995). Sapphire Bound! In K. Crenshaw, N. Gotanda, G. Peller, & K. Thomas (Eds.), *Critical Race Theory: The key writings that formed the movement* (pp. 426–437). New York, NY: The New Press.

Barnes, S. L. (2006). Whosoever will let her come: Social activism and gender inclusivity in the Black Church. *Journal of the Scientific Study of Religion, 45*(3), 371–387.

Baszile, D. T. (2008). Beyond all reason indeed: The pedagogical promise of critical race testimony. *Race Ethnicity and Education, 11*(3), 251–265.

Beusman, C. (2013, June 27). Why is Rachel Jeantel being treated like she's the one on trial? *Jezebel. Com*. Retrieved from http://jezebel.com

Crenshaw, K. (1991). Mapping the margins: Intersectionality, identity politics, and violence against women of color. *Stanford Law Review, 43*(6), 1241–1299.

Dancy, T. E. (2012). *The Brother Code: Manhood and masculinity among African American males in college*. Charlotte, NC: Information Age.

Hill-Collins, P. (1986). Learning from the outsider within: The sociological significance of Black feminist thought. *Social Problems, 33*(6), S14–S32.

hooks, b. (1981). *Ain't I a woman: Black women and feminism*. Boston, MA: South End Press.

hooks, b. (1999). *Remembered rapture: The writer at work*. New York, NY: Henry Holt and Company.

Hull, G. T., Bell-Scott, P., & Smith, B. (1982). *All the women are White, all the Blacks are men, but some of us are brave*. New York, NY: The Feminist Press.

Johnson, J. (2013, June 28). Love her or hate her, Rachel Jeantel is a star. *CNN.Com*. Retrieved from http://www.cnn.com

Jones, C., & Shorter-Gooden, K. (2003). *Shifting: The double lives of Black women in America*. New York, NY: Harper Collins Publishers.

Kutateladze, B., Lynn, V., & Liang, E. (2012). *Do race and ethnicity matter in prosecution?* (1st ed.). New York, NY: Vera Institute of Justice.

McKittrick, K. (2006). *Demonic grounds: Black women and the cartographies of struggle*. Minneapolis, MN: University of Minnesota Press.

Mueller, B. (2013, July 20) Marissa Alexander case emerges as symbol after Zimmerman verdict. *Los Angeles Times*. Retrieved from http://articles.latimes.com

Perkins, L. M. (1983). The impact of the cult of true womanhood on the education of Black women. *Journal of Social Issues, 39*(3), 183–190.

Rennison, C. M., & Welchans, S. (2002). *Bureau of justice statistics special report: Intimate partner violence.* (NCJ 178247). U.S. Department of Justice, Office of Justice Programs.

Rothman, N. (2013, August 19). Are the media turning Trayvon Martin's mother into Cindy Sheehan? *Mediate.Com.* Retrieved from http://www.mediaite.com/tv/is-the-media-turning-trayvon-martins-mother-into-cindy-sheehan

Yancy, G. (2008). *Black bodies, white gazes: The continuing significance of race.* Lanham, MD: Rowman & Littlefield.

Yarbrough, M., & Bennett, C. (2000). Cassandra and the "sistahs": The peculiar treatment of African American women in the myth of women as liars. *The Journal of Gender, Race & Justice, 3*, 625–657.

EFUA AKOMA

16. RESPONDING TO TRAYVON MARTIN'S DEATH

A Grassroots Approach

In the aftermath of Hurricane Katrina in 2005, eighty-two per cent of Black Americans believed achieving racial equality was not likely to happen in the near future. Once President Obama won office and began serving as the 44th Commander in Chief of the United States of America in 2009, this percentage dropped to 45% (Brooks, 2012). Then in February of 2012, a tragedy occurred when George Zimmerman targeted young Black male Trayvon Martin as a threat. Zimmerman indicated to the police that he stalked Martin because fit his stereotypical image of how a threat is defined, a young Black male (John-Hall, 2012, Kirk. 2012, Pignataro 2012). This begs the question, if this stereotypical image is all it takes to be deemed a threat, where does this leave all the other young Black males?

In light of the verdict pronouncing Martin's killer not guilty, more than just young Black males are forced to come to terms with the reality of living in a country that oftentimes does not provide safety for Black people. Around the country a lack of justice has been noticed when acts against Black communities take place. Americans also continue to bear witness to the murder of Blacks and that the killing of Martin is not an isolated incident. In fact, the numbers are staggering. In 2012, Black men, women and children were killed all over the U.S. at rates as high a 1 person killed every 28 hours at the hands of the police, security guards and self-appointed law enforcers like Zimmerman (Akuno, & Eisen, 2013). Has having a Black President positively impacted race relations given these statistics? This data tells us no, and other research confirms this as well. Areas such as educational attainment, career advancement, net worth, and health outcomes still illustrate vast disparities between whites and minorities (Lum, 2009).

Once President Obama took office, many people began espousing ideology of existing in a post-racialist state (Lum, 2009). To say this means race is no longer an indication for social ordering (Lopez, 2010) and that civil rights laws are no longer necessary (Parks & Rachlinski, 2009). In an address at Howard University in 1965, Lyndon Johnson talked about the insufficiency of viewing freedom as freedom as equality.

> You do not wipe away the scars of centuries by saying: Now you are free to go where you want, do as you desire and choose the leaders you please. You do not take a person who for years has been hobbled by chains and liberate him,

bring him to the starting line of a race and then say, "You are free to compete with all the others" and still justly believe you have been completely fair.

Forty-seven years after Johnson's speech, young Martin's death teaches U.S. citizens that the freedom to go where you want is not a guaranteed or protected right for some. We do not live in a post racialist era, and we continue to accumulate wounds to add to the scars of the past as race based stereotyping remains a central part of the landscape of America.

Black youth in the U.S. express major differences in how race is perceived in comparison to their white counterparts. In fact, Black youth are skeptical about any post-racial ideology (Cohen, 2011). Historically there has been a shared understanding among Blacks and other people of color and ample evidence that the American government has not proven a reliable source to protect civil liberties. In the wake of Martin's death, grassroots organizations created campaigns, compiled data and strategized how to make substantive change in Black communities (Akuno, 2012; Atkinson, 2013; Collins, 2013). This chapter reveals issues facing Black Americans in the 21st century and a grassroots organizational call for change.

BLACKS KILLED IN THE US: PROVIDING THE REAL DEAL

The Malcolm X Grassroots Organization (MXGM)

Those who analyze the routes to Black success have oftentimes been polarized in their approaches. The two main routes have been assimilation/integration-incorporating elements of the dominant culture into your worldview (Parillo, 2012; Shelton & Emerson, 2010) or Black nationalism-building and sustaining Black unity (Kaplan, 2011). MXGM is a Black Nationalist nationwide grassroots organization that believes Blacks, most of whom are working class people, need to construct their own realities ("About MXGM", n.d.). In order to plan where you need to go, you must know where you presently are. To understand where Black communities are, this organization produced a series of documents to be used to mobilize communities to initiate change in a number of ways. In addition to the creation of these reports, this organization has a track record of creating programs, campaigns and tools used for empowering Black communities across the U.S. such as *Let Your Motto Be Resistance: A Handbook on Organizing New Afrikan and Oppressed Communities for Self-Defense, CopWatch, Know Your Rights Information, The People's Self Defense Campaign*, the *No More Martins Campaign Appeal, Justice for Tatiana 'Jasira' Lima* and the *Jackson Plan* (Details of all of these campaigns can be found on their website http://mxgm.org).

The campaign around determining the extent to which Black communities are experiencing attacks leading to the death of men, women, and children resulted in the first report titled *Trayvon is All of Us* which called for President Obama to address the epidemic of Black murders through a national plan for racial justice (Akuno,

2012). It was also created to provide concrete numbers of Blacks who are losing their lives every day in the U.S. at the hands of police officers, security guards, and self-appointed law enforcers like Zimmerman.

National and local media coverage often underreports missing and killed minorities and in recognizing this deficiency, MXGM began compiling its own data to understand the extent to which Black communities are affected (Akuno, & Eisen, 2013b). This initial report detailed that between January and April of 2012, 30 Blacks were killed. Of the 30 killed, twelve were innocent of any illegal behavior and were not a threat and another eight were emotionally disturbed or displaying strange behavior. Of the remainder, it appeared all but two could have been addressed without the use of deadly force (Akuno, 2012).

The second document, *No More Trayvons! Demand a National Plan of Action for Racial Justice* of "No More Martin's Campaign" updated the first report by compiling the numbers of deaths from January 2012 through June 30, 2012. The report revealed 120 men, women and children were killed which means every 36 hours, a Black person was killed. These killings have been termed extrajudicial because they were committed without trial or any due process, against all international law and human rights conventions. Of those killed, eleven percent were under the age of 18, twenty-nine per cent were under 21 and sixty-nine per cent were under 31 years old. Mental health and substance abuse issues accounted for 23% of these deaths, 40% had suspicious behavior or appearance or traffic violations and 20% began with 911 calls to assist with domestic violence issues. In considering how these encounters were initiated, of the 120 that began as criminal activity, only thirty-seven per cent met that criterion. Of the 120 killed, only eighteen percent were likely armed based on police reports, witnesses, and investigations (Akuno, & Eisen, 2013a).

In April of 2013, MXGM released "Operation Ghetto Storm: 2012 Annual Report on the Extrajudicial Killings of 313 Black people by Police, Security Guards and Vigilantes" that compiled all of the killings in 2012. This third document provided continued evidence that in the face of the outcries for justice after Martin's murder, even with increased scrutiny on the actions against Black people, every 28 hours, a Black man, woman, or child was killed in the U.S. in 2012. This mounting evidence illustrates a systemic practice of targeting and killing Blacks in America in alarming numbers without a trial, jury, or judge and little if any accountability for those committing these violations of human and constitutional rights against this population (Akuno, & Eisen, 2013a).

While MXGM has concentrated its work around the killings of Blacks, additional evidence also exists to shed light on other ways in which Blacks are also targeted. At the end of 2011, the Black prison population was 37% of all prisoners (Carson, & Golinelli, 2013), yet this group only constitutes 13% of the U.S. population. Current statistics also illustrate that 21% of Black males by the time they turn 30 will be in prison compared to 2.3% of their white counterparts (Harrison & Beck, 2004). Compounding this situation is the reality that Black males are more likely to serve time in prison than they are to attend college (Western & Pettit, 2010).

MXGM stresses the need to address these issues on a number of levels. The initial *Martin in All of Us* report called for the following:

1. They call on all the organizations defending the human dignity and rights of Black people to collaborate on producing an independent national database of these executions.
2. We must demand that the priorities of Homeland Security be shifted from resources currently used to bolster the military industrial complex to focus on areas most useful for human for development such as education, health care and the development of sustainable energy and technologies.
3. At the same time, Homeland Security grants to police departments should be conditional on institutional overhaul that deprograms racist policies, rules of engagement, training and rewards.
4. Redirect Homeland Security Funds to establish and institutionalize local community mental health programs.
5. Overhaul policies that encourage and justify harassment, assault and murder by non-trained, non-accountable citizens, such as "stand your ground".
6. Eliminate all the policies and procedures on all levels of government and in all state agencies that sanction the racial profiling of Black and other discriminated and targeted groups.
7. Stop the War on Drugs and end the mass incarceration of Black people.
8. Challenge the cultural and legal climate that demonizes Black people and encourages racist attacks by security guards and vigilantes by instituting a massive public education campaign that addresses the historic legacy of white supremacy and institutional racism and educates the public about their fundamental human rights.
9. Finally, the Obama administration must create and institute a *"National Plan of Action for Racial Justice"* to fulfill the governments obligations under the Convention to Eliminate all forms of Racial Discrimination (CERD) by creating a permanent Inter-Agency Working Group to implement all of the aforementioned demands to protect Black and other historically oppressed groups from racial discrimination, targeted violence, and summary executions (Malcolm X Grassroots Movement, 2012).

A critical step in addressing these issues is organizing Black communities to end their reliance on responding to these killings but protecting the communities so these killings do not occur. To promote this change, they created an organizing tool, *Let Your Motto Be Resistance: A Handbook on Organizing New Afrikan and Oppressed Communities for Self Defense.* MXGM recognizes they are not the only groups in the U.S. affected by these actions and thus calls for an alliance with Indigenous peoples, Latinos, Arabs, Asians, and progressive whites to challenge all of the aforementioned issues and engage in the proposed solutions.

It is clear that Black communities are confronted with serious issues with which they must deal. Because previous reliance on the criminal justice system from the very initial stages of profiling, to arrests, violent attacks leading to deaths, and conviction rates do not operate equally for everyone in the U.S., change must happen. MXGM has provided much needed data highlighting the extent of the problem for 2012. Others must join in these efforts.

REFERENCES

Akuno, K. (2012). *Trayvon Martin is all of us. Malcolm X Grassroots Movement*. Retrieved from http://mxgm.org

Akuno, K., & Eisen, A. (2013a, July 17). No more Trayvons! Demand a national plan of action for racial justice. *Malcolm X Grassroots Movement*. Retrieved from http://mxgm.org

Akuno, K., & Eisen, A. (2013b, April 7). Operation ghetto storm: 2012 annual report on the extrajudicial killings of 313 black people by police, security guards and vigilantes. *Malcolm X Grassroots Movement*. Retrieved from http://mxgm.org

Atkinson, K. (2013, June 28). Grassroots organizations launch 'CopWatchNYC'. *New York Amsterdam News*. Retrieved from http://amsterdamnews.com

Brooks, R. (2012). A linked fate: Barack Obama and Black America. *Politics and Power*. Dissent 59.3.

Carson, E., & Golinelli, D. 2012. *Prisoners in 2012–advance counts*. Retrieved from Bureau of Justice Statistics: http://www.bjs.gov

Cohen, C. (2011). Millennials & the myth of the post-racial society: Black youth, intra-generational division & the continuing racial divide in American politics. *Daedalus, 140*(2), 197–205.

Collins, S. (2013, November 20). Kevin Powell launches national grassroots organization; BK Nation Debuts in the district. *The Washington Informer*. Retrieved from http://www.washingtoninformer.com

Harrison, P., & Beck, A. (2004). Prisoners in 2004. *Bureau of Justice Statistics Bulletin*. Retrieved from http://www.bjs.gov

John-Hall, A. (2012, April 9). Of hoodies and mistreatment—Perception trumps reality for young males in hoodies. *Philadelphia Inquirer*.

Johnson, L. B. (1965, June 4). *To fulfill these rights*. Washington, DC: Howard University.

Kirk, S. (2012). Hoodies don't make the man. *The* (OH) *Columbus Dispatch*, p. 14.

Lopez, I. (2010). Post-racial racism: Racial stratification and mass incarceration in the age of Obama. *California Law Review, 98*(1023).

Lum, L. (2009). The Obama era: A post racial society. *Diverse: Issues in Higher Education, 25*(26), 14–16.

Malcolm X Grassroots Movement. (2012, April 6). *Trayvon Martin is all of us*. Retrieved from http://mxgm.org/trayvon-martin-is-all-of-us/

Parillo, V. (2012). *Strangers to these shores: Race and ethnic relation in the United States, 2010 Census update* (Xth ed.). Boston, MA: Allyn & Boston.

Parks, G. S., & Rachlinski, J. J. (2009). Implicit bias, election'08, and the myth of a post-racial America. *Florida State University Law Review, 37*, 659.

Pignataro, J. T. (2012, March 29). 'Hoodies up' for Trayvon\hundreds wearing hooded sweatshirts march to city hall to protest fatal shooting of unarmed black teenager in Florida. *The Buffalo News*, p. 7.

Shelton, J. E., & Emerson, M. O. (2010). Extending the debate over nationalism versus integration: How cultural commitments and assimilation trajectories influence beliefs about Black power. *Journal of African American Studies, 14*(3), 312–336. U.S. Department of Justice. *Office of Justice Programs*. Retrieved from http://www.bjs.gov

Western, B., & Pettit, B. (2010). *Incarceration and social inequality*. Retrieved from American Academy of Arts and Sciences: http://www.amacad.org

KIRK JAMES & JULIE SMYTH

17. IF GEORGE ZIMMERMAN WERE FOUND GUILTY, WOULD THE CRIMINAL JUSTICE SYSTEM BE CONSIDERED JUST?

A Racial Analysis of American Criminal Justice in the Aftermath of Trayvon Martin

Issues relating to criminal justice have long divided the United States, creating a nearly bipolar perception of justice among its citizens (Alexander, 2010; Ryan, 2013). The Trayvon Martin verdict was no different - feelings ranged from disappointment, disbelief and anger, to relief, validation, and even jubilation. But to African Americans and other racialized minorities, Martin's death became emblematic of the extreme outcomes of racial profiling enmeshed in a history of criminal laws arbitrarily targeting Black men (Best, 2013; NeJame, 2013; Siddiqui, 2013).

The lack of consensus in the deliverance of justice, begs the following questions: what would it say about America's criminal justice system if George Zimmerman was convicted of Martin's murder? Would justice be celebrated? Would it be viewed as a well-oiled machine that convicts the guilty and acquits those who are innocent? While these questions are theoretical and somewhat rhetorical, this chapter aims to examine the ubiquitous correlation between Blackness and criminality in America by illuminating the criminal justice system through both historical and contemporary lenses. More specifically, this chapter investigates how legislative policies and policing disproportionately targets, and subsequently funnels, poor Black men, women, and children into the criminal justice system. How did we become a society where being Black, specifically being Black and male, became criminal? This examination posits that the criminal justice system is inherently racist and therefore unjust. It further challenges Americans to utilize the loss of Martin as a tipping point in our analysis and application of justice.

EMANCIPATION?

To comprehend the relationship between race and criminal law one must study the historic connection between defining crime, criminal law, and race. The idea that color itself can create or denote criminal behavior is deeply rooted in our history. (Finkelman, 2003, p. 206)

K.J. Fasching-Varner et al. (Eds.), Trayvon Martin, Race, and American Justice, 107–111.

The passage of the Thirteenth Amendment is hailed as a monumental achievement in ending legalized inequality and the subhuman treatment of Blacks in America. While its passage theoretically ended slavery, it also served to birth another peculiar institution – slavery was made unconstitutional "except as punishment for crime whereof the party shall have been duly convicted" (U.S. Const. amend. XIV).

The 'Black Codes' were laws passed by Southern States in response to the Emancipation. They were intended to criminalize, and control newly freed Blacks (Alexander, 2010). W.E.B. Du Bois (1910) venomously attacked the codes as nothing more than neo-slavery. Cohen (1991) stated, "the main purpose of the codes was to control the freedman" (p. 28). It became a crime to be Black and unemployed. The Codes further forbade Blacks from occupations outside those of a farmer or servant, unless they were able to pay a hefty annual tax. Laws were passed that permitted beatings, incarceration, and unpaid labor if Blacks broke what were often economic and socially oppressive contracts with whites (Alexander, 2010; Paige & Witty, 2009). If a newly freed Black family lacked financial means, their children could be taken and placed in the unpaid apprenticeships of white businesses. 'Pig Laws' were aimed at the theft of any farm animal with a value determined at more than ten dollars. Poor, hungry, and often homeless, Blacks arrested under Pig Laws were often sentenced to grand larceny charges and could receive up to a five-year jail sentence. Laws were also enacted that prohibited Blacks from looking whites in the eye, and in some states it was even a crime for a Black man to walk on the same side of the road as a white person. Finally, it was also against the law for a Black person to testify during any court proceedings involving whites (Finkelman, 2003; Muhammad, 2010).

These laws created a boom in the prison population. Once arrested and convicted, the formerly freed Blacks were leased out by the criminal justice system to labor in coal mines, railroads, and, of course, plantations. This 'convict leasing system' allowed states to lease out their mostly Black prison population as laborers for a fee, which became popular and profitable for both states and businesses throughout the South (Alexander, 2010; Mancini, 1996; Oshinksy, 1996).

For such a clearly prejudiced system to flourish in light of the Emancipation, the public had to also buy into the criminality and inferiority of Blacks (Alexander, 2010). As such, the images and narratives told of Blacks pre-Emancipation were generally that of a trusting, submissive and docile people. The term *quashee* was used by white slave owners to describe Black men as, 'gay, happy-go-lucky, frivolous, and cheerful' (Beckles, 1996, p. 9). White supremacy and the institution of slavery were further rooted in this attributed identity.

Post-Emancipation, the attributed identity of Blacks in America shifted. Social scientists, who long theorized Black inferiority during the heydays of slavery, were galvanized to observe and quantify the behavior of freed Blacks. Hoffman's landmark 1896 publication, *Race Traits and Tendencies of the American Negro,* saturated public consciousness with the imagery of Black men as criminal. His research negated the proximity of slavery to its subjects, negated the present social and economic plight of Blacks, but nonetheless proclaimed that, "crime, pauperism, and sexual immorality" (p. 217) are tendencies of Black people. Proponents of this doctrine could then substantiate their belief by highlighting the prevalence of Black men in the criminal justice system.

As a rule, the colored criminal does not enjoy the racial anonymity that cloaks the offenses of individuals of the white race. The press is almost certain to brand him, and the more revolting his crime proves to be, the more likely it is that his race will be advertised. In setting the hallmark of his color upon him, his individuality is in a sense submerged, and instead of a mere thief, robber, or murderer, he becomes a representative of his race, which is in turn made to suffer for his sins (Sellin, 1928, p. 63).

ONE HUNDRED YEARS LATER

Eerily reminiscent of the Black codes of 1865, the 'war on drugs' precipitated the current period of mass incarceration. In 1972, the U.S. prison population stood at close to 200,000, but today there are approximately one and half million people incarcerated, and nearly five million are on probation or parole (Carson & Golinelli, 2013; Maruschak, 2012). Perhaps more disturbing than the vast number of people incarcerated, is its extremely disproportionate racial composition. In 2007, approximately 900,000 prisoners were African American (Mauer & King, 2007). In 2009, the Bureau of Justice Statistics reported that non-Hispanic Blacks accounted for nearly 40% of the total federal and state prison population; however, the 2010 census reported that Blacks comprised less than 14% of the U.S. population. Even more startling is the fact that more African American men are under some form of criminal justice supervision today than were enslaved in 1850 (Alexander, 2010).

This drastic and racially disproportionate swell in the prison population is often attributed to an increase in crime, particularly drug-related crimes among people of color. However, the usage and sale of drugs is found to be consistent amongst whites and Blacks, yet the rate of African Americans convicted of drug offenses is 49% higher than their white counterparts (Alexander, 2010; Mauer & King, 2007). So, why are Blacks arrested and sentenced to prison at exponentially greater rates than whites?

A politically-driven media campaign in the mid-1980s portrayed Black men and women as the poster-children of the war on drugs, harkening back to the antiquated attributed identity of Blacks as criminal. In 1985, President Reagan hired media staff to paint the portrait of the war on drugs as a Black problem. Images of Black drugs dealers, 'crack whores,' 'crack babies,' and the decay of inner-city neighborhoods' permeated public consciousness (Alexander, 2010). This ideology was used to portray Blacks as criminal while at the same time denouncing any social or economic correlations to crime. President George H. W. Bush hailed this sentiment when he stated, "We must raise our voices to correct an insidious tendency - the tendency to blame crime on society rather than the criminal" (Becket & Sasson, 2004, p. 53).

In 1995, the conduction of a survey asked people to close their eyes and envision a drug user. The results were published in the *Journal of Alcohol and Drug Education* found that 95% of participants pictured a Black drug user, while only 5% envisioned other races. In actuality, research indicates that in 1995 only 15% of drug users in America were Black (Alexander, 2010; Holzer & LaLonde, 1991).

The unrelenting media coverage, which racialized the war on drugs, further compounded draconian laws and sentencing policies. In 1987, to ensure that individuals convicted of a criminal offense would serve at least 85% of their time in prison, the federal government enacted Truth in Sentencing legislation. These laws minimized early-release eligibility based on good behavior (Alexander, 2010). By 1994, more than ten billion dollars was allocated to states that were willing to implement some facet of Truth in Sentencing. Federal aid to construct new state prisons further enticed the implementation of stringent sentencing policies. As such, by 1995 almost 30 states passed some form of Truth in Sentencing (Dyer, 2000).

Sentencing laws continued to become more punitive, and prison populations increased exponentially due to the onset of 'three-strikes' legislation. This legislation, aimed at attacking repeat offenders, allowed prosecutors to request a life sentence for a third 'serious or violent' felony conviction (Bloomberg & Lucken, 2010). The implementation of these laws varied, but some states considered drug offenses 'serious or violent.' By 1997, the federal government and at least twenty-four states implemented some form of 'three-strikes' legislation (Walker, 1998).

Today, the most contemporary example of the young Black man as criminal is New York City's 'Stop and Frisk' policing strategy. Though they account for only 4.7% of New York City's population, young Black and Latino males between the ages of 14-24 accounted for 41.6% of the 685,724 stops in 2011. Firearms were confiscated in less than .5% of stops (New York Civil Liberties Union, 2011). Nine out of 10 people stopped by the New York Police Department (NYPD) are neither arrested nor ticketed. While these findings usurp the illusion of young Black men as criminal, many people still support policies such as 'stop and frisk.' This clearly demonstrates that the attributed identity of young Black men as criminal trumps empirical research, and is in some sense a greater determinant for criminal justice policies and legislation.

CONCLUSION

George Zimmerman's "not guilty" verdict elicited a wide range of emotions from the American public – many thought that justice was not served. However, as demonstrated in this chapter, even a guilty verdict would have done little to correct a history of arbitrarily criminalizing color. Slavery was once a legalized institution protected by laws. Post Emancipation, the infamous Black Codes and the convict-leasing system created an identity of Blacks as "criminal." Today, the mass incarceration of people of color and the criminal justice system as a whole are not only protected by laws, but are further substantiated by the public perception of Black men as criminal.

If we are truly a nation that proclaims justice as a core principle, then America must correct this insidious tendency to criminalize color. George Zimmerman's "not guilty" verdict is not the true obstruction of justice, but rather it is our entire criminal justice system. America will only be united when the roots of our criminal justice system are exposed, and hundreds of years of injustice are used to inform a system that can be truly just and representative of all.

REFERENCES

Alexander, M. (2010). *The new Jim Crow: Mass incarceration in the age of colorblindness*. New York, NY: New Press.

Beckett, K., & Sasson, T. (2004). *The politics of injustice: Crime and punishment in America* (IInd ed.). Thousand Oaks, CA: Sage.

Beckles, H. (1996). *Black masculinity in Caribbean slavery*. Kingston, JA: University of the West Indies.

Best, X. (2013, August 11). 'Up to no good': The racial profiling of Trayvon Martin and Abdulrahman Awlaki. *Truth-Out*. Retrieved from http://truth-out.org

Blomberg, T. G., & Lucken, K. (2010). *American penology*. New Brunswick, NJ: AldineTransaction, Transaction publishers.

Carson, E. A., & Golinelli, D. (2013). *Prisoners in 2012: Advance counts*. Retrieved from Bureau of Justice Statistics: http://www.bjs.gov

Cohen, W. (1991). *At freedom's edge: Black mobility and the southern white quest for racial control*. Baton Rouge, LA: Louisiana State University Press.

Du Bois, W. E. B. (1910). Reconstruction and its benefits. *American Historical Review, 15*(4), 784.

Dyer, J. (2000). *The perpetual prisoner machine: How America profits from crime*. Boulder, CO: Westview Press.

Finkelman, P. (2003). *Defending slavery: Proslavery thought in the old south: A brief history with documents*. Boston, MA: Bedford/St. Martin's.

Hoffman, F. L. (1896). *Race traits and tendencies of the American Negro*. New York, NY: Macmillan.

Holzer, H., & LaLonde, R. (2000). Job stability and job change among young unskilled workers. D. Card & R. Blank (Eds.). *Finding jobs: Work and welfare reform*. New York, NY: Russell Sage Foundation.

Mancini, M. (1996). *One dies, get another: Convict leasing in the American South, 1866-1928*. Columbia, SC: University of South Carolina Press.

Mauer, M., & King, R. (2007, July). Uneven justice: State rates of incarceration by race and ethnicity. *The Sentencing Project*. Retrieved from http://www.sentencingproject.org

Maruschak, L. M. (2012). *Probation and parole in the United States, 2011*. Retrieved from Bureau of Justice Statistics: http://www.bjs.gov

Muhammad, K. G. (2010). *The condemnation of blackness*. Cambridge, MA: Harvard University Press.

NeJame, M. (2012, May 30). Trayvon Martin shooting wasn't a case of racial profiling. *CNN Opinion*. Retrieved from http://www.cnn.com

Paige, R., & Witty, E. (2009). *The Black-white achievement gap: Why closing it is the greatest civil rights issue of our time*. New York, NY: Amicom.

Oshinsky, D. M. (1996). *Worse than slavery: Parchman farm and the ordeal of Jim Crow justice*. New York, NY: Free Press.

Ryan, M. (2013, July 15). System has failed: Crowds react to George Zimmerman verdict. *USA Today*. Retrieved from http://www.usatoday.com

Sellin, T. (1928). The Negro criminal: A statistical note. *Annals of the American Academy of Political and Social Science, 140*(1), 52–64.

Siddiqui, S. (2013, July 30). Bill to end racial profiling given new life by Trayvon Martin outcry. *The Huffington Post*. Retrieved from http://www.huffingtonpost.com

New York Civil Liberties Union. (2011). *Stop and frisk*. Retrieved from http://www.nyclu.org

Walker, S. (1998). *Sense and nonsense about crime and drugs: A policy guide* (IVth ed.). Belmont, CA: West/Wadsworth.

JENNIFER M. GÓMEZ

18. EBONY IN THE IVORY TOWER

Dismantling the Stronghold of Racial Inequality from the Inside Out

MYTH OF A POST-RACIAL SOCIETY

It is January 2012. In a discussion with psychology doctoral students and psychologists regarding President Obama, joy and pride, accompanied by the long-awaited ability to exhale, abounded. We finally had realized an American post-racial society.

As a psychology scholar, I wondered if perhaps this discussion was a social experiment on the rhetoric that can accumulate in groups that are ripe with hierarchies and steeped in tradition. After all, negative opinions toward Blacks have increased since President Obama was elected (Lybarger & Monteith, 2011). I chose to voice my viewpoint, not intending to speak for all Black Americans, but communicating that while Black, President Obama is upper class, light-skinned, educated, and Hawaiian, therefore, he did not elicit the same stereotypes that a darker-skinned, physically bigger, Black man who grew up in an inner-city would have. I was met with silence- the utter refusal to deal with the harsh realities of the effects commonly held stereotypes of Black men can have on a society. Bigoted beliefs, hate, racist ideology, and inequality are not harmless. They can be strong contributors to racially motivated murders, like that of teenager Trayvon Martin. Especially here within the elite circular confines of the ivory tower where education provides higher class and status, fighting for social justice means having change affect some of the country's most influential. I wonder then what it would take for scholars to openly and readily acknowledge that racism is still as strong as it has ever been, with denial of that reality feeding racism with strength, power, and, most frighteningly, immunity?

SOCIETAL EXPECTATIONS OF RACISM

The myth of the post-racial society pervades. The history of racism in the U.S. has dictated society's understanding of bigotry. Slavery, Jim Crow, and the backlash during the Civil Rights movement provided the societal backdrop for racial slurs, segregation, lynchings, police brutality, and white supremacy. That history remains the basis for society's understanding of racism. Overt racism is largely viewed as unacceptable (Dovidio, 2001); covert racism is often unnoticed or ignored.

K.J. Fasching-Varner et al. (Eds.), Trayvon Martin, Race, and American Justice, 113–117.
© *2014 Sense Publishers. All rights reserved.*

Despite overt and covert racism, an extremely intelligent and qualified Black man was elected as President for two terms and has not suffered the fate of far too many high profile Black leaders of the past, including Medgar Evers, Martin Luther King, Jr., Harry and Harriette Moore, and Malcom X. These changes are *steps* towards success. Blacks in America are still subject to inequality (Gómez, forthcoming). Thus, it is not surprising that the same racist ideology that contributed to these assassinations is found, overtly or covertly, in the murder of Trayvon Martin. The challenge becomes how to retain the ground we have made, while fighting for the freedom we have yet to fully realize. We have not succeeded until we possess equality in all respects: access to high-quality education, jobs, and careers; pay that is comparable to whites; ability to live and work in neighborhoods that are not overrun with violence; access to quality physical and mental health care; self-esteem, without the necessity of double-consciousness (DuBois, 1903); absence of internalized self-hatred; true equality that *embraces* differences. In short, to live in a world without bigotry, where racially motivated murders, like that of Martin, no longer exist.

CURRENT RACIST MANIFESTATIONS

Systemic: The Structure of Racism in Academia

In many ways, academia mirrors societal inequality, with Black scholars and viewpoints often subjugated. For instance, psychological research determines the lens through which we examine psychological processes, such as conceptualizing human distress as biologically rather than contextually caused. Further, the peer review process in publication reinforces mainstream views, which inhibits the dissemination of theoretical and empirical work that challenges, contradicts, or simply differs from the dominant frame.

Additionally, systemic racism has been infused in some classrooms beginning with desegregation (hooks, 1994). In academia, systemic racism takes the form of classroom dynamics that: ignore the reality of groups who are and are not represented in academia; ignore the reality of the history of American racial oppression; ignore the reality of the current state of American racial oppression; and ignore the reality of the benefit of white and/or class privilege that professors themselves hold.

Interpersonal: Minoritizing Minority Voices

Voices of Black scholars are often muted as a result of two frameworks, microaggressions and chilly climate. Microaggressions (e.g., Sue, 2010) are perpetrated by members of the dominant culture who have the power to impose their reality (Sue, Capodilupo, Nadal, & Torino, 2008); interpersonal microaggressions include microinvalidations, such as *The Trayvon Martin case was not about race* (e.g., Sue, 2010). 'Chilly climate' refers to conscious or unconscious sexism in academia that impacts daily work, promotions, income, and status (Freyd & Johnson, 2010).

Though chilly climate references gender bias, it can explain the treatment that Blacks experience in the university—societally lowered status. Microaggressions and chilly climate can work in conjunction to undermine Blacks' success in academia.

Black students are faced with bigotry from colleagues and superiors in the academic setting. Phrases that reference the underlying assumption of Africa as the 'Dark Continent' oppress students who are already visibly and/or culturally different from the majority of their peers, resulting in a cultural, as opposed to intellectual, 'imposter syndrome' (Gómez, 2013). This common assumption of inferior intelligence (Sue, Capodilupo, & Holder, 2008) is personified here; a Black university student shared her career aspirations with her professor, who responded, "Do you really think people here want to listen to a Black woman judge?" This sentiment has similarities with the Zimmerman acquittal, portraying the dominant view that Blacks' viewpoints, leadership, and even lives are devalued.

After developing a reputation from professors and peers as being intelligent and insightful, one instructor degraded a Black psychology doctoral student, describing her as 'attacking and aggressive," loosely referencing—and prejudicially misinterpreting—her engagement in typical academic discourse as justification. This is an example of the use of coded language that conveyed the instructor's underlying prejudice, as they are synonyms to stereotypes of Blacks being violent and criminal (Sue et al., 2008). The power of these stereotypes, along with their ability to transcend contexts, influences not only academic feedback, but racially-motivated violence as well, such as in the murder of Martin.

JUSTICE IN THE IVORY TOWER

The moral dilemma of fighting for racial justice within academia is that by virtue of membership, we are in collusion with a system that is knowingly and unknowingly problematic in its systemic and interpersonal practices of inequality. This association can be perceived as approval of the system and could perhaps be used to mask the problems within the system (e.g., a Black professor, like a Black U.S. President, can be distorted as evidence of a post-racial environment).

The elitism in the ivory tower makes less possible change that is sought from the outside; further, higher education, particularly in psychology and related disciplines, is ostensibly a place where examination of the world in which we live dominates our thinking. Thus, while a self-aggrandizing culture can develop and be super-imposed upon the learning culture, academia is fundamentally an institution of learning that encourages and awards investigative, critical questioning of societal dynamics that condone murder of youth like Martin, for example.

Academia is populated with avenues in which we can fight to change the status quo within a culture that is fraught with white, male, heteronormative assumptions of normality and success (Gutierrez y Muhs, et al., 2012). The changes made in academia can engender change in society more broadly—through research, pedagogy, and community building.

The lens in which research is conducted can be limiting when the culture around the research is itself narrow. Nevertheless, the underlying tenet of psychological research is the pursuit for understanding the truth of the human condition. Being faithful to our experience of truth, while incorporating the sociocultural context into our research, etches a new reality in the field that aligns closer to the reality for many underrepresented groups. By conducting research that documents inequality and/or is culturally relevant, such as Cultural Betrayal Trauma Theory (Gómez, 2012), our work creates a bridge between the state of the field and the experience of people from diverse social locations and cultural categories. This knowledge can provide fuel for the broader societal fight for social justice.

Along with research, pedagogy offers a way to effect tangible change. By teaching students how to think, creating classrooms where the totality of students' identities are encouraged, and fostering the genuine belief that students' viewpoints do matter despite racially-motivated negative feedback, we can create a next generation of scholars who will fight for social justice during an era where violent and nonviolent discrimination prevails. Teaching in culturally informed ways, such as utilizing media that contradicts stereotypes, and addressing the inequality ever-present in what students are taught in psychology and society, can encourage inclusion of underrepresented students. This means actively challenging students' perceptions of Blacks, students' perceptions of minorities, and the common assumptions that many privileged whites adhere to and impose upon others as reality. This engendering of critical thinking is beneficial to Black and non-Black students, as internalized, interpersonal, and institutional racist ideology prevails. Thus, classrooms can serve as havens for mutual intellectual and spiritual growth that transforms education into freedom (hooks, 1994).

Fostering this sense of belonging is one way to engender change from the inside, but is not enough given the oppression within the academy. Through aligning ourselves with committed Black scholars, scholars of color, and white allies both within and across institutions, community building is beneficial for our success, our longevity, our given department, our chosen field, academy, the society, and us. Though fighting for racial justice within academia can be very isolating, there is an ever-growing community of scholars who have been or are currently battling the same war for social and racial justice. Volumes like the current one create a virtual dialogue of understanding, goals, strategies, and hope that engender self-care and motivation to continue. By actively challenging and dismantling the inequality present in academia, we are joining a community of professionals who are making lasting change.

Gaining critical mass on small scales (e.g., within departments) and larger scales (e.g., within the field) means that the ability to ignore dismisses or minimizes the magnitude of the enduring academic, and societal inequality is greatly diminished. Most importantly, acculturation into the academic milieu, when it costs us our souls, our integrity, our spirit, our motivation, and our will is not only not worth it, but is antithetical to creating the kind of inclusive community for which we are striving.

Retaining our souls, remaining grounded outside the academy, and actively striving for self-empathy in the struggles we are facing is vital to the collective health of change. Within this transcendent community, we act as runners in a social justice relay race: through research, pedagogy, and community-building, reaching the finish line cannot be the goal; we race throughout our lives, then pass the baton along to the next generation of fighters.

CONCLUSION

There is an abundance of evidence that documents the oppression of Blacks in America (Gómez, forthcoming). Blacks continue to be subject to unique, unquestionably severe, and long-lasting oppression that once justified slavery and currently maintains the status quo, as exemplified by the murder of Martin, and the subsequent acquittal of the murderer. Nevertheless, it is important to have the fight for racial justice be intertwined with the fight for broader social justice (e.g., racism towards other groups; anti-gay legislation; able-ism) because the underlying sickness is the same: belief in superiority justifies the belief in domination (Lorde, 1983); together, we dismantle a system that capitalizes on inequality. In this way, fighting for racial and social justice in academia engenders change: not hierarchically, from the top down; not grassroots, from the bottom up; but rather horizontally, from the inside out.

REFERENCES

Books, B. (1994). *Teaching to transgress: Education as the practice of freedom.* New York, NY: Routledge.

Dovidio, J. F. (2001). On the nature of contemporary prejudice: The third wave. *Journal of Social Issues, 57*, 829–849.

DuBois, W. E. B. (1903). *The souls of Black folk.* New York, NY: Bantam Books.

Freyd, J. J., & Johnson, J. Q. (2010, February 8). *References on chilly climate for women faculty in academe.* Retrieved from University of Oregon: http://pages.uoregon.edul

Gómez, J. M. (2012). Cultural betrayal trauma theory: The impact of culture on the effects of trauma. In *Blind to Betrayal.* Retrieved from https://sites.google.com

Gómez, J. M. (2013). The "Imposter Syndrome"? Dealing with racism from fellow graduate students in psychology. *Psych Discourse—News Journal of the Association of Black Psychologists, 47*(1), 23.

Gómez, J. M. (forthcoming). Microaggressions and the enduring mental health disparity: Black Americans at risk for institutional betrayal. *Journal of Black Psychology.*

Gutierrez y Muhs, G., Niemann, Y. F., González, C. G., & Harris, A. P. (2012). *Presumed incompetent: The intersections of race and class for women in academia.* Logan, UT: Utah State University Press.

Lorde, A. (1983). There is no hierarchy of oppressions. *Bulletin: Homophobia and Education, 14*(3/4), 9.

Lybarger, J. E., & Monteith, M. J. (2011). The effect of Obama saliency on individual-level racial bias: Silver bullet or Smokescreen? *Journal of Experimental Social Psychology, 47*, 647–652.

Sue, D. W. (Ed.). (2010). Microaggressions, marginality, and oppression: An introduction. In *Microaggressions and marginality: Manifestation, dynamics, and impact.* Hoboken, NJ: John Wiley & Sons, Inc.

Sue, D. W., Capodilupo, C. M., & Holder, A. M. B. (2008). Racial microaggressions in the life experience of Black Americans. *Professional Psychology: Research & Practice, 39*, 329–336.

Sue, D. W., Capodilupo, C. M., Nadal, K. L., & Torino, G. C. (2008). Racial microaggressions and the power to define reality. *American Psychologist, 6*, 277–279.

ROGELIO SÁENZ

19. FIFTY YEARS OF THE DEFERMENT OF THE DREAM FOR RACIAL JUSTICE

From Hattie Carroll to Trayvon Martin

It has been half a century since Dr. King delivered his monumental "I Have a Dream" speech at the March on Washington on August 28, 1963.

Many Americans laud the improvements in race relations that have occurred in the United States since then. Many Americans proclaim that we now live in a post-racial, color-blind society, where race is no longer significant. After all, these individuals claim, for the first time in our nation's history, we elected a Black man to the U.S. presidency.

Of course the hatred that many Americans and even members of Congress have lashed against President Obama clearly shows that racism is alive and well today. Certainly, South Carolina Republican Representative Joe Wilson's "You lie!" bellow, which interrupted President Obama's health care reform speech to Congress on September 9, 2009, not only was cloaked in racism but showed a disrespect for the office (see Dowd, 2009). Many other current events and indicators evince the continued significance of race.

This chapter provides an overview of the injustice concerning the deaths of African Americans Hattie Carroll and Trayvon Martin that occurred half a century apart. The similar outcomes of the two trials associated with these deaths serve as reminders that despite some improvements that have occurred in race relations, much has also not changed since Dr. King revealed his dream on that eventful day.

THE DEATH OF HATTIE CARROLL

On the evening of February 8, 1963, many of Maryland's prominent citizens turned out for the Spinsters' Ball, a white-tie affair, held at the Emerson Hotel in Baltimore (Frazier, 2005). One of these guests was William Zantzinger, a rich white 24-year-old tobacco farmer, accompanied by his wife, Jane.

Prior to their arrival at the ball, they had started drinking at a restaurant where they were eventually refused more drinks due to disorderly behavior (Douglas, 2009). They subsequently arrived at the ball where the couple continued to drink heavily with the husband exhibiting obnoxious behavior, which included striking women and workers with his cane. In the wee hours of the morning at approximately 1:30 a.m.,

K.J. Fasching-Varner et al. (Eds.), Trayvon Martin, Race, and American Justice, 119–123.

Zantzinger approached Hattie Carroll, a Black 51-year-old barmaid and mother of 11 children, and loudly demanded a drink as she was serving another customer (Slade, 2013). He became increasingly agitated and began yelling racial epitaphs at her when she did not serve him immediately. As she was getting his drink, he lifted his cane and struck Carroll on her right shoulder (Goshko, 1963, p. 3). Witness reports indicated that instantly after being struck, Carroll became unsteady and said, "This man has upset me so that I feel deathly ill," (Goshko, 1963, p. 3). Her condition worsened with her speech becoming "thick, slurred and incoherent" (Goshko, 1963, p. 3). After being transported by ambulance to Baltimore's Mercy Hospital, she died there several hours later from a brain hemorrhage (Goshko, 1963).

Zantzinger was apprehended as Carroll was taken to the hospital and homicide charges were added after her death. Specifically, the second-degree murder charge was complicated because Carroll suffered from atherosclerosis, hypertension, and an enlarged heart (Slade, 2013). The three-judge panel that would try Zantzinger acquitted him of the second-degree murder charge and charged him, instead, with manslaughter along with three assault charges. Zantzinger's request to have his trial moved from Baltimore was granted. The trial was set to take place in Hagerstown, Maryland, on June 19, 1963. Eight days later, on June 27, the panel of three judges found Zantzinger guilty of manslaughter in the death of Carroll. The sentencing stage of the trial was postponed.

On the same historic day of the March on Washington when Dr. King delivered his "I Have a Dream" speech, approximately 70 miles northwest in Hagerstown, Maryland, the three-judge panel announced the sentence of Zantzinger for manslaughter in the death of Carroll. The panel delivered a mere slap on the wrist of Zantzinger—six months in jail along with fees summing to $625. To add insult to injury, Zantzinger was allowed to harvest his tobacco crop before reporting to jail (Slade, 2013).

This event was overshadowed by the March on Washington and the electrifying orator describing his dream. Sociologists of the time did not call attention to the case and for the most part have overlooked it. Nonetheless, Bob Dylan wrote a song titled "The Lonesome Death of Hattie Carroll" which brought the case to the national consciousness. In the conclusion of the song, Dylan chides Lady Liberty for the miscarriage of fairness in the case. Dylan (1964) wrote:

Oh, but you who philosophize disgrace
And criticize all fears
Bury the rag deep in your face
For now's the time for your tears

Dylan used poetic license in the song including dropping the letter "t" from "Zantzinger," among other exaggerations and inaccuracies (see Frazier, 2005; Slade, 2013).

As an epilogue, Zantzinger had another run-in with the law involving race. In 1991, he was convicted for charging poor African American tenants rent for dilapidated housing he had not owned since 1986 (Slade, 2013), a conviction for which he received more jail time and had to pay a greater sum in fines than he did for the death of Carroll (Frazier, 2005). He died at the age of 69 on January 3, 2009 (Douglas, 2009).

In the pre-Civil Rights era the death of Carroll and the lenient sentence of Zantzinger were not uncommon. Indeed, several other high-profile unpunished deaths of African Americans occurred a few months after Carroll's death that year: the murder in June of civil rights activist Medgar Evers in Jackson, Mississippi and the deaths in September of four young girls, Addie Mae Collins, Denise McNair, Carol Robertson, and Cynthia Wesley, killed in the Birmingham, Alabama, church bombing. There were other similar high-profile deaths within the decade before (Emmett Till in Mississippi in 1955) and the decade after (Dr. King in Memphis in 1968 and George Jackson in San Quentin Prison in 1971) Carroll's death along with countless other lower profile deaths.

Even though the volume of such deaths has declined compared to that era, they have not disappeared.

THE DEATH OF TRAYVON MARTIN

Nearly fifty years after the death of Hattie Carroll, on the evening of February 26, 2012, African American teenager Trayvon Martin was walking back to his father's fiancée's home from a convenience store (Alcindor, 2012). The setting: a gated community in Sanford, Florida. He attracted the gaze of George Zimmerman, a white-Peruvian man and self-appointed neighborhood watchman. Zimmerman focused his attention on Martin and followed him. He called 911 and although the dispatcher instructed Zimmerman to stay in his vehicle until authorities arrived, he continued pursuing Martin. A struggle broke out between the two culminating in Zimmerman fatally shooting Martin.

This event appeared to be a straightforward case. An armed 28-year-old man fatally shoots an unarmed teenager walking home after going to the store. We well know that such cases are anything but straightforward when race is involved. Indeed, due to Florida's stand-your-ground law, it took 44 days for Zimmerman to be charged and only after a special prosecutor was asked to review the case (Alcindor, 2012).

The trial of Zimmerman, which began on June 10, 2013, was to be decided by a jury consisting of five white women and one Latina woman. The defense relied on the time-tested strategy of racial profiling to show that Martin was a hoodie-clad troublemaker—there was talk of marijuana and school problems—who did not belong in the neighborhood in which a man who felt threatened killed him (Blow, 2013). The defense closed with a snowy-image video showing Martin making his purchase at the convenience store before his encounter with Zimmerman. The video resembled the countless others that we regularly see capturing criminals in the act. Put simply, Martin was put on trial and criminalized in Zimmerman's trial (Cobb, 2013).

The jury had three options: to find Zimmerman guilty of second-degree murder; guilty of manslaughter; or find him innocent. On the evening of July 13, 2013, a little over a month after the start of the trial, the jury found Zimmerman innocent in the death of Martin.

As an epilogue on Zimmerman, he has attracted media attention in scrapes with the law following his acquittal. While two have involved vehicular speeding, a third in early September 2013 concerned questioning on allegations of domestic violence against his wife, who has filed for divorce, and her father (Alvarez, 2013), but did not result in charges.

CONCLUSIONS

As we are in a reflective state of mind given the 50th anniversary of Dr. King's "I Have a Dream," it is important to call attention to the senseless deaths of Hattie Carroll and Martin and the trial outcomes of Zantzinger and Zimmerman, which occurred a half century apart. Although the lives of Carroll and especially that of Martin were pointlessly cut short, Zantzinger spent only six months in jail for the death of Carroll in 1963, while Zimmerman will not spend any time in the death of Martin today. While some things have improved concerning race relations since the eventful day of August 28, 1963, many others, unfortunately, have not.

In the interim, we have seen a transformation of racism from the overt, in-your-face hate spewed by proud card-carrying racists to the 'kinder' and 'gentler' form where individuals use 'nice' talk and actions to support and sustain the racism and inequality that is deeply etched at the structural level, in the form of our laws and institutions (Bonilla-Silva, 2001, 2013; Feagin, 2006, 2013). In the contemporary context, many whites and Americans, in general, are secure in believing that we are now color-blind and live in a post-racial society—we have gotten past the significance of race.

Accordingly, it is not surprising to observe whites and African Americans—as well as other groups of color depending on the issue—holding nearly diametrically opposed views regarding issues such as the police beating of Rodney King, the trial outcome of O.J. Simpson, views on the continued existence of racial discrimination and inequality, opinions regarding the continued need for affirmative action, and so forth (see Blow, 2012; Smith, & Seltzer 2000).

As the demography of the United States progressively shifts along racial and ethnic lines, we are already seeing increasingly vigorous efforts to limit the access of people of color, particularly African Americans and Latinos, to the political process and opportunity structure. In this manner white privilege and white space are protected in the midst of a growing population of color and, eventually, a declining white population. The erection of gates, fences, and walls alongside the enactment of ordinances and laws to keep 'those people' ("the other") out of 'our' neighborhoods, communities, and country represent measures to maintain white privilege and white space (Moore, 2007; Saenz et al., 2011). Similarly, efforts to racially profile people serve the same purpose. These forces—formed, supported, and maintained by a color-blind ideology—allowed Zimmerman's defense team to convince the jury that Martin was a troublemaker who was up to no-good in a place where he did not belong—rather than as a frightened unarmed teenager pursued by an armed man. The story that the defense related fit neatly in the white narrative concerning "the criminal Black man" (Feagin, 2013).

Thus, today, drawing on Langston Hughes (Rampersad & Roessel, 1994), we continue to see the deferment of Dr. King's dream for racial justice.

REFERENCES

Alcindor, Y. (2012, December 12). Trayvon—Typical teen, or troublemaker. *USA Today*, p. 1A.

Alvarez, L. (2013, September 9). Police question Zimmerman about a domestic dispute. *New York Times*. Retrieved from http://www.nytimes.com

Blow, C. M. (2012, April 6). From O.J. to Trayvon. *New York Times*. Retrieved from http://www.nytimes.com/

Blow, C.M. (2013, July 15). The whole system failed Trayvon Martin. *New York Times*. Retrieved from http://www.nytimes.com

Bonilla-Silva, E. (2001). *White supremacy and racism in the post-civil rights era*. Boulder, CO: Lynne Rienner.

Bonilla-Silva, E. (2013). *Racism without racists: Color-blind racism and the persistence of racial inequality in America*. 4th ed. Lanham, MD: Rowman & Littlefield.

Cobb, J. (2013, July 14). Blood on the leaves. *The New Yorker*. Retrieved from http://readersupportednews.org

Douglas, M. (2009, September 13). W.D. Zantzinger, Subject of Dylan song. *New York Times*, pp. B8.

Dowd, M. (2009, September 13). Boy, Oh, Boy. *New York Times*, p. 17.

Dylan, B. (1964). *The lonesome death of Hattie Carroll*. Retrieved from http://www.bobdylan.com

Feagin, J. R. (2006). *Systemic racism: A theory of oppression*. New York, NY: Routledge.

Feagin, J. R. (2013). *The white racial frame: Centuries of racial framing and counter-framing* (IInd ed.). New York, NY: Routledge.

Frazier, I. (2005, February 24). Life after a lonesome death. *The Guardian*. Retrieved from http://www.theguardian.com

Goshko, J. M. (1963, June 21). Zantzinger witnesses describe attack. *The Washington Post*, p. 3.

Moore, W. (2007). *Reproducing racism: White space, elite law schools, and racial inequality*. Lanham, MD: Rowman & Littlefield.

Rampersad, A. (Ed.), & Roessel, D. (Assoc. Ed.). (1994). *The collected poems of Langston Hughes*. New York, NY: Vintage.

Sáenz, R., Menjívar, C., & Garcia, S. J. E. (2011). Arizona's SB 1070: Setting conditions for violations of human rights here and beyond. In J. Blau & M. Frezzo (Eds.), *Sociology and human Rights: A bill of rights in the twenty-first century*. Newbury Park, California: Pine Forge Press.

Slade, P. (2013). *True lies: The lonesome death of Hattie Carroll*. Retrieved from http://www.planetslade.com

Smith, R. C., & Seltzer, R. (2000). *Contemporary controversies and the American racial divide*. Lanham, MD: Rowman & Littlefield.

TAMARA F. LAWSON

20. THE *RES GESTAE* OF RACE

The Implications of "Erasing" Race

The George Zimmerman murder trial provides a high profile example of how issues surrounding race can be construed differently inside and outside the courtroom. Much of the public attention and media coverage of the case focused on facts prior to the deadly encounter, such as the fact that the Trayvon Martin, was allegedly followed by the defendant both from his vehicle and on foot, and also that the defendant was told by the police not to follow the victim at all. For some, these facts created a public perception that the unarmed teen victim was either unfairly targeted, criminally profiled, or racially stereotyped because he was a Black male teen in that neighborhood, a neighborhood that had recently experienced a rash of residential burglaries by Black male teens. Yet, inside the courtroom the defense objected to direct or indirect references to Zimmerman having a racial motive, and the prosecution echoed that the case was not about race.

One of the undisputed yet controversial facts in the George Zimmerman murder trial was the race of the alleged victim; Trayvon was an African American male. Prior to the opening statements at trial, the Zimmerman defense team filed a motion urging that any mention by the prosecution of the word "profiling" would inappropriately inject race into the case and thus be unfairly prejudicial. That motion serves as the stimulus for this chapter and necessitates a broader discussion of the issues at stake when a pre-trial motion to exclude race is filed in a case involving an inter-racial murder, such as this case with a white Hispanic defendant and an African American victim. The motion was purportedly attempting to urge the court to indirectly adopt an artificial standard of colorblindness, which is jurisprudentially inconsistent with existing precedent that permits the relevant use of race among the totality of the circumstances within a criminal case.

Thorough legal analysis mandates that there is no fact that is *per se* off limits or automatically inappropriate to consider. The legal concept that all the facts are important and thus all must be properly included for the jury to evaluate is captured in the Latin term *res gestae*. Evidence is considered *res gestae* "when: it is so closely connected to the charged offense as to form part of the entire transaction, or it is necessary to give the jury a complete understanding of the crime, or when it is central to the chain of events (Allen v. State of Oklahoma, No. F-2005-471, Court of Criminal Appeals, 2005)." In more basic terms *res gestae* can be described as all circumstances surrounding and connected with the crime at issue. During the

K.J. Fasching-Varner et al. (Eds.), Trayvon Martin, Race, and American Justice, 125–128.

Zimmerman trial there was an attempt to convince the public, and even the court, that race was a fact that was somehow "off limits" or "improper" to consider in criminal cases. Arguably, the efforts to exclude or limit the use of race in the Zimmerman trial were done solely to gain tactical advantage because exclusion was not required under the law. In fact, Zimmerman's arguments were contrary to existing legal precedent. The following examples demonstrate that the use of race is not prohibited in the American criminal justice system and that race is commonly used: (1) as a factor to establish a defendant's motive or state of mind in crimes with inter-racial facts, (2) as a factor within the totality of circumstances towards finding reasonable suspicion or probable cause to detain or arrest a suspect, (3) as a factor in evaluating the reliability of eye witness testimony in cross-cultural identification cases, or (4) as a factor in the reasonable perception of a deadly threat in self-defense scenarios. Particularly in cases of self-defense, it has been found that the race of the participants of the deadly encounter has impact on the case. The preliminary findings complied by *The Tampa Bay Times* and The Urban Institute both separately conclude that killings of African American victims are more likely to be found justified than killings of white victims in Florida and other stand-your-ground states (Childress, 2012).

The multiple ways in which race is currently employed in court is not without criticism or commentary, but the relevant use of race to fully inform the jury regarding the totality of the circumstances in criminal cases has been repeatedly accepted by appellate courts, including the United States Supreme Court. Some scholars further assert that dealing with race "head on" in criminal cases and making race a conscious issue for the jury to evaluate, instead of a subliminal one unwittingly motivating the analysis, is the only effective way to minimize the risk of a (racially) skewed result from the jury. The implications of excluding race, or even minimizing its significance, can negatively impact a case in a way that risks the fairness and/or accuracy of the ultimate verdict.

"The *Res Gestae* of Race" seeks to illustrate how race, in conjunction with all the other facts, can be an integral part of the case and should be treated as such. In an accurate assessment of any criminal case, *all* the facts matter. Further, the specific contours of each fact, as well as the lens through which each fact is viewed matters; the absence of important facts can dictate drastically different evidentiary inferences and generate completely different verdicts. In criminal trials generally and in the George Zimmerman murder case specifically, the victim's race is a part of the complete story of the crime and an integral and necessary fact for the jury to evaluate among the totality of the circumstances. The inclusion of all the relevant facts is most critical in murder cases where the deceased victim-witness is unable to tell his or her version of the events. The *res gestae* concern is exacerbated in cases involving self-defense that typically present intense factual disputes to establish either a murder or a justified killing. The controversial murder charge filed against Zimmerman for killing Martin highlights the importance that each and every fact plays in a controverted case. The absence, limitation, or de-emphasis of any one fact could have consequences on the outcome.

Many approach discussions about race as a political "hot potato" or somehow bigoted. However, that need not be the case. Although it may be strategically preferable for the defense or prosecution to ignore, minimize, or even wholly avoid issues of race in a particular criminal case, there is seldom a strong legal rationale for it. Some litigants avoid issues of race solely due to the lack of knowledge of the empirical research on implicit bias and its subtle yet consistent impact on jurors. However, strictly from an evidentiary stand-point, when analyzing what happened before, during, and after the deadly encounter of an alleged murder, the victim's race is simply one fact among the totality of the circumstances that also must be analyzed, just like age, and gender, the location of the crime scene, and all the corresponding forensic evidence. A thorough analysis of the Zimmerman murder case can no more ignore Trayvon's race than it can ignore that it was raining the night of the killing. The fact that it was raining is relevant for the jury to consider why Trayvon might have had the hood of his hooded-sweatshirt on – was the hood on to conceal his identity in a convert way making him appear reasonably more suspicious or was the hood on to protect his head from the rain? In the same way, the fact that Trayvon matched the race, gender, and age of the suspected residential burglars in the neighborhood may have informed Zimmerman's perception of Trayvon as "suspicious," and/or fueled Zimmerman's state of mind toward Trayvon that he was one of the individuals "who always get away." All these facts matter, and have significance on the reasonableness of Zimmerman's perceptions and related actions as to whether his act of killing was criminal or justified. Each fact works in concert to form the complete story of the crime. From the complete story that is presented to the jury, including facts that are highly contested and in dispute, the jury is charged as the ultimate finder of fact to determine whether, beyond a reasonable doubt, a crime occurred. However, without the complete story, the accuracy of the jury is compromised and the "justice" in the American criminal justice system is jeopardized. An attempt to urge courts to employ a colorblind ideology to issues of evidentiary relevance is a perilous path to traverse.

REFERENCES

Alper, T. (2005). Stories told and untold: Lawyering theory analysis of the first Rodney King assault trial. *Clinical Law Review, 12*(1).

Barnes, M. L. (2013). Reflection on a dream world: Race, post-race and the question of making it over. *Berkley Journal of African American Law and Policy, 11*(1), 6–18.

Capeheart, J. (2013, July 12). Race and the George Zimmerman Trial. *The Washington Post.* Retrieved from http://www.washingtonpost.com

Chestek, K. D. (2011). Competing stories: A case study of the role of narrative reasoning in judicial decisions. *Legal Communication & Rhetoric, 9*, 99.

Childress, S. (2012, July 31). *Is there racial bias in "stand your ground" laws?* Retrieved from http://www.pbs.org

Fletcher, G. P. (1988). *A crime of self-defense: Bernard Goetz and the law on trial.* Chicago, IL: University of Chicago Press.

Harris, D. A. (2003). Using race or ethnicity as a factor in assessing reasonableness of the fourth amendment activity: Description yes; prediction, no. *Mississippi Law Journal, 73*, 423–475.

Harvard Law Association. (1988). Race and the prosecutor's charging decision. *Harvard Law Review, 101*(1520), 546–1547.

Johnson, K. R. (2010). How racial profiling in America became the law of the land: *United States vs. Hignoni-Ponce* and *Whern vs. United States* and the need for truly rebellious lawyering. *The Georgetown Law Review, 98*(4), 1006–1077.

Jones, R. L. (2007). A more perfect nation: Ending racial profiling. *Valparaiso University Law Review 41*(2), 621–658.

Lawson, T. F. (2012). A fresh cut in an old wound—A critical analysis of the Trayvon Martin killing: The public outcry, the prosecutor's discretion and the stand your ground law. *University of Florida Journal of Law and Public Policy*.

Ledwon, L. (1995). *Law and literature: Text and theory*. New York, NY: Routledge.

Lee, C. (2013). Making race salient: Trayvon Martin and implicit bias in a not yet post-racial society. *North Carolina Law Review, 91*(1555).

Lee, C. K. Y. (1996). Race and self-defense: Towards a normative conception of reasonableness. *Minnesota Law Review, 81*(367), 404–406.

Lyon, R. (2009). Media, race, crime and punishment: Re-framing stereotypes in crime and human rights issues. *DePaul University Law Review, 58*(741).

Martin, S. T., Hundley, K., & Humburg, C. (2012, June 2). Race plays complex role in Florida's "stand your ground" law. *Tampa Bay Times*. Retrieved from http://www.tampabay.com

Matsuda, M. (1987). Looking to the bottom: Critical legal studies and reparations. *Harvard Civil Rights–Civil Liberties Law Review, 22*(323).

Monahan, J., & Walker, L. (2002). *Social science in law: Cases and material*. New York, NY: Foundation Press.

Richardson, L. S., & Goff, P. A. (2012). Self-defense and the suspicion heuristic. *Iowa Law Review, 98*(293), 293–336.

Roman, J. K. (2013, July). Race, justifiable homicide and stand your ground laws: Analysis of FBI supplementary homicide report data. Retrieved from Urban Institute: http://www.urban.org

Ruthland, M. (2012, June 20). Sanford police chief Bill Lee fired in wake of Trayvon Martin case. *Miami Herald*. Retrieved from http://www.miamiherald.com

SECTION 4

VISION OF A SOCIALLY JUST SOCIETY: LESSONS TRAYVON MARTIN TEACHES

DONTE DENNIS

SHOULD I FEAR?

Reflections from a Student

Dear President Obama & America,

We have a problem. A large portion of our society today seems to think that people regardless of race, gender or age get the same opportunities, but sadly this is not the case. Since the founding of this country individuals of color have seldom been treated with fairness or equality. From the perspective of African Americans or Native American groups, although we live in the same society as other races, people of color in this country are still negatively stereotyped.

Even more frightening is that people of color have adopted these negative stereotypes. They have become conditioned to believe individuals' appearance, namely skin color, means that they are 'dangerous'. They then decide to take action on these assumptions and when society attempts to hold them accountable, they are let off scot-free after the 'dangerous' individual is killed. This happens over and over again – as if it is a cycle.

I am about the same age as Trayvon Martin and to see someone who could have been just like me, someone who had plans set out for his future, whose life was taken because he looked 'dangerous' is not right. He could have very well left the house to take a break from studying or decided to get something for a family member, and was killed because he looked 'dangerous'. But what made him 'dangerous'? Martin's description matched that of more than half of my neighborhood and me.

So now I am left wondering what should I do to keep myself safe? Should I throw away all of my hoodies? I certainly cannot change my skin color or gender, nor would I want to. So what could I possibly do to keep myself from dying at the hands of someone who finds me 'dangerous' and decides to take action that would or could result in the death of another unarmed Black boy?

A young Black male,
Donte Dennis

K.J. Fasching-Varner et al. (Eds.), Trayvon Martin, Race, and American Justice, 131.

JESSICA SCOTT

21. REPRESENTATION MATTERS

Changing Images of Black Masculinity in America

Thousands of people have had years of their lives wasted in prison – years they would have been free if they had been white. (Alexander, 2010, p. 114)

The death of Trayvon Martin is an urgent illustration that not only have years of freedom been lost to an inordinate number of Black men in this country, but that years of life have also been tragically curtailed. Martin is one example among many of young Black men who have been the subjects of extrajudicial killings or institutionalized police violence that continue to be terrifying echoes of the murder of Emmett Till and post-emancipation lynching in the American South (Davis, 1981). The murder of Martin, the subsequent acquittal of George Zimmerman, and the discursive presence of the case in the media illustrate that Black masculinity in America has been constructed as a threat. In order for racial justice to become a reality in the United States, the way the dominant culture sees and represents young Black men must shift.

Walker's classic text *The Color Purple* is capable of serving as a model for transformative community relationships. For the past several years I have taught a unit during which we read the text and watch the film version of *The Color Purple*. For many students the differences between the two versions seem insignificant. Even using Martin as a "real-life" example of the costs of such cinematic representations of Black masculinity, students remain convinced that, for them, the "purpose" of the book is to convey the story of a woman overcoming the violence and oppression of men, and the book has been successful enough. For me, Black masculinity hangs in the balance of the liminal space between film and text.

The knowledge that Zimmerman possessed about Martin was that he was young, Black, and male. Zimmerman described Martin as a "teenager" wearing a hoodie (Zimmerman Calls, n.d.). This knowledge resulted in his assessment of Martin as someone who didn't belong in the gated community and who looked like he was "on drugs." Regardless of whether or not Zimmerman shot Martin *because* he was a young Black man, the meanings of Black masculinity as they have been constructed in America resulted in Zimmerman's decisions to follow, watch, and pursue Martin in a way that resulted in Martin's death. The knowledge that Martin was a teenager did nothing to mitigate the threat that his body posed in Zimmerman's imagination.

K.J. Fasching-Varner et al. (Eds.), Trayvon Martin, Race, and American Justice, 133–137.

Constructions of the threat of Black masculinity, which result in very real dangers to the lives and liberation of Black men in America, are gendered as much as they are raced and classed. And, because they rely upon the centrality of sexualized terror, particularly in relation to white femininity (Davis, 1981), confronting these images demands an analysis embedded in awareness of the intersecting relationships of such constructions. Otherwise, "analyzing an instance of injustice as *solely* racial, gendered, or economic in nature is likely to result in an inadequate understanding of causes, injuries, and solutions" (Juang, 2005, p. 708).

Limited representations of Black masculinity through "controlling images" (Collins, 2005) translate into denial of recognition of the humanity of Black men (Juang, 2005). The narrow representational outlets of professional athletics and hip hop spaces within which the Black male body become commodities that serve the interest of wealthy white investors (Collins, 2005; Farrow, 2010) and are not adequate for honoring the complexity of Black men's lives.

Racial injustice is "not merely a problem of negative images that can be remedied by creating more positive portrayals" (Juang, 2005, p. 709). However, structures of racial injustice are ineffective without being shored up by an ideological underpinning of cultural messaging, which reinforces the threat posed by "the image of the feared Black male body [which] also reappears across entertainment, advertisement, and news" (Collins, 2005, p. 153). Otherwise, the practices involved in suppressing particular groups of people are visibly discriminatory and by becoming visible, have failed to evolve as effective tools for suppression in an era of "color-blindness" (Alexander, 2010). This is why what Davis (1981) has christened the "myth of the Black rapist" was necessary in order to justify the lynching of Black men after emancipation. Justifications for lynching took several forms before finally foregrounding the necessity to protect white womanhood from the threat of Black men who were constructed as sexually unrestrained: "Racial profiling is based on this very premise – the *potential* threat caused by African American men's bodies. Across the spectrum of admiration and fear, the bodies of Black men are what matters" (Collins, 2005, p. 153).

Such "controlling images" (Collins, 2005) limit the possibilities for Black men to be recognized in their most authentic and complex human selves. Collins writes, "Black men are well represented within this industry of media violence, typically as criminals whose death should be celebrated, and often as murder victims who are killed as 'collateral damage' to the exploits of the real hero" (p. 101). These images are ubiquitous to the point of becoming hegemonic, and they have resulted in "a fear reinforced by media imagery that has helped to create a national image of the young Black male as a criminal" (Alexander, 2010, p. 113). Collins (2005) spoke to the representations specific to particular experiences, but projected onto racialized bodies, they affect the experiences of men of color who are not criminals, but may continuously be perceived as criminal: "For middle-class Black men who lack the actual experiences of prison and street culture, mass media representations of gangstas as authentic symbols of Black masculinity help fill the void. They may not be actual gangstas, but they must be cognizant that they could easily be mistaken as criminals" (p. 240). Black masculinity has been constructed as a threat, but Martin's death is a sobering reminder that the real danger lies in being perceived as a threat (Staples, n.d.).

While Walker was criticized for her representation of violent and abusive Black men in *The Color Purple*, the written word offers a rehabilitation of Albert, a damaged character, who is reintegrated through the transformation that occurs as a result of the liberation of the protagonist and primary narrator of the novel, Celie. At the end of the text, Celie and Albert sit together on the porch spending the evenings exploring a shared intellectual curiosity that causes them to raise questions about African philosophies and practices, gender roles, and love, sewing together, and learning one another in a way that neither had thought possible or desirable.

Celie heals from the trauma of sexual, physical, and emotional abuse at the hands of her stepfather, Pa, and her husband, Albert, through the radically transformative love of Shug Avery, the woman who is first Albert's and then Celie's lover. Celie's story of overcoming abuse, learning to love herself, and her reunion with her sister, from whom Pa separated her, provides the primary narrative arc for the text, communicated through letters written from Celie to God. However, Celie is not the only character who is hurting. Though her husband abuses her, his character also allows the reader to see the generational pain inflicted through expectations of masculinity in the text. Albert's father forbids Albert's marriage to Shug Avery, destroying Albert's potential for happiness. Albert then attempts to exact similar expectations of masculinity on his son Harpo, who was happily married to Sofia until Albert instructed him to abuse Sofia to make her submissive.

This violence is not, however, without a context. The violence of racism is a looming, but often absent, presence in the text. Its sinister implications are manifest in both the arrest and imprisonment of Sofia and in the death of Celie's father, whose life was cut short by a lynching mob as a consequence of his economic success, and whose history must be uncovered after Pa's death. While Pa could be any opportunistic man who married a wealthy young widow, the violence of the lynching mob was reserved for Black men after emancipation (Davis 1981).

Celie's fear of Albert was justified in a way that Zimmerman's suspicions about Martin never were. However, the ability for Albert to be seen and recognized as a whole man with potential to become a better version of himself is a result of Celie's liberation. The film version, though, offers a much narrower representation of Black masculinity as a largely threatening presence, the destruction of which is the cost for Celie's liberation. Albert's menacing behavior dominates the majority of the film. Though he appears intermittently, he is always at a distance even after Celie's departure. When Celie does see him, she continues to be visibly frightened by him, even after he has been destroyed by the curse she issues at her departure from his house. At the end of the film, Albert is vanquished from the community and must watch the happiness of the other characters from a distance. Equally, one of the few times when Black men are not behaving in a threatening way in the film is when they are attempting to help a desperate Miss Millie get her car out of reverse in order to return home after dropping Sofia off to spend Christmas day with her family. Miss Millie perceives the men who offer their help as a threat, and the very real risk of being a Black man in the proximity of white womanhood (Davis, 1981) is made tangible through her cries for them to stop trying to attack her.

The structure of Walker's text is set in a community where very few white people are present, but where the violence of racism is the legacy inherited by characters whose lives have been circumscribed by violence; it allows us to address the process of healing from such violence, the recuperation of a Black masculinity that is, by the conclusion of the text, allowed to be fully human in its expression, and the resilience of a community that heals external and internal wounds communally rather than through the escape of some members or the expulsion of others. I believe that the generational violence experienced by the men in Albert's family is a violence that would be mitigated enormously in a racially just society, but in order to create that racially just society, "controlling images" of Black masculinity (Collins 2005) need to be interrupted, challenged, and expanded to include actual experiences and greater possibilities for the lives of African American men.

The differences between Walker's text and its film representation are startling and important given the context of racial injustice in our contemporary moment. Without a representational mode through which men of color are permitted to be seen as whole individuals with a range of motivations, emotional complexities, and desires for themselves and their communities, threatening and violent representation of men of color will remain a model for the way that the lives of Black men in America are seen. If space for representation and recognition of complex Black masculinity had existed in the popular imagination of the United States, Zimmerman might have been able to look at Martin without perceiving him as a threat, and Martin might still be alive. Shifts in the criminal justice system, the venue where the value of Martin's life came up short compared to the threat he allegedly posed, and where young Black men are incarcerated at alarmingly disproportionate rates when compared to other demographics (Alexander, 2010; Collins, 2005), will be difficult, if not impossible without a shift in the way that Black men are represented in the American imaginary. Walker's womanist vision of the world has the possibility to heal us all from the psychological violence of structural injustices, but its commodification by Hollywood filmmaking results in the same representation of Black men that fed Zimmerman's unjustified description of Martin as "suspicious"; "up to no good"; "on drugs" (Zimmerman Calls, n.d.), and that allowed a jury to refuse recognition of Martin's person as one deserving of justice in life and in death.

REFERENCES

Alexander, M. (2010). *The new Jim Crow: Mass incarceration in the age of colorblindness*. New York, NY: The New Press.
Collins, P. (2005). *Black sexual politics: African Americans, gender, and the new racism*. New York, NY: Routledge.

Davis, A. (1981) *Women, race, and class*. New York, NY: Vintage Books.

Farrow, K. (2010). Is gay marriage anti-black??? In R. Conrad (Ed.), *Against equality: Queer critiques of marriage* (pp. 21–32). Lewiston, ME: Against Equality Publishing Collective.

Juang, R. (2005). Transgendering the politics of recognition. In S. Stryker & S. Whittle (Eds.), *The transgender studies reader* (pp. 706–720). New York, NY: Routledge.

Spielberg, S. (Director-Producer), Guber, P., & Peters J. (Producers). (2003). *The color purple* [DVD]. Los Angeles, CA: Warner Brothers.

Staples, B. (n.d.). *Just walk on by*. School World. http://www.myteacherpages.com/

Walker, A. (1982) *The color purple*. New York, NY: Harcourt Brace.

Zimmerman calls non-emergency line. (n.d.). In *USA Today*. Retrieved from http://www.usatoday.com

ADRIENNE MILNER

22. POST-RACE IDEOLOGY IN BLACK FACE

*What Trayvon Martin Teaches About Color-blind Racism and White
People's Love for Martin Luther King, Jr. and Barack Obama*

Why do white people love Dr. Martin Luther King, Jr. and Barack Obama? These leaders can be pointed to as symbols of the perception that the United States is and should be a post-racial nation. Support for King and Obama enables white people to maintain a facade of color-blindness while simultaneously displaying a personal approval of Blacks (i.e.: "I'm not racist, I voted for Obama"). It appears easier to condemn discrimination than to acknowledge privilege.

In the wake of Trayvon Martin's murder, the popular and idealized notion that the U.S. either is, or should be, a color-blind society must be confronted. The events surrounding Martin's killing and George Zimmerman's acquittal evidence the persistence of racism, and confirm why color-blind messages put forth by King and Obama, which are neither feasible nor desirable, are commonly adopted by white people. Zimmerman's contention that the shooting was not racially motivated, and the white general public's acceptance of this claim, demonstrates the way in which color-blind racist ideology continues to mask the importance of race and prevent social justice.

In this chapter, I discuss King's and Obama's color-blind racial ideology to demonstrate how these leaders garner support from white people while simultaneously being othered by them, ultimately furthering racial divides and resulting in greater inequity. I specifically explain how the concept of post-racialism, promoted by King and Obama, functions to appease white people, reaffirming ideology associated with white privilege, and the perpetuation of racism and discrimination. I then address how prevailing color-blind ideology consistent with that of King's and Obama's messages has served to conceal the very racism which resulted in the conceptualization of Martin as suspicious in a housing complex in which he was staying, the initial failure of the police to charge Zimmerman with a crime, and Zimmerman's successful legal defense.

KING, OBAMA, AND POST-RACIALISM

In 2011, the Thalia Surf Shop in Laguna Beach, offered 20% off all Black colored items to commemorate Dr. Martin Luther King, Jr. Day (Caparell, 2011), while the campus cafeteria at the University of California Irvine served chicken and waffles

K.J. Fasching-Varner et al. (Eds.), Trayvon Martin, Race, and American Justice, 139–144.

(Jackson, 2011). Despite King's hope to diminish the significance of race, these events highlight the impulsive association many Americans make between King and his Blackness, as well as the stereotypes attached to Black individuals in America.

Though not all white people revere King, his broad public support is evidenced by the creation and observance of a federal holiday in his honor, as well as a national willingness to teach about him in mainstream schools. Public acceptance of King is in stark contrast to that of other civil rights leaders, such as Malcolm X, who did not promote a color-blind agenda, demonstrating that King's nonviolent and inclusive approach continues to be more palatable for white people than other methods utilized to address civil rights issues. King has been cast as the face of color-blindness, though ironically, the way in which Americans think about him as a racialized individual reifies the fact that the U.S. will continue to be a racist rather than raceless society.

Turner (1996) argued that although King supported affirmative action and was more color-aware than color-blind, conservatives have oversimplified and decontextualized his views to support a color-blind agenda. In particular this has been achieved by citing King's famous line from his "I Have a Dream" speech. The line reads, "I have a dream my four little children will one day live in a nation where they will not be judged by the color of their skin but by the content of their character." With this line racists are able to frame color-blindness positively, claiming, 'if it's good enough for King, it's good enough for us' (Culp, 1994).

At worst, those who use King's words to promote a color-blind agenda may do so knowingly to maintain a racist social structure, while those who support the notion of color-blindness with the best intentions contribute to concealing a prevailing system of privilege and disadvantage based on skin color. Bonilla-Silva (2003) explained that with the emergence of color-blind racism, "whites have developed powerful explanations—which have ultimately become justifications—for contemporary racial inequality that exculpate them from any responsibility for the status of people of color (p. 2)." Color-blind racism allows white people to maintain their advantages without having to articulate at whose expense.

White people have used the election of Obama to the U.S. presidency to further reinforce the notion that America is a color-blind society. Obama's racial identity can be described in a myriad of ways; Black, white, biracial, African American; he has, however, often been primarily defined as 'the first Black President,' demonstrating continuing vestiges of the one-drop rule. This characterization of Obama also demonstrates the inability of white people to separate the persona and accomplishments of leaders of color such as King and Obama from their race.

Pundits from across the political spectrum argued that Obama's victory indicated that race did not play a major role on Election Day; however, polling data suggests that there was a significant relationship between race and voting patterns. Considering public disapproval of the wars in Iraq and Afghanistan and the economic conditions surrounding the election (Hill, Herron, & Lewis, 2010), Lewis-Beck and Tien (2009) estimated that in what should have been a landslide, Obama only won comfortably because 11.5% of whites did not vote for him because of his race. Piston (2010) found that across the nation, white voters punished Obama for his race but not his party affiliation where negative racial stereotypes considerably eroded white support for Obama. However, Obama was still able to win the election by earning 96% of Black voters' support, 13% of the electorate (Kuhn, 2008; Edge, 2010), further demonstrating the continuing importance of race in American.

An examination of Obama's campaign strategy also highlights the perpetuity of racism in American. While other Black politicians often brought their minority group status to the forefront of their campaigns, Obama took a race-neutral approach where instead he preached a message of unity and togetherness (Marable, 2009). To mobilize and empower Blacks, for instance, Jesse Jackson focused his presidential announcement speech on race; Obama's announcement speech centered on bi-partisanship and ending foreign wars, making no mention of race. Obama, furthermore, explained how he embodied all races in his "A More Perfect Union" speech as a strategy for minimizing racial divides, addressing white voters' concerns that he had a "Black" agenda, and quelling the influence of the controversial remarks made by Reverend Jeremiah Wright (Frank, 2008). This is not to say, however, that the media and American public also accepted Obama's color-blind campaign. In fact, even though Obama minimized his race to connote a "post-Black" type of leadership, critics continuously racialized Obama.

The phenomenon of Americans' inability to dissociate Obama from his racial characteristics, despite his consistent effort to de-racialize himself, directly relates to the concept of color-blind racism in that it enables white people to maintain racial privilege while claiming that race is no longer a factor in individual and institutional decision making processes. Metzler (2010) explained the logic and consequences behind labeling Obama's election a victory for post-racialization in America:

Electoral decisions that claim to be "color-blind," such as the election of President Obama, are as steeped in racist ideology as the ones that predated the civil rights era in that they continue the frontal assault on the racial reality and thinking that permeate much of American social and political institutions without acknowledgment or apology (p. 400).

Obama's attempt to minimize race plays into the white ideology of color-blindness, which ultimately perpetuates racism. In order words, Obama's image furthers white supremacy by giving credence to the impossibly attainable ideals of non-racism and a world in which individuals 'don't see color.' Ironically, the way in which Obama garners the support of white people by downplaying his race demonstrates this impossibility.

MARTIN AND POST-RACIALISM

Throughout his first term and following his re-election, Obama maintained a nuanced way of speaking about race that appeased whites, refrained from discussing racial issues, and resisted requests from civil rights leaders to target resources into communities of color and to reduce disparities experienced by Blacks and Hispanics (Jacobs & King, 2010). Days after Zimmerman was acquitted of Martin's murder, however, Obama finally publically acknowledged that the U.S. was not a post-racial society stating, "Trayvon could have been me 35 years ago." He also referenced King requesting that Americans ask themselves: "Am I judging people as much as I can, based on not the color of their skin, but the content of their character?" (Lewis, 2013, p. 3). Obama's remarks surprised whites and the mainstream media but confirmed what people of color already knew—that the U.S. is not and will not become a color-blind society.

Zimmerman, his supporters, and many among the white general public contended that the shooting was not racially motivated. Martin's murder and Zimmerman's acquittal demonstrate, however, that social justice is unlikely to be achieved when color-blind ideology veils racial injustices. Zimmerman and his family pointed to the fact that Zimmerman, a multiracial minority, supported the Black community in the past to support the claim that race did not play a role in the murder. Hanchard (2012) explained that this confusion about what constitutes racism is testament to prevailing color-blind ideology; so-called multiculturalism and multi-racism are treated as markers of equality where, in reality, someone identifying as non-white or someone who has previously worked on behalf of people of color is not excluded from racism.

Since police originally determined that there was no evidence to contradict Zimmerman's story that he killed Martin in self-defense, and Zimmerman was not charged with any crime, scholars have rooted the Martin killing within a racialized context in which young Black males are killed without ramifications for those responsible. Serino, the Sanford Police Department's lead investigator, utilized color-blind ideology in order to diminish the racial injustice of the murder, telling the FBI that he believed Zimmerman's actions were not race-based, but rather were inspired by Martin's clothing, and specifically the hoodie which Martin was wearing to protect himself from the rain (Reid, 2012). Interestingly, Serino's comment was rooted in racial stereotypes linking hoodies with images of hoodlums and gang members, and these images are associated with young men of color. It is unlikely that Zimmerman would have deemed a white person, elderly person, or a woman wearing a hoodie to be suspicious, and Serino would not have accepted Zimmerman's suspicions of these people because of their clothing.

Further evidencing how the shooting and acquittal were race-based, Hancock (2012) explained that the murder confirmed the restriction of Blacks' basic freedoms. In this case the restriction centered on freedom of movement where Martin was unable to move through a space in which he belonged without being targeted as suspicious and killed without repercussion. Hanchard (2012) highlighted the importance of race in the Martin case by examining Martin's death within state sanctions such as Florida's stand-your-ground law that authorize and legitimize the murder of Blacks by private citizens through a racial hierarchy that supports the protections of the privileged when they kill the disadvantaged.

CONCLUSION

The events surrounding Martin's murder shatter the popular and idealized notion that America is, or should become, a color-blind society. Race remains one of, if not the most (Spivey, 2003) important factor in determining individuals' life chances. Crenshaw et al. (1998) contended that racialism is a better alternative to color-blindness because despite the downfalls of classifying individuals by skin color, a racialized framework leaves room to acknowledge racism; a color-blind agenda does not. Once the color-blind ideology of King and Obama is abandoned in favor of a racialized framework, which allows for an understanding of how hegemonic beliefs about race and power benefit whites, racial injustices such as Martin's murder will be recognized as such. In turn, greater societal justice will be achieved when white people acknowledge race as an unmistakable factor in the perpetration and punishment of violence, as was clearly the case for Martin and Zimmerman.

REFERENCES

Bonilla-Silva, E. (2003). *Racism without racists: Color-blind racism and the persistence of racial inequality in the United States.* New York, NY: Rowan & Littlefield.

Caparell, A. (2011, January 18). Store blasted for advertising discounts on 'black' items in honor of Martin Luther King day. *New York Daily News.* Retrieved from http://articles.nydailynews.com

Crenshaw, K., Gotanda, N., Peller, G., & Thomas, K., (Eds.). (1998). *Critical race theory: The key writings that formed the movement.* New York, NY: New Press.

Culp, J. M., Jr. (1994). Color-blind remedies and the intersectionality of oppression: Policy arguments masquerading as moral claims. *New York University Law Review, 69*(1), 162–196.

Edge, T. (2010). Southern strategy 2.0: Conservatives, white voters, and the election of Barack Obama. *Journal of Black Studies, 40*(3), 426–444.

Frank, D. A. (2008). The prophetic voice and the face of the other in Barack Obama's "A More Perfect Union" address, March 18, 2008. *Rhetoric and Public Affairs, 12*(2), 167–194.

Hanchard, M. (2012). You shall have the body: On Trayvon Martin's slaughter. *Theory and Event, 15*(3).

Handcock, A. (2012). Trayvon Martin, intersectionality, and the politics of disgust. *Theory and Event, 15*(3).

Hill, S. J., Herron, M. C., & Lewis, J. B. (2010). Economic crisis, Iraq, and race: A study of the 2008 presidential election. *Elections Law Journal, 9*(1), 41–62.

Jackson, N. (2011, January 27). UC Irvine says fried chicken and waffle dinner on Martin Luther King Jr. day was insensitive. *Los Angeles Times.* Retrieved from http://articles.latimes.com

Jacobs, L. R., & King, D. S. (2010). Varieties of Obamaism: Structure, agency, and the Obama presidency. *Perspective on Politics, 8*(3), 793–802.

Kuhn, D. P. (2008, November 5). Exit polls: How Obama won. *Politico.* Retrieved from http://www.politico.com

Lewis, P. (2013, July 19). "Trayvon Martin could have been me 35 years ago," Obama says. *The Guardian.* Retrieved from http://www.theguardian.com

Lewis-Beck, M. S., & Tien, C. (2009). Race blunts the economic effect? The 2008 Obama forecast. *Political Science and Politics, 42*(1), 687–690.

Marable, M. (2009). Racializing Obama: The enigma of post-black politics and leadership. *Souls: A Critical Journal of Black Culture, Politics, and Society, 11*(1), 1–15.

Metzler, C. (2010). Barack Obama's Faustian bargain and the fight for America's racial soul. *Journal of Black Studies, 40*(3), 395–410.

Piston, S. (2010). How explicit racial prejudice hurt Obama in the 2008 election. *Political Behavior, 32*(4), 431–451.

Reid, J. (2012, July 15). Zimmerman investigator blamed black officers for leaks, 'pressure' to file charges. *MSNBC*. Retrieved from http://thegrio.com

Spivey, D. (2003). *Fire from the soul: A history of the African-American struggle*. Durham, NC: North Carolina Academic Press.

Turner, R. (1996). The dangers of misappropriation: Misusing Martin Luther King, Jr.'s legacy to prove the color-blind thesis. *Michigan Journal of Race and Law, 2*(1), 101–130.

EDITHA ROSARIO

23. THE LEGAL EDUCATION GAP

How a High School Legal Education Can Lay the Foundation for a Just Society

George Zimmerman's acquittal resulted in a call from activists and academics across the country to repeal stand-your-ground laws. What followed was a movement that began in Florida to eliminate a legal mechanism that has racist applications and bias in favor of perpetrators and produced unjust outcomes (Alvarez, 2013). Yet many Americans were confused or ill informed about the other legal concerns at issue. Such unfamiliarity is in part responsible for the sense of disempowerment many communities felt regarding stand-your-ground and Zimmerman's acquittal. While these communities recognize and are deeply affected by the disparities in the criminal justice system, they often lack the tools to construct practical reforms to achieve the justice they desire.

This observation is not meant to ring the bell of paternalism; rather, it is the beginning of an inquiry into how to empower communities most affected by the murder of Martin and his perpetrator's acquittal. As a progressive new lawyer and veteran educator, I teach a criminal law course at Bard Early College New Orleans (BECNO) for a class composed primarily of high school students of color who come from non-selective public high schools. The program is located in Louisiana, where more people are incarcerated than anywhere else in the world (Chang, 2012, para. 1). In New Orleans, one in fourteen Black men is imprisoned, and one in seven is imprisoned, paroled, or on probation (Chang, 2012, para. 7). My students have a personal and practical stake in understanding a criminal justice system that acutely affects them and their communities.

When we discussed the Zimmerman trial in my class, I communicated my professional opinion that under the law, Zimmerman should have been convicted of at least manslaughter. But I was not surprised to discover that my students presumed it was solely the *fault* of law that led to Zimmerman's acquittal. They did not consider the jury's lack of legal knowledge in the outcome. Their perspective illustrates the reality that very few Americans understand how trials are conducted or the legal issues in the balance. This perception results in a lack of power to determine the parameters of justice.

I refer to this phenomenon as the "legal education gap." While the phrase may evoke the myriad of concerns in modern American law schools, in this context

K.J. Fasching-Varner et al. (Eds.), Trayvon Martin, Race, and American Justice, 145–149.

it refers to the contrast between a lawyer's expertise and a citizen's lack of such knowledge. I offer one model to empower communities most affected by disparities in the criminal justice system—a criminal law education at the high school level.

This chapter is a call to academics to consider practical routes of addressing the legal education gap by instructing the young people most affected by it. Without a fundamental understanding of the criminal justice system and how it interacts with other aspects of social and cultural life, my students and our communities are powerless against the forces that create unjust outcomes.

THE GAP

I became acutely aware of the legal education gap in the fall of 2013. My students asked me to explain the Zimmerman verdict—or what happened to Martin, as they called it. Many wanted to quell the fears the unjust outcome inspired: that society and the criminal justice system were afraid of young people of color and did not respect them. As is the practice in a class focused on critical thinking, I directed the questions back to the students:

What do you think were the legal issues in the case against George Zimmerman?
Murder. Race. Racial profiling. Stand-your-ground. Self-defense?
With what did the prosecution charge Zimmerman?
Manslaughter. Murder. Both? Second degree killing.
What is the difference?
I don't know.

I did not expect the students to identify these nuances of law, but wanted to assess the boundaries of their understanding. While most of them had paid very close attention to the trial, they remained confused about the legal mechanisms at play, and the adults in their lives often could not help to make sense of it.

I posit that the confusion is, in part, the result of the decreasing importance of civics education in U.S. public schools. Political science and civics classes are designed to provide students with the opportunity to engage with, and learn about, the American legal and political system (Galston, 2004, p. 264). Galston (2004) reported that civics classes are in a decline—a single offering takes the place of "the three courses in civics, democracy, and government that were common until the 1960s" (p. 264). Galston (2004) also reported that the main measure of civics education is the National Assessment of Educational Progress (NAEP). The NAEP (2010) measured civics knowledge of representative samples of fourth, eighth, and twelfth graders (p.1). The most current NAEP study shows a drop in the twelfth-grade score between 2006 and 2010. Civics knowledge among students is waning.

Galston (2004) contended the decentralization of the public school system further complicates civics education (p. 264). In New Orleans, for example, charter schools make up the majority of schools (Cowen Institute for Public Education Initiatives, 2013, p. 2). Charters are often for-profit schools functioning under the guise of the "public" umbrella, whereas traditional public schools are in the decline. Both the decentralization of public schools and the drop in the NAEP score indicate we are educating a less civic-minded populace, in New Orleans and nationally.

In addition, American legal education is specialized, providing lawyers with the exclusive power to understand, and ultimately determine, the metes and bounds of justice. According to Schrup and Provenzano (2013):

> The legal profession is a highly conventionalized discourse community that can be entered only after intense socialization in the ways of its expert members. (pp. 81-82)

This specialization contributes to and encourages the legal education gap. If a legal education remains solely the province of lawyers, communities will maintain a dependency on the agents of the system to develop legal structures that deeply impact their lives. It is a tragic irony that those most affected by injustices in criminal law, particularly in Louisiana, are the least empowered to change their condition.

A SOLUTION & A CALL FOR MORE

I encountered the relationship between law, education, and self-empowerment as an alternative high school teacher in Chicago. My students were predominantly people of color and came from low socio-economic back groups; and, as I shared their background, they trusted me to help them outside the classroom to access the proper resources to deal with the social and economic problems that kept them in crisis. But without a legal education, it was difficult to craft long-term solutions. The students remained dependent on systems and processes they did not understand or respect.

Since then, I have used my legal training and my teaching experience to implement a strategy of educating high school students in criminal law to guide them in discovering *their own* agency to respond to the social and economic injustices propagated by the criminal justice system. While education is not enough to enact social change, it is a necessary prerequisite to action.

At BECNO, my class is premised on the principle that students cannot achieve agency or self-governance within an unjust society if they cannot trace the network that determines justice. Freire (1993) expressed this need for student-centered learning that focuses on liberation and transformation (p. 35). While it is not possible or even desirable to educate high school students in the minutiae of legal training, BECNO's pedagogy is an ideal method through which to teach the complex, inquiry-based approach in criminal law. BECNO is a dual-enrollment program founded in 2008 as part of Bard College's Early College Initiative that provides college coursework to approximately 150 Orleans Parish students who attend the supplemental program during their school day. Students earn high school and college credits in courses that challenge them to engage in inquiry-based learning and higher-level thinking through a variety of college level texts. The program's pedagogy, based on Bard College's Institute for Writing and Thinking, is designed to promote "practical,

147

hands-on instruction in a collaborative learning environment [which] demonstrates for teachers how they can lead their students to discover rather than just setting out to find answers" (Bard, 2013).

My students' inquiry into the social and economic injustices of the criminal justice system included: investigating the different categories of homicide in Louisiana and their respective sentences; theorizing about the moral imperatives behind such categorization; identifying the role of race, gender, and social class in prosecution rates; and evaluating whether and how the death penalty could ever be justly implemented. Through this work, students reflected on their understanding of the criminal justice system. They also considered the ethical dilemmas of incarceration and their impact on the community and situated their experiences within their conclusions.

When my students expressed their fears about Martin's murder, I challenged them to analyze the social and legal factors that led to Zimmerman's acquittal and the social division that followed. Specifically, I contextualized the justice system's treatment of young men of color through the Supreme Court decision *Miller v. Alabama*, which held that a sentence of mandatory life without parole for juveniles is unconstitutional without an individualized sentencing hearing to determine whether the sentence is appropriate (p. 2455). The Court reaffirmed the principle stated in *Roper v. Simmons* (2005) and *Graham v. Florida* (2010), that "children are constitutionally different from adults for purposes of sentencing" (p. 2464). In *Miller*, the Court cites to psychological studies on the differences between adult and juvenile brain development to show that while juveniles are more inclined to take risks, they are disposed to reform of any deficiencies of youth later in life (p. 2464). This propensity for reform, therefore, is a consideration unique to young people, and an individualized sentencing hearing must consider a young defendant's age, family, home, and the circumstances of the offense before he is relegated to a life sentence without parole (pp. 2468).

My students explored the psychological studies and the reasoning in *Roper*, *Graham*, and *Miller*, and consequently related the idea that "children are different than adults" to how the media portrayed Martin during Zimmerman's trial. We explored many media posts that asserted opinions like the following:

> Martin was no 'child.' He was not yet a legal adult, but at 17 years of age he could, with a parent's permission, kill and die for the United States military. And 17-year-olds, particularly when they are six feet tall, intoxicated on drugs, and physically fit, as was Martin, can and do kill and die in the streets of America. (Kerwick, 2013, para. 3)

My students discerned that Court's articulation of the difference between children and adults was a response to the unjust social distortion of young people of color into adults. They concluded Martin was treated in the same way as juvenile defendants, and that his age, family, home, and circumstances were considered in determining whether *his aggressor* was guilty. Ultimately, *Miller* exposed my students to legal authority that validated their experience and allowed them to grapple with the complexities of legal reasoning in postulating solutions.

CONCLUSION

During the semester, the Louisiana Supreme Court ruled in *State v. Tate* that *Miller* was not retroactive and did not apply to the young people previously sentenced to life without parole (p. 1). My students responded, not with cynicism, but with a desire to generate the next steps in restoring justice to these young people. I offer these experiences to demonstrate how a criminal law class helped my students analyze and identify the legal and social forces that influenced Zimmerman's acquittal. While the specifics of how to expand similar courses in public schooling are beyond the scope of this chapter, such inquiry is vital to the pursuit of justice in our communities. My students and their peers will inherit the Louisiana criminal justice system and its imperfections. Providing them with a legal education ensures that they will work to reform it into the just legal system we all deserve.

REFERENCES

Alvarez, L. (2013, August 11). Florida sit-in against 'Stand your ground.' *New York Times*. Retrieved from http://www.nytimes.com

Chang, C. (2012, May 29). Louisiana is the world's prison capital. *The Times-Picayune*. Retrieved from http://www.nola.com

Cowen Institute for Public Education Initiatives. (2013). *The state of public education in New Orleans: A 2013 report.* Retrieved at http://www.coweninstitute.com

Freire, P. (1970). *Pedagogy of the oppressed* (XXth ann. ed.). New York, NY: Continuum Books.

Galston, W. A. (2004). Civic education and political participation source novice towards mastery in written legal analysis and advocacy. *Political Science and Politics, 37*(2), 263–266.

Graham v. Florida, 130 S. Ct. 2011, 2026 (2010).

Institute for writing and thinking: Mission. (n.d.). In *Bard College*. Retrieved from http://www.bard.edu

Kerwick, J. (2013, July 15). Trayvon martin: A child, or a thug wannabe? *The New American*. Retrieved from http://www.thenewamerican.com

Miller v. Alabama, 132 S. Ct. 2455 (2012).

The National Assessment of Educational Progress. (2010). *Civics 2010: National assessment of educational progress at grades 4,8 and 12*. Retrieved from http://nces.ed.gov

Roper v. Simmons, 543 U.S. 551, 569 (2005).

Schrup, S. O., & Provenzano, S. E. (2013). The conscious curriculum: From novice towards mastery in written legal analysis and advocacy. *Northwestern University Law Review Colloquy, 108*, 80–101.

State v. Tate, 2012–2763 (La. 11/5/13).

JAMES L. HOLLAR

24. WHAT IF ZIMMERMAN HAD BEEN A DRONE?

A Social Justice and Science Fiction Lesson Plan

Allow me a moment to express a concern regarding the use of Trayvon Martin's death as a teaching moment within the classroom. This apprehension was first raised in the fall of 2013 at an education conference in Seattle, Washington. I was troubled by multiple educators' (including my own) use of Martin and his death. Indeed, it may seem incredulous to you now that I bring such a tragedy into a curriculum usually reserved for robots and aliens. It is, however, important for me to consider the meaning of this mixing of tragedy and curricula along with you.

My discussion here begins with some science fiction inspired questions: What if Zimmerman had been a drone? Would the result of the encounter between Zimmerman and Martin been different if Zimmerman, instead of being a man with a gun (and a complex mixture of experiences and the prejudices that grew out of them), had been some kind of advanced surveillance device? Although rhetorical, these questions make for a provocative discussion about the role technology may play in shaping our humanity. More simply, a student may begin such a discussion by saying, "If Zimmerman had been a drone, Trayvon Martin would be alive today." Though simplistic, such an answer complicates the equally simplistic notion that surveillance is always an impediment to our freedoms.

Perhaps in this "What if?" discussion we can learn what it is about our society that led to this tragedy and what, if anything, can be done to help ensure it never happens again. But here educators, myself included of course, must tread carefully when discussing the death of a young person. I feel strongly, however, that science fiction material in schools has a responsibility to take the "descriptive of today" axiom seriously. In doing so, we can urge students to connect issues of race, gender, and class with classroom discussions involving our future, and more specifically, what technology can do and can not do for us.

With Bradbury's short story "The Pedestrian" (1951), such connections can be made powerfully between science fiction tropes and first, the surveillance, and then killing of Trayvon Martin. In this chapter I offer teachers a rationale for using Bradbury's story, a two-day lesson plan, as well as some reflections from the use of the story within my own research in two classes of a Science Fiction elective courses at a Wisconsin high school in the spring of 2012.

K.J. Fasching-Varner et al. (Eds.), Trayvon Martin, Race, and American Justice, 151–155.
© *2014 Sense Publishers. All rights reserved.*

THE STORY

In Bradbury's "The Pedestrian," a man is marked as different by an automated police car for walking at night. The character, Leonard Mead, is identified as different as well because he does not have a television, a wife, or a profession. The story is often anthologized in textbooks; I used it as an introduction to Bradbury's *Fahrenheit 451* when I taught a sophomore English class. I taught it as others did I am sure, with an emphasis on the price of progress theme. I asked students to consider the following questions: What might these markers tell us about the society in which Bradbury was living in 1951? Why does Bradbury choose these specific markers?

Consider the possibilities of teaching this story through a social justice lens by focusing on the markers of difference at work when Zimmerman marked Martin. Questions like these would follow those from above: What markers of difference spur more monitoring in our modern society? How, for example, did Martin's 'color' mark him as suspect in the eyes of Zimmerman? Could technological advancements in how society monitors people lessen how race marks certain people as suspicious? It is these types of questions that must be hacked into science fiction curricula by teachers concerned with raising issues of justice for their students. Going beyond the additive content integration, a shift towards a social justice multicultural education perspective makes the construction of both identity and difference visible in a way that we too often ignore in the classroom.

THE LESSON

Day 1

Entry Task: Prompt #1	Write about your experiences being monitored or interacted with by police and/or other figures of authority outside of the home. Why would our answers be different?
	Read The Pedestrian
Answer & Discuss Questions	1. Why is hyper-surveillance such a common trope in science fiction? Although this answer is perhaps obvious, try to delve beneath it a bit.
	2. Other than concern with surveillance, about what do you think Bradbury is warning us? How does he draw our attention to these issues?
	3. How is Leonard Mead marked as different in this society? What about him does the robot-cop consider as aberrant behavior and/or choices? What do you think Bradbury has in mind by choosing these things in particular?
Homework: Prompt #2	What are the markers of your identity? Are these markers in your control or not? Explain.

DISCUSSION OF TEACHING PRACTICE

Prompt one began a dialogue with the students on difference. Student responses were evenly split between thinking whether their experiences would be different or not. In terms of the explanations of these responses, most interesting were the discussions of both youth and race. Of those who thought their responses would be similar, a few specifically mentioned that being "teenagers" would tie their experiences together. Of the students who thought their responses would be different, only four mentioned that "race" would be a factor. In addition to the evenness in experiences being similar or different, the dearth of students considering race as a factor in difference was interesting. Indeed, the students were surrounded by youth in the classroom, but they were also surrounded by whiteness (at least in these particular classrooms) in a similar way. For example, in the first period classroom of twenty-seven teenagers, there were only five students of color. But when these students moved out into the hallways they saw much more racial diversity. The question becomes, do these students of color and whiteness bring this awareness of the school's diversity into this more racially segregated space, and how would this impact my ability to infuse course content and discussions with more complex notions of difference?

With prompt two, I again used a journal prompt as a way to elicit student responses. As both an alternative to and preparation for whole-class discussions, these prompts connected the students to the story at hand through their own experiences. In the earlier prompt, I asked students to consider their experiences as a way to think about the story. I then used a worksheet question to have them consider how these experiences compared to their classmates. In the second prompt, students considered the markers of their identity and then later were asked if particular markers produced more monitoring. As a less intrusive way to ask concrete questions, the prompts helped prepare students for whole-class discussions that were grounded in the lives of the students.

LESSON CONTINUED

Day 2

Small Group Work	1. What markers of difference spur more monitoring in our society?
	2. How do different people experience being monitored differently? For example, how do women experience monitoring differently than men do?
	3. As a group, come up with a list of statements that state these differences, For example: Youth tend to be monitored more than the elderly.
	4. Could technological advancements in how society monitors people lessen such differences in how people are monitored? Why or why not?
Whole-Class Discussion	5. How would more advancement surveillance impact this kind of monitoring?
	6. What about the Trayvon Martin killing? How about surveillance helping us to know what really happened?

DISCUSSION OF TEACHING PRACTICE CONTINUED

In discussion questions four, five and six on day two, I made explicit the connection between the issues raised by Bradbury and contemporary issues involving race like "driving while Black," New York City's "stop and frisk" policies, and Martin's death. Although we did not have the chance to delve into the Martin-Zimmerman connections too deeply since the case had yet to go to trial, I present a sampling of student comments here to provide a path for other teachers to follow.

In asking students to consider the possibility of a positive outcome to more advanced monitoring systems, I both returned to issues raised in my first journal prompt and, more significantly, urged students to add issues of race, gender, and class into the more traditional science fiction classroom discussion of increased technology's impact on human freedom. As for question four above, responses were mixed. The largest group of twenty-two similar students responded that technological advancements could lessen differences in monitoring. Here is a sample response I collected:

> Yes, because with mass monitoring, everyone is being watched instead of just a select few. It would be fairer than only selecting a small group of suspicious people to watch.
> The next grouping, made up of twelve students, discussed some version of a "Yes, but only if" response. Here is a sample response I collected:
> Motion sensitive cameras would lessen the differences, everyone who moves would be monitored. Drones would not because they would probably be programmed to look for certain indicators.

The last group comprised nineteen students who commented that such advancements would either have no impact or make such disparities even greater. Here is one of those responses:

> Technology is a reflection of humanity, so if it is a drone that looks for markers that are programmed by humans it would be influenced by their prejudice.

These kinds of responses underscore for me another way to encourage young people to consider the future that lay before them in terms of difference, especially those differences that can be monitored by others.

CONCLUSION

I hope these ideas offer teachers a way to discuss Martin and the meaning of his death that will both honor his life and help us consider closely what it means to live in a society where a young African American man can be marked as "up to no good" as soon as he walks outside.

As an educator, I am left with yet another question: What if I had the chance to teach this material again? I would add to the above an attempt to link Zimmerman's bi-racial identity, and the how his "not white" status was used to excuse his racialized surveillance of Martin, to the argument several of the Science Fiction students made for and against the increased monitoring technology as free (or not) from bias, because it would still be controlled by humans.

It is into an ever-diversifying future we step into each day and the future we depict, whether on the page or on the screen, will either represent a way to understand this or a way to hide from it. Science fiction as a genre has a long history of simultaneously deracing humanity while using the scary green alien as metaphor to depict a whole host of anxieties and anger towards people of color. Thus, a central concept within Science Fiction curricula must be the serious examination of identity and difference. Such conversations are difficult as teachers must not re-inscribe the "othering" that particular students already experience in the classroom and larger society. Although talking about difference is seldom a safe activity within schools, the Science Fiction classroom offers a space to consider these ideas through the symbolic language of robots and aliens.

Finally, I return to my initial concern. I hope I can learn as much from Martin as I hope to teach with his help. What is the lesson then that Martin can teach us? For me, it is how important these words by James Baldwin remain today: "There is never time in the future in which we will work out our salvation. The challenge is in the moment; the time is always now (Baldwin, Stanley, & Pratt, 1989)."

REFERENCES

Baldwin, J., Standley, F., & Pratt, L. (1989). *Conversations with James Baldwin*. Jackson, MS: University Press of Mississippi.
Bradbury, R. (1966). *The pedestrian: A fantasy in one act* (Ist ed.). New York, NY: Samuel French Inc. Retrieved from http://www.samuelfrench.com

SECTION 5

WHAT CAN WE POSSIBLY TELL OUR CHILDREN?
POST-VERDICT CONVERSATIONS

SECTION 5

WHAT CAN WE POSSIBLY TELL OUR CHILDREN?
POST-VERDICT CONVERSATIONS

BROOKE BELL

FIXING THE JUSTICE SYSTEM BIT BY BITE

Reflections from a Sixth Grade Student

Now that the trial is over and we know that George Zimmerman was not punished for killing Trayvon Martin, I wonder why? In my home, I am always punished when I do wrong things. What makes George Zimmerman any different? In Louisiana, we often say, "Food is my friend." I know this essay is supposed to be about the Trayvon Martin case so you are probably wondering why I am discussing food. There is a very good reason for this, and not because I am hungry; in fact, thinking about this case makes me lose my appetite. When I think about what happened to Trayvon Martin and what did not happen to George Zimmerman, I think the shooting was only the first problem. No punishment was a second problem. Both problems could be fixed over lunch.

There were two people: the seventeen-year-old boy, Trayvon Martin, and the twenty-nine-year-old neighborhood watch man, George Zimmerman. Many times during this case, they brought up the fact that Trayvon was walking down the street wearing a hoodie. Apparently, hoodies send Mr. Zimmerman into attack mode. Besides the hoodie, Trayvon only had Skittles and a drink. Since food is our friend, it seems the hoodie sent Mr. Zimmerman over the deep end.

This case shows that my parents apparently do better a better job at punishing bad behavior than our courts. This case also shows that our justice system does not always work, and how having a lot of clever people does not always fix a problem. There were lots of lawyers, a judge, a jury, and news people. They didn't fix the problem. None of it helped.

I recently learned in Teaching Tolerance of a lunch event called "Mix It Up," where people eat lunch with people who are different. As people eat together, they are supposed to find what they have in common, helping people learn how not to judge or stereotype other people. Before making a decision, if all the people in the case would have been required to participate in a "Mix It Up" lunch the two problems could have been solved. Maybe they could have better understood how it feels to always be under suspicion. They might have been able to imagine how things felt to Trayvon on the night Mr. Zimmerman followed him around for no reason. Mr. Zimmerman could have learned that he was judging people and not giving them a chance. The jury could have gotten to know George Zimmerman and found out that he was not a hero and they might see that some people are believed all the time, just because, and other people are accused all the time, just because. Bite by bite, as they eat lunch, people would become more compassionate and the justice system would become fairer.

K.J. Fasching-Varner et al. (Eds.), Trayvon Martin, Race, and American Justice, 159.
© 2014 Sense Publishers. All rights reserved.

SHANA SIEGEL

25. WHITE IS THE NEW BLACK, COLONIALISTS ARE THE NEW COLONIZED

Folktales of White Western Victimization as Cover for Pathology

In many important ways the reactions to the Zimmerman verdict, and post-verdict demonstrations by media commentators, right-wing politicians, and the general public in the US, mirror reactions in Canada to First Nations' assertions of land, treaty, and human rights through the Idle No More movement. These reactions both inform and are informed by folktales that have been perpetuated and passed down at least through a millennium in which successive generations of white westerners have perpetrated atrocities against non-western/non-white peoples, as well as non-human life forms, and the natural world.

FOLKTALES AND WHITE WESTERN PATHOLOGY

White western folktales in the multicultural U.S. and Canada promote constructions of nationhood that privilege white westerners and their versions of reality over all other groups. The longstanding themes promoted by these folktales reflect a number of problematic patterns of thought and behavior in the white, western worldview that are perpetuated at a considerable cost to everyone.

Denial of Pain and Suffering

One of the long-standing themes involves the outright denial of the pain and suffering of others as well as, and perhaps primarily, the denial of any responsibility in alleviating this pain and suffering. One way this is done is by attempting to shift the blame by any means possible. Thus, when confronted with criticisms of white supremacy in the US criminal justice system, Newt Gingrich suddenly became fascinated with Zimmerman's Latino ethnicity, and the topic of Black-on-Black violence in Chicago (CNN, 2013). Similarly, when faced with First Nations' protests over land and treaty rights violations in Canada, commentator and academic Barry Cooper (2013) reminded Canadians that Native peoples had fought with each other before Europeans arrived, and had also been newcomers to the Americas at some point in history. In both cases the purpose was to detract attention away from ongoing systems of white supremacy/settler colonialism by showing how 'other

K.J. Fasching-Varner et al. (Eds.), Trayvon Martin, Race, and American Justice, 161–165.

people' also have done 'bad' things, and thereby implying that white westerners and their systems of oppression were being unfairly singled out for criticism.

Other versions of this theme hold that injustices are all past history, and thus discussing them not only opens old wounds, but is itself a form of injustice. In media reactions to protests surrounding both the Zimmerman verdict and to the Idle No More movement, protesters complaining about ongoing injustices were chastised for not 'getting over' the 'past,' as well as for 'tearing us apart' at a time that we need to be 'brought together' (Arrowood & Powell, 2013; Edwards, 2013; Gwynne, 2013; Bemmel, 2013; Blatchford, 2013; Henderson, 2013). In white western folktales, then, merely reminding white westerners of past and ongoing injustices is treated as an intentional act of aggression aimed at damaging relations, while the only thing that counts as being 'brought together' is absolute obedience (forcibly or voluntarily achieved) to white, western norms of status quo white supremacy and settler colonialism.

Selective Interest in 'Law and Order'

Interestingly then, at the same time white westerners try desperately to distance themselves from the systems of racial and colonial oppression in which they are complicit, they insist that non-white/non-western peoples, who are most victimized by these systems, shut up and submit fully to them. Such antics are most clearly visible in white western folktales regarding exactly who is violating the law. For example, media commentators and members of the general US public insisted that Martin was clearly up to no good (Gwynne, 2013). Yet, the only objective 'threat' posed by Martin was that he was a young Black man walking freely down the street in a predominantly non-Black neighborhood – violating longstanding, yet unconstitutional and unjust, norms of racial segregation designed to protect white westerners against just such social contact.

The older and larger gun-toting Zimmerman, who had a long history of violence and racism, and who continued to stalk, physically confront, and then kill teenage Martin despite explicit instructions from law enforcement authorities *not to do this,* was treated as the victim/hero by these same commentators. Similarly, those who protested the verdict were treated as a threat to law and order, though the only threat they actually posed was that of forcing a national conversation on white supremacy in the US criminal justice system; the system that acquitted the vigilante killer was not treated as a threat. There were many parallels to these reactions in Canada, where federal and provincial governments have routinely violated Canadian Supreme Court rulings—as well as binding international human rights laws—mandating consultation with First Nations peoples prior to impacting their land and treaty rights. As if these laws simply did not exist, non-violent First Nations protesters who asserted their land and treaty rights were presented as lawless criminals and even 'terrorists' (Canadian Press, 2013). Police officials who refused to move against First Nations protesters were treated as lawless cowards, and the government and business interests that routinely violate these laws, and frequently resort to violence in the process, were held up as the epitome of lawfulness (Canadian Press, 2013; Blatchford, 2012 & 2013).

Other Folktale Themes

Many other folktale themes are observable throughout the political and media commentary on these two cases, including themes of equating the non-equitable, inverting reality, making unrealistic assertions of victimhood, and psychologically projecting the crimes or shortcomings of white westerners onto others. For example, media commentators such as Gingrich and Geller characterized non-violent protesters as an angry, irrational and uneducated "lynch mob" and/or likened Obama's mild expression of sympathy for the Martin family as a verbal "public lynching" (CNN, 2013; Arrowood & Powell, 2013). By equating the non-equitable, white western commentators inverted the reality of racialized oppression in the US, presented a killer as a victim, and presented the victims – Martin, the Martin family, the protesters, and all people of color – as perpetrators. Such characterizations further displayed psychological projection, since it was Gingrich who displayed irrationality and ignorance in his inability to fathom ongoing systems of racialized oppression in the US, and since white westerners – not people of color – have been the primary participants in lynch mobs throughout US history.

Similarly in Canada, commentators characterized not just First Nations protesters asserting their land and treaty rights, but all First Nations peoples as lazy, insatiable parasites who will leech off the Canadian government and people until there is nothing left (Ivison, 2013; Blatchford, 2012). Yet, Canada has been built upon the ongoing, often violent colonization and dispossession of First Nations peoples from their lands and resources, and conservative Canadians frequently argue in favor of (illegally) abolishing all land and treaty rights and forcibly assimilating First Nations peoples as a means of taking the remainder of their lands and resources (Cooper, 2013). Commentators also routinely complain that non-violent First Nations rail and road blockades resulting in travel delays are holding Canadians 'hostage' (Blatchford, 2012) – as if momentary inconveniences to white westerners are not merely equitable with, but somehow more offensive than ongoing colonialism and dispossession.

Assertions of Victimhood as Cover for Pathology

As mentioned, projections and other psychological tactics promoted by white western folktales allow white westerners to pretend that *they* are victims, and that the ongoing oppression that is inflicted upon all other groups is not perpetration, but self-defense against past, present and future imagined victimizations. We saw such claims, quite literally, in Zimmerman's defense, just as we saw this in the reactions to the Idle No More movement and, the violent RCMP raid of a peaceful anti-fracking encampment on Elsipogtog First Nations' territory in New Brunswick.

Such projective assertions of white western victimization reflect more than just an anger about white western peace "being shattered and business interrupted" (Charmichael & Hamilton, 1967, 10), and more than just a fear that, if given a chance, non-white/non-western peoples might perpetrate against white westerners the same acts that the latter have perpetrated against them (Martinot, 2003). Such assertions also reflect more than a deep and pervasive cultural pathology; they reflect a much more terrifying threat: a deep and pervasive fear among white westerners of having to face themselves and their society for all that they have done and become.

Members of white western society have built their collective identities upon the fantastical, delusional idea that they are the pinnacle of human 'progress' and 'civilization,' despite persistent observations to the contrary (Forbes, 2008; Douglas, 1852). In order to do so, they have spent several centuries externalizing the parts of themselves that do not fit into this delusion, projecting them upon other peoples, and then seeking to control and annihilate these other peoples (and thus these parts of themselves) through the forcible subjugation and/or annihilation of these other peoples (Szasz, 1970; Gay, 1993; Hardtman, 1998). As long as they can claim victim status, they can assert self-defense, and can thus put off facing their monstrous perpetrations and the deep, repressed and sublimated trans generational pain and suffering underpinning them.

CONCLUSION

A number of scholars have remarked on the pathology of white western culture, whose members, in denying and repressing their own past, suffer enormously from the loss of their identity, their history, and much of their humanity (Deloria, 1969; Baldwin, 1965; Wise, 2005). While their pain may be real, their screams of victimization are not, and they must be confronted at every opportunity. Failing to do so does a disservice not only to white westerners and/or our own humanity, but to all living things on the planet. The processes that rationalize and justify the ongoing racial and colonial oppression of Black, Brown and First Nations' peoples in North America are one and the same with the processes that rationalize and justify the ongoing decimation of the planet, all living things upon it, and its ability to support life.

REFERENCES

Arrowood, E., & Powell, B. (2013, July 19). "Race-baiter in chief:" Right-wing media react to Obama's Trayvon Martin Remarks. *Media Matters*. Retrieved from http://mediamatters.org

Baldwin, J. (1965, August). The white man's guilt. *Ebony Magazine*, 47–48.

Blatchford, C. (2012, December 27). Christy Blatchford: Inevitable puffery and horse manure surrounds hunger strike while real Aboriginal problems forgotten. *National Post*. Retrieved from http://fullcomment.nationalpost.com

Blatchford, C. (2013, January 7). Christy Blatchford: Politicized policing around Idle No More blockades puts rule of law at risk. *National Post*. Retrieved from http://fullcomment.nationalpost.com

Bemmel, A. (2013, April 1). Alexis Van Bemmel: Racist responses to Idle No More tied to misinformation about Canada's past. *Straight*. Retrieved from http://www.straight.com

Canadian Press. (2013, January 16). Idle No More: Manitoba newspaper gives thumbs down to corrupt, lazy Aboriginal 'terrorists'. *The Star*. Retrieved from http://www.thestar.com

Carmichael, S., & Hamilton, C. V. (1967). *Black power: The politics of liberation in America*. New York, NY: Vintage Books.

CNN. (2013, July 15). Race relations in wake of Zimmerman verdict. Retrieved from http://transcripts.cnn.com

Cooper, B. (2013, January 26). Aboriginals have no claim to sovereignty. *Vancouver Sun*. Retrieved from http://www.vancouversun.com

Deloria, V., Jr. (1969). *Custer died for your sins: An Indian manifesto*. New York, NY: Avon Books.

Douglas, F. (1852/1999). What to the slave is the fourth of July? In P. Forner (Eds.), *Frederick Douglass: Selected speeches and writings*. Chicago, IL: Lawrence Hill.

Edwards, D. (2013, July 14). Rove: Obama 'ripped us apart' by sympathizing with Trayvon's parents [Video file]. *Raw Story*. Retrieved from http://www.rawstory.com

Forbes, J. D. (2008). *Columbus and other cannibals*. New York, NY: Seven Stories Press.

Gay, P. (1993). *The cultivation of hatred: The bourgeois experience, Victoria to Freud, Vol. III*. New York, NY: W.W. Norton & Co.

Gwynne, K. (2013, July 17). Four unhinged, offensive reactions to the Zimmerman verdict. *AlterNet*. Retrieved from http://www.alternet.org

Hardtmann, G. (1998). Children of the Nazis: A psychodynamic perspective. In Y. Danieli (Eds.), *International handbook of multigenerational transmission of trauma*. New York, NY: Plenum Press.

Henderson, Matt. (2013, January 19). Idle No More commenters could use some lessons in critical thinking. *Winnipeg Free Press*. Retrieved from http://www.winnipegfreepress.com/

Ivison, J. (2013, January 7). John Ivison: Whatever the Canadian state cedes to Theresa Spence, it will never be enough. *National Post*. Retrieved from http://fullcomment.nationalpost.com/

Martinot, S. (2003). Patriotism and its double. *Peace Review*, *15*(4), 405–410.

Szasz, T. (1970). *The manufacture of madness*. Syracuse, NY: Syracuse University Press.

Wise, T. (2005). *White like me: Reflections on Racism from a privileged son*. New York, NY: Soft Skull Press.

CRYSTAL SIMMONS, HANNAH BAGGETT &
SHARONDA R. EGGLETON

26. HOODIES IN THE CLASSROOM

Examination of Racial Profiling in the Trayvon Martin Shooting and
Implications for Education

Harrell (1999) asserted that the formal education system is a primary mode of transmission of racist ideology. As such, it is important to consider the impact of the discourse around racism and the experiences of people of color on the dispositions (Villegas, 2007) of teacher candidates. This chapter will therefore focus on how teacher candidates (n=25; 23 white, 21 female) defined and interpreted racism and racial profiling and their perceptions of profiling in educational contexts over the course of two focused, one-hour professional development sessions.

As university instructors at a predominately white institution (PWI) in the Southeast, we (two African American women and one white woman) take note of consistent, persistent comments that our teacher candidates make when prompted to reflect on race and ethno-racial status. We are former public school teachers who have worked in diverse school settings, and we are especially sensitive to the need to develop white teacher candidates' competencies in teaching diverse populations (Howard & Aleman, 2008). We believe that it is through the lens of our teacher candidates' reflections about both their formative personal experiences and their field experiences in pre-service teacher education that racism must be tackled. Specifically, in light of the Trayvon Martin shooting, we were interested in conducting two focused professional development sessions to understand how our teacher candidates responded, reacted, and contributed to the discourse about racism and racial profiling within the social sphere and in their future classrooms.

Prior to planning the first session, we reflected upon our experiences teaching at the university level, and chose exemplary quotes to represent beliefs that our teacher candidates exhibited over the course of several semesters:

> I am not here to talk about those issues; I am only going to be concerned with teaching my subject.

Such comments have layered my experience as a graduate and teaching assistant in the College of Education at a PWI in the southeastern region of the United States. However, it is through nine years of classroom teaching experience that we have gained an understanding that there is a growing need to provide teacher candidates with opportunities to explore and understand *'those'* issues.

K.J. Fasching-Varner et al. (Eds.), Trayvon Martin, Race, and American Justice, 167–172.
© *2014 Sense Publishers. All rights reserved.*

It's not About Race

As I reflect upon my own experiences working in a low-income school with predominantly African American and Latino populations and compare it to the mindset and perspectives of some of my white teacher candidates, I'm worried and fearful that stereotypes and deficit labels will continue to be placed on students of color. It is therefore imperative that teacher preparation programs prepare their teacher candidates for cultural diversity and issues concerning race and racism (Howard & Aleman, 2008; Ladson-Billings, 1995; Sleeter & Grant, 2003; Tatum, 1997; Villegas, 2007).

I'm not Interested in that Political Stuff

As a white former high school teacher in a predominately African American school, and a teacher for social justice, I am concerned by what I perceive as white teacher candidates' propensity to exhibit belief systems that are not adaptive for teaching diverse populations. Specifically, many of the teacher candidates in my classes do not recognize racial inequality, hold deficit views of students of color; embrace 'colorblindness' as an approach to diversity, and fail to recognize the privileges granted to whiteness as an ethno-racial status and cultural normative (Johnson, 2002; Lewis, 2001; Milner, 2003; Sleeter, 2001; Tatum, 1997).

SESSION ONE

After general introductions were made in our first session, we asked teacher candidates in small groups to generate original definitions of racism and racial profiling. We hypothesized that they would define racism in terms of individual, overt acts (i.e. use of the "n" word), rather than cultural, aversive, or structural racism (Clark & O'Donnell, 1999; Jones, 1997). We also hypothesized that some candidates would generate accurate definitions of racial profiling, but would not necessarily agree that Martin was racially profiled. When we compared their definitions to those that are commonly used in the research literature (Ramirez et al, 2003; Wellman, 1977, as cited in Tatum, 1997), both of our hypotheses were confirmed: candidates' definitions were aligned with those pertaining to individual racism, but all definitions omitted elements of the systemic nature and the inherent power associated with racism. Also, when candidates discussed their broad reflections about racial profiling and its role in the shooting, the cross-section of opinions reflected the rhetoric in the broader public sphere. Some stated that Martin had been murdered due to the color of his skin. Others said that race did not play a part in his death and that George Zimmerman did not profile Martin. And still others asserted that all people are profiled, and gave examples of white people being labeled as 'preppy', 'redneck', or 'nerds'. When prompted to reflect about the verdict, candidates' comments again reflected the broader public response in that some believed justice had been served based on the evidence presented. Others held a more nuanced view of the case and acknowledged that the 'colorblind' approach of the justice system marginalizes the experiences of people of color. A relatively small number of teacher candidates expressed dismay about the verdict and seemed to recognize that Martin was racially profiled, and that the verdict did not hold Zimmerman accountable for his murder.

As a closing to the first session, we asked teacher candidates to answer four guiding questions related to racial profiling as they completed their fieldwork (observation, tutoring, and student teaching) in local schools over the next several weeks.

In our initial approach to conducting the second professional development session, we anticipated that we would ask teacher candidates to do a free-write about a time that they felt racially profiled. It was our hope that many white candidates would have ended up with a 'blank page', in that they would have never experienced racial profiling. We discussed the possibility that this realization could be powerful, especially when juxtaposed with statistical information and video interviews about how often students of color felt profiled or stereotyped at school. We anticipated this realization would assist in furthering their recognition of white privilege. However, after reviewing the demographic makeup of our session of almost all white candidates and some of the responses to our initial questions about racial profiling, we decided to de-center the focus on candidates' experiences. Despite establishing baseline definitions for racism and racial profiling, we were fearful that white candidates might have written about instances when they felt discriminated against by people of color. We decided that a conversation about "reverse racism" and the fundamental misconceptions that accompany this perspective were beyond the scope of our professional development agenda. In retrospect, we question that decision, and admit that a conversation about why white people cannot experience racism would be powerful and valuable. However, at the time, our initial instinct was to send them to the field with some guiding questions, and to write their reflections to share during our second session, in lieu of writing about their own experiences.

SESSION TWO

In the second session, we asked candidates, again in small groups, to share their reflections with one another about the following questions:

How might students of color be profiled or stereotyped in the classrooms in which you are observing/have observed/been a student?
What differences do you see in instructional practices across various student groups?
What differences do you see differences in disciplinary practices across student groups?
What differences do you see in student-teacher interactions across student groups?

As teacher candidates shared their reflections about profiling and stereotyping in classrooms, it was apparent that candidates perceived that students of color (e.g. African American and Latino students) were viewed as deficient in relation to mainstream school 'norms'. Not surprisingly, Asian students, along with white students, were characterized as high achievers, a notion that supports the model minority myth (Lee, 2008). One teacher candidate shared, "Students of color are stereotyped as rowdy, lazy, lacking intelligence and coming from a low socio-economic status home with parents that do not care." We drew parallels from these candidates' observations to the ways in which Zimmerman stereotyped Martin as a suspicious youth in the wrong neighborhood. We also saw these stereotypes in the media's response to the shooting. During and after the trial, some in the media used Martin's hoodie as a way to characterize him as a thug. This hoodie became an implicit symbol of the perceived delinquency of youths of color, specifically African American males. It became a way for certain media personalities to equate Blackness with criminality – without actually talking about race or invoking racial epithets or slurs. We know, however, that a huge cross-section of students, and adults, wears hoodies on a regular basis.

With respect to instructional practices, teacher candidates observed that teachers held lowered expectations for students of color. In the same way, Rachel Jeantel was characterized by the media as being inarticulate and unintelligent, and speculated about her performance in school. Teacher candidates perceived that disproportionate numbers of students of color were missing from Honors and AP courses. In turn, candidates perceived that students of color tended to be in classes that supported rote learning and memorization. One teacher candidate noted in her observation, "I've noticed that students of color in lower academic groups are not often challenged at all in school. The instructional practices are easy and just used as busy work." Interestingly, one student did note that during her observation, she observed no differences in instructional practices. However, she asserted that because "we have a minority president," teachers should not make assumptions regarding the ability levels of students of color. She argued, "Obviously he [Obama] is very intelligent, so why don't teachers assume minorities are like him?"

Teacher candidates also observed differences in disciplinary practices, which included the perception that students of color were more harshly disciplined than white students. All of the collected responses (n=17) referenced the unfair treatment and punishment of students of color. As one teacher candidate posited, "Plain and simple, white kids don't get in trouble and Black kids do." Teacher candidates also acknowledged that African American males were more likely to be targeted and disciplined than white males: "The teacher used gentle constructive disciplinary actions with two white males, yet used insults, yelling, and intimidation when a Black male needed correction." As the details of the case unfolded, the public learned of Martin's numerous suspensions from school. The lack of critical analysis of the mainstream discussions of disciplinary practices reinforced the stereotypes of Martin as a thug and a criminal. One teacher candidate, however, made a compelling observation regarding her perception of white female teachers' disciplinary practices with African American males. She perceived that these teachers were hesitant to discipline this particular group of students because they did not want to be viewed as racist.

Ten out of the seventeen reflections attributed differences in student-teacher interactions across student groups to a shared commonality of race and ethnicity. Many of the teacher candidates reported that they perceived that white teachers were better able to understand white students, and African American teachers could get along better with African American students. Of these ten responses, half of the candidates acknowledged the importance of teachers' reflection upon their own cultural biases and how these biases have the potential to impact relationships and instructional practices. These responses leave us with the sense that some candidates have moved beyond essentializing, and have begun to understand the nuances of student-teacher relationships (Howard, 2008). As a teacher candidate poignantly observed:

> Student-teacher interactions may be limited to students and teachers that have the same gender, race, and socioeconomic class. This is a natural occurrence, but as teachers we have a responsibility to reach all students. Sometimes as teachers, we overlook students that are different than us out of fear, lack of knowledge or lack of knowledge of our own social patterns.

"Colored Students"

The Trayvon Martin shooting and two professional development sessions highlight that our teacher candidates' beliefs are not indicative of a post-racial society. By examining the topic of racism and racial profiling through an educational lens, we hoped to present teacher candidates with an opportunity to understand how these issues may translate into students' experiences in the classroom. As we reflected on this experience as teacher educators, we were most struck by the fact that several teacher candidates used the term "colored" to describe students they observed. Their casual use of this term is an example of the embedded racist attitudes and experiences they bring to their work as teachers. Unchallenged, these aversive actions have the potential to create barriers in their future classrooms, and could potentially serve to marginalize their future students of color. We wonder about Martin's teachers and the barriers he may have experienced in classrooms, including the disciplinary actions taken against him.

We also remarked on the different levels of critical consciousness (Ladson-Billings, 1995) that the white teacher candidates displayed over the course of the two sessions. In moving forward in our work as teacher educators, we anticipate taking a deeper look at the white teacher candidates who do come to our classes with a degree of cultural awareness, because we find this is the exception to the rule. We wonder if, in creating space for their voices, they can help to "write the wrong" from a different perspective—one that may seem more legitimate, unfortunately.

REFERENCES

Clark, C., & O'Donnell, J. (Eds.). (1999). *Becoming and unbecoming white: Owning and disowning a racial identity*. London, UK: Bergin & Garvey.

Harrell, C. J. P. (Ed). (1999). The meaning and impact of racism. In *Manichean Psychology* (pp. 1–51). Washington, DC: Howard University Press.

Howard, T. C., & Aleman, G. R. (2008). Teacher capacity for diverse learners: What do teachers need to? know? In M. C. Smith, S. Feiman-Nemser, D. J. McIntyre & K. E. Demers (Eds.), *Handbook of Research on Teacher Education* (pp. 157–174). New York, NY: Routledge.

Johnson, L. (2002). My eyes have been opened: White teachers and racial awareness. *Journal of Teacher Education, 53*(20), 153–167.

Jones, J. M. (1997). Racism: What is it and how does it work? In J. M. Jones (Ed.), *Prejudice and Racism* (IInd ed.) (pp. 365–410). Washington, DC: McGraw Hill.

Ladson-Billings, G. (1995). Toward a theory of culturally relevant pedagogy. *American Educational Researcher Journal, 32*(3), 465–491.

Lee, S. (2008). Model minorities and perpetual foreigners: The impact of stereotyping on Asian American students. In M. Sadowski (Ed.), *Adolescents at school: Perspectives on youth, identity, and education* (IInd ed.) (pp. 75–83). Cambridge, MA: Harvard Education Press.

Lewis, A. E. (2001). There is no "race" in the schoolyard: Colorblind ideology in an (almost) all White school. *American Education Research Journal, 38*(4), 781–811.

Milner, H. R. (2003). Teacher reflection and race in cultural contexts: History, meaning, and methods in teaching. *Theory into Practice, 42*(3), 173–180.

Ramirez, D. A., Hoopes, J., & Quinlan, T.L. Defining racial profiling in a post-September 11 world. *American Civil Law Review, 35*(2), 1195–1223.

Sleeter, C. E. (2001). Preparing teachers for culturally diverse schools: Research and the overwhelming presence of whiteness. *Journal of Teacher Education, 52*(2), 94–106.

Sleeter, C., & Grant, C. (2003). *Making choices for multicultural education: Five approaches to race, class, and gender* (IVth ed.). New York, NY: John Wiley & Sons, Inc.

Tatum, B. (1997). *"Why are all the black kids sitting together in the cafeteria?": And other conversations about race*. New York, NY: Basic Books.

Villegas, A. (2007). Dispositions in teacher education: A look at social justice. *Journal of Teacher Education, 58*, 370–380.

Wellman, D. (1977). *Portraits of white racism*. Cambridge, MA: Cambridge University Press.

MARCUS BELL

27. RACE IS, RACE ISN'T

Trayvon Martin, Stop and Frisk, and the Salience of Racial Profiling in
"Post-Racial America"

Not *Guilty*. Three little syllables, two simple words, one American tragedy. On July 14, 2013, George Zimmerman was acquitted on all charges in the killing of Trayvon Martin. Less than a month later, on August 12, 2013, a federal judge ruled that New York City's controversial stop-and-frisk policy violated the constitutional rights of various minority groups. While seemingly – and perhaps, legally – unrelated, the Martin tragedy and the ruling on stop-and-frisk, as well the discourse surrounding them, both highlight the cognitive dissonance, the pervasive ignorance, and the ideological contradictions that permeate the so-called 'national conversations about race.' This chapter is about racial discourse and the various ways it minimizes, justifies, and ultimately reproduces racial inequality (Fairclough, 1995; Gee, 1999). In the pages to follow, I will elaborate upon the discursive strategy of using racial crime statistics to justify the criminal suspicion of Blacks and Latinos (Yancy, 2008), while simultaneously minimizing the importance of race as a relevant factor in the processes that result from this suspicion. I label this particular strategy the 'race is, race isn't discursive frame.' After briefly discussing this discursive strategy in greater detail, I will provide multiple examples of how it was employed in the discourse surrounding the Martin tragedy and the stop-and-frisk ruling. I will conclude with a brief discussion on how this type of discourse minimizes the salience of racial inequality and exacerbates the perception that the United States of America has entered a post-racial epoch (Kaplan, 2011).

A DISCURSIVE FRAME

It is a well known and documented fact that young Blacks and Latinos are overrepresented in various forms of street crime, including serious offenses such as aggravated assault, armed robbery, and homicide (Desmond & Emirbayer, 2010; Mauer, 2006; Rios, 2011; Tonry, 2011). Despite the fact that, in absolute terms, the majority of Blacks and Latinos will never commit any of these offenses, their demographic overrepresentation as perpetrators of crime leads many U.S. citizens to erroneously believe that most Blacks and Latinos are criminals to be feared. Although the stereotype of Black criminality – and more recently, Latino criminality – have been a mainstay in the United States for quite some time (Muhammad,

K.J. Fasching-Varner et al. (Eds.), Trayvon Martin, Race, and American Justice, 173–177.

2010; Sellin, 1928), today the U.S. is said to be post-racial (Kaplan, 2011; Parks & Hughey, 2011).

Despite our ostensible post-racialism, racial profiling is a ubiquitous reality in the contemporary United States (Glover, 2009). Although concentrated on younger and more impoverished and particularly male Blacks and Latinos (Rios, 2011), even older members of these demographic groups, including those of high status and socioeconomic standing, are not immune to the humiliating, devastating, and sometimes, lethal effects of racist profiling. Perhaps more troubling is that, despite the use of racial crime data to justify the suspected criminality of Blacks and Latinos, those who sanction racist profiling will often deny the salience of race as being meaningful to its practice. That is, race is relevant in the criminal suspicion and systematic targeting of Blacks and Latinos because they are overrepresented in crime data. Somehow simultaneously, race is not relevant because we live in a post-racial society where all individuals, regardless of race, are treated as individuals and judged according to their own merit. In the rationalizations for both the killing of Martin and the defense of stop-and-frisk policies, the race is, race isn't discursive frame was on full display.

Trayvon Martin

Was race, in any shape or form, a factor in the killing of Martin? This was and continues to be one of the more pressing questions surrounding this tragic event. Unfortunately, the law itself was not so inquisitorial. Legally, race was not to be given any formal or explicit consideration. The legal indifference to the salience of race in the suspicion, tracking, and killing of Martin was most powerfully demonstrated when the presiding judge in the trial of George Zimmerman ruled that it was inadmissible to use the term "racial profiling" to describe the events that led up to Martin's death. Zimmerman's defense attorneys, many legal analysts, and even the prosecution proclaimed that this tragic incident was not about race (Bloom, 2013). Through multiple interviews following the not guilty verdict, we would learn that the jury thought the same way.

The legal and ideological position that race played no factor in the killing of Martin begs the question, why was he deemed suspicious in the first place? If it can be legally stipulated that Zimmerman profiled Martin, then what was the nature of this profiling, especially considering that race has been eliminated as a possible motivation? In critically analyzing the discursive subtext of the various justifications given for the actions of Zimmerman, the answer to this question seems incredibly clear - race. To some, it was the attire that Martin wore; he was wearing a hoodie. To some, it was the behavior of Martin; he was walking too slowly. However, the most common – and most revealing – rationalization of the suspicion of Martin, was a string of unsolved break-ins in the community, all ostensibly perpetrated by young, Black, males. These justifications for Zimmerman's profiling of Martin are exemplars of the race is, race isn't discursive frame.

First, the notion that it was the hoodie, and the hoodie alone, which rendered Martin as suspicious in the eyes of Zimmerman, does not meet the standard of critical scrutiny. Never mind the fact that it was raining; if hoodies, *as hoodies,* are cause for concern in regards to potential criminality, then college campuses across the country are hotbeds for future and current criminals. It was not the hoodie per se, but it was the hoodie draped over the head of a young Black body (Yancy, 2008). Most tellingly, it was suggested on more than one occasion that Zimmerman was justified in his suspicion of Martin because of the slew of recent break-ins suffered by the community at the hands of young Black males. Unless Martin was responsible for these particular offenses, then it becomes difficult to see why these alleged crimes were relevant to the events that led up to Martin's death. What purpose did mentioning the alleged criminal activity of other *young Black males* serve other than a reminder that Martin, too, was a *young Black male*? These justifications for the actions of Zimmerman typify the race is, race isn't discursive frame, a frame that was on full display less than a month later when stop-and-frisk policies took center stage in the national discourse.

Stop and Frisk

In a Washington Post OP-ED entitled, "'Stop and frisk' is not racial profiling," New York City Mayor Michael Bloomberg utilized the race is, race isn't discursive frame to rationalize, justify, and defend New York City's stop-and-frisk policies. Throughout the opinion piece, Mayor Bloomberg clearly articulated the racial dimensions that factor into the NYPD's police practices. The mayor highlighted the focus of the police department on poor minority neighborhoods, the overrepresentation of Blacks and Latinos as victims of violent crime, and the overrepresentation of Blacks and Latinos as perpetrators of violent crime. According to Mayor Bloomberg, the 'facts' are that "Ninety percent of all people killed in our city — and 90 percent of all those who commit the murders and other violent crimes — are Black and Hispanic (Bloomberg, 2013)." According to Mayor Bloomberg, to ignore the reality of what these 'facts' represent is a deadly form of political correctness. Here, *race is* meaningful because the fact is clear—Blacks and Latinos are far more likely to engage in criminal activity.

What is most compelling about this particular opinion piece, and similar arguments in support of stop-and-frisk, is that these racial crime database justifications for stop-and-frisk are meant to serve as a defense against charges of racial profiling. That is, in justifying the unilateral suspicion of Black and Brown bodies, racial crime statistics are used to signify the logical nature of that very suspicion. Yet, when properly identified and criticized as racial profiling, the role that race plays in this 'logical' suspicion is minimized, obfuscated, or eliminated altogether. For example, in the very same opinion piece in which Mayor Bloomberg laments the political correctness that obscures or masks the "fact" that Blacks and Latinos are overrepresented in various forms of violent crime, he also waxes nostalgically in a self-congratulatory manner about the law he signed in 2004 that formally banned racial profiling. Here, despite the invocation of racial crime statistics, *race isn't* meaningful because racial profiling has been banned in New York since 2004. This cognitive dissonance, this racial ignorance, is in no way unique to the mayor of New York (Mills, 2007).

The real facts regarding stop-and-frisk are that in its design, its implementation, and its impact, race is a central feature to its existence. The discursive strategies used to justify its continued practice highlight this point. Supporters claim that stop-and-frisk is not about race, but rather, it is merely designed to reduce crime. While a sad reality, they state, it must be acknowledged that Blacks and Latinos are disproportionately affected by this practice because of disproportionately high Black and Latino crime rates. But if individual Blacks and Latinos are not being stopped and frisked because of their race – the epitome of racial profiling – then why are larger crime rates in Black and Brown communities relevant to these particular individuals being stopped? In other words, unless the specific individual being stopped is suspected of committing the very crimes that lead to the disproportionate crime rates of Blacks and Latinos, then there must be another explanation, other than race, for the stop taking place. To date, no serious alternative explanation has ever been offered. Again, *race is* important because Blacks and Latinos commit more crimes, but *race isn't* important because racial profiling is an anathema to our new post-racial society. Just as in the Trayvon Martin tragedy, this discursive frame reproduces racial inequality while promoting the ideology of post-racialism (Fairclough, 1995; Gee, 1999; Kaplan, 2011).

CONCLUSION

In this chapter, I introduced the *'race is, race isn't* discursive frame.' This frame entails the simultaneous *usage* and *denial* of race in discourse surrounding racial phenomena. Racial crime data are used to justify the criminal suspicion of Black and Latino males. The impact of race is minimized as a relevant factor in the very profiling being rationalized by racial crime data. While crime data were the discursive focus in this paper, the race is, race isn't discursive frame is applicable to other domains, such as poverty and education. As a result of this discursive sleight of hand, there is a dissonance that allows racial inequality to be reproduced, while also engendering and exacerbating the ideological belief that the United States has entered a state of post-racialism. As the Martin tragedy and stop-and-frisk policies clearly demonstrate, unless this discursive frame and the actions that result from it are identified, challenged, and ultimately eliminated, Blacks and Latinos will continue to face racial discrimination within the geopolitical space of a "post-racial" society. For countless people of color, not only our democracy is at stake, but it is literally a matter of life and death. To correct Mayor Bloomberg, when it comes to racism, white ignorance is deadly.

REFERENCES

Bloom, L. (2013, July 15). Zimmerman prosecutors duck the race issue. *The New York Times*. Retrieved from http://www.nytimes.com

Bloomberg, M., R. (2013, August 18). "Stop and frisk" is not racial profiling. *The Washington Post*. Retrieved from http://articles.washingtonpost.com

Desmond, M., & Emirbayer, M. (2010). *Racial domination, racial progress: The sociology of race in America*. New York, NY: McGraw Hill.

Fairclough, N. (1995). *Critical discourse analysis: The critical study of language*. London, England: Pearson Education Limited.

Gee, J. P. (1999). *An introduction to discourse analysis: Theory and method*. New York, NY: Routledge.

Glover, K. S. (2009). *Racial profiling: Research, racism, and resistance*. Lanham, MD: Rowman & Littlefield.

Jackman, M. R. (1994). *The velvet glove: Paternalism and conflict in gender, class, and race relations*. Berkeley, CA: The University of California Press.

Kaplan, H. R. (2011). *The myth of a post-racial America: Searching for equality in the age of materialism*. Lanham, MD: Rowman & Littlefield.

Mauer, M. (2006). *Race to incarcerate*. New York, NY: The New Press.

Mills, C. W. (2007). White ignorance. In S. Sullivan & N. Tuana (Eds.), *Race and epistemologies of ignorance*. Albany, NY: State University of New York Press.

Muhammad, K. G. (2010). *The condemnation of blackness: Race, crime, and the making of modern urban America*. Cambridge, MA: Harvard University press.

Parks, G. S., & Hughey, M. W. (Eds.). (2011). *The Obamas and a (post) racial America?* New York, NY: Oxford University Press.

Rios, V. M. (2011). *Punished: Policing the lives of black and Latino boys*. New York, NY: New York University Press.

Sellin, T. (1928). The Negro criminal. A statistical note. *Annals of the American Academy of Political and Social Science, 140*, 52–64.

Tonry, M. (2011). *Punishing race: A continuing racial dilemma*. New York, NY: Oxford University Press.

Yancy, G. (2008). *Black bodies, white gazes: The continuing significance of race*. Lanham, MD: Rowman & Littlefield.

NICHOLAS D. HARTLEP & DAISY BALL

28. WRITING THE WRONG

Fighting Against the "American Justice" System

In our chapter we *write the wrong* by responding to today's criminal justice system (Bedi, 2003; Omi & Winant, 1994). We identify and address the racial wrongs that the Trayvon Martin case reveals and connect that analysis of the case with the *Simon v. State* case. We argue that Asian Americans are oppressed by the criminal justice system vis-à-vis the "model minority" stereotype that racializes them (Hartlep, 2013a, 2013b, 2014; Lee, 2009). It is important to examine Asian American victimization because while national data indicates that juvenile arrests have decreased in the last 20 years, and when the data is disaggregated by race, Asian American youth are the only group to show an increase in arrests during this period (KCCD, 2008). Our focus and interest is on the relevant connections between how African Americans and Asian Americans are disenfranchised by the legal system, though we know that disenfranchisement occurs among all non-white groups.

THE AMERICAN CRIMINAL JUSTICE SYSTEM IN COUNTER-STORY

Our argument is grounded in the theoretical and conceptual frames of "racial projects" (Bedi, 2003; Omi & Winant, 1994), which Omi and Winant (1994) define as formal systems enacted by those in power to create and maintain racial groups. The criminal justice system is a "racial project" adversely impacting a range of racial minorities, not just African Americans. The counter-story we tell is crucial because society reports statistics and criminality in a colorblind fashion (New Century Foundation, 2005).

To demonize African Americans and naturalize inequality and race-based discrimination, politicians often use master-scripts and majoritarian stock-stories (Hartlep, 2014; Lyotard, 1984). These hegemonic narratives cast African Americans as dangerous, culturally inferior, and more likely to be found in prison cells than in college classrooms (Justice Policy Institute, 2002). Conversely, while African Americans are stigmatized as being unintelligent criminals, Asian Americans are presented as academic and civic model minorities, intelligent, law-abiding citizens who, by dint of their own hard work, are upwardly mobile in the United States (see Hartlep, Forthcoming; Petersen, 1966). These inaccurate meta-narratives, however, are highly problematic (Hartlep, 2013b).

K.J. Fasching-Varner et al. (Eds.), Trayvon Martin, Race, and American Justice, 179–184.
© 2014 Sense Publishers. All rights reserved.

The "Asian-American-as-model-minority" narrative reinforces the criminal justice 'racial project' because, if Asian Americans are understood to be law-abiding citizens, then the criminal justice system cannot be accused of being racist against African Americans. In other words, the system is justified by the master narrative that if Asian Americans are *not* breaking laws and ending up in our nation's jails and prisons, then African Americans must deserve to be imprisoned because they are prone to criminality. We need to build more prisons—so the narrative goes—to house these criminals, and we need more police to protect law-abiding citizens. Predictably, the racial project absolves the criminal justice system from critical self-reflection—for example, from acknowledging that the system depends upon a constant source of criminals to fill its prisons in order to make money and maintain the *status quo* of racial, social, political, and economic relations in the United States.

Counter-stories

Fundamentally, counter-stories only make sense when they are told in relation to that which they are countering (Bamberg & Andrews, 2004). Therefore, we aim not only to counter-narrate the injustice that the criminal justice system represents, but also to contextualize Asian Americans' maltreatment by the system in relation to African Americans' experiences. Our counter-narrative and analysis are important responses to hegemonic understandings of the American criminal justice system, not only because "[v]iolence is a growing issue among Asian American youth; Asian American youth have the highest percentage of juvenile violent crime—21% in contrast to Blacks (17%), whites (16%) as well as a steady increase in arrests" (KCCD, 2008, p. 4), but also because "[t]he last 20 years or so has seen Asian Americans become the fastest-growing targets for hate crimes and violence" (Le, 2013, para 3).

THEORETICAL FRAMES USED FOR UNDERSTANDING: RACIAL PROJECTS AND IMPLICIT RACIAL BIAS

Racial Projects

Within their work on race formation, classification systems, and relations in the United States, Omi and Winant (1994) set forth their conception of "racial projects" as formal systems put into place by the powers that be to create and maintain distinct racial groups. They cite slavery, Jim Crow, and exclusionary immigration policies as examples. According to Winant (1998), not all racial projects are "racist." For a racial project to be racist, it must do the following: "*A racial project can be defined as racist if it creates or reproduces hierarchical social structures based on essentialized racial categories*" (p. 63, italics added). The criminal justice system is a racial project insofar as it is seen as a normal system within society despite its having been operationalized by those in power to create and maintain distinct racial groups, while profiting economically. Prisons are now run by corporations that have privatized them, making prisons a multi-billion dollar industry in the United States (Lee, 2012).

Implicit Racial Bias

Implicit racial bias can be understood as "the bias in judgment and/or behavior that results from subtle cognitive processes (e.g., implicit attitudes and implicit stereotypes) that often operate at a level below conscious awareness and without intentional control" (NCSC, n.d.). There is much literature demonstrating that implicit racial bias has implications within the criminal justice system, such as in sentencing and jury selection, as well in our daily lives (e.g., see Levinson, 2007; Levinson, Cai, & Young, 2010; Levinson & Smith, 2012).

A CASE STUDY OF CRIMINAL (IN)JUSTICES

1. *Anthony Simon and Steffen Wong.* The stereotype of the Asian male as martial artist emerged in the 1970s (Lee, 2003) alongside a spate of martial arts films, a popular genre from the late 1960s to the present day. This stereotype was the motivating factor behind the 1982 murder of Steffen Wong, a Chinese American, by Anthony Simon, an elderly white man. According to Lee (2003), the two men each owned one-half of a duplex, and had exchanged words in the past. Tensions between the two mounted because of the changing demographics of the neighborhood; Simon had expressed concerns about becoming surrounded by Asian neighbors (Lee, 2003). As Wong entered the duplex in which he lived, Simon shot and killed Wong. Simon claimed in testimonies during the trial that he fired in self-defense. He assumed that because of Wong's race, Wong was a martial arts expert. As outlandish as this argument may seem, it was convincing enough to lead the jury to acquit Simon on all counts. Implicit racial bias was clearly at play.

2. *George Zimmerman and Martin.* The stereotype of the African American male as criminal has emerged as yet another system of control, as defined by the (white) majority. While it is no longer permissible to outwardly exclude or discriminate based upon race, *it is* permissible to exclude and discriminate based upon criminal status and/or perceived threat (Alexander, 2010). The African American male-as-criminal stereotype fueled the events that occurred on February 26, 2012. As Martin walked home through his neighborhood after a quick run to the local 7-11, Zimmerman, an armed white-Hispanic patrolling the neighborhood in his vehicle, noticed Martin making his way home, and called 911 to report a "suspicious person." Although the 911 operators instructed Zimmerman not to pursue Martin, Zimmerman did not listen but exited his vehicle and trailed Martin on foot. Minutes later, Martin and Zimmerman crossed paths, and an altercation took place. Zimmerman fired at Martin who died from a gunshot wound to the

chest (Rudolf & Lee, 2012). In trial testimony from a series of character witnesses called by the defense, Zimmerman was painted as a concerned watchman doing his duty by keeping the neighborhood safe from criminal African American youth. Apparently, the characterization of "concerned citizen" was more effective than that of an unarmed African American juvenile being accosted by an armed man: Zimmerman was eventually acquitted. Did the jury believe Zimmerman because of their implicit racial biases? The jury was all female and nearly all white.

WRITING THE WRONG: OUR RESPONSE TO THE AMERICAN CRIMINAL JUSTICE RACIAL PROJECT

Writing the wrong in response to the American criminal justice racial project is one of the only ways to curb the normalization of racism in the United States (Berry & Stovall, 2013; Hayes & Hartlep, 2013). Ideology and hegemony are key tools in processes of normalization of racism. All knowledge, necessarily, arises from some point of view and is thus expressed accordingly. Following Smith (1972), ideological accounts come from processes that involve "procedures which people use as a means not to know" (p. 3). That is, knowing involves both seeing and acknowledging as well as not seeing and overlooking. As Berry and Stovall (2013) noted, "In response to the question *whose knowledge is most worth knowing*, the normalization and ordinariness of race and racism in the US curriculum would nearly silence the experiences of young Black men" (p. 594, emphasis in original).

In the U.S., the worldview of the racial minority is not a salient one. Interpretations of events, therefore, tend to be in line with the dominant ideology, which includes ideas about value—who are valuable members of society, and who are disposable? Whose ideas count, and whose do not? Whose story is to be believed, and whose story is to be ignored? Citing Lorde, Berry and Stovall (2013), stated that racism is "the belief in the inherent superiority of one race over all others and thereby the right to dominance" (pp. 595-596). From this, they argued, the story we tell about Martin follows the lines of the dominant ideology; because of this, Martin—his life and his story—never had a chance. "Martin was shot and killed not because of anything he did or failed to do appropriately. Martin's life ended because the knowledge most worth knowing in U.S. social, educational, and legal contexts demonizes his persona and deems it normal and ordinary to view him as a threat" (Berry & Stovall, 2013, p. 595). This may help explain why it took 46 days and a "public uproar" calling for a police investigation until Zimmerman was finally arrested (Cobb, 2012).

As with African Americans, the 'knowledge' that U.S. society holds about Asian Americans is silenced—just in the opposite direction. It is hegemonic to say that Asian Americans are "model" minorities. Does this mean they are not in need of equal protection by the State? Does this mean that their knowledge and their experiences are less important within the dominant racial frame? (Feagin, 2010).

REFERENCES

Alexander, M. (2010). *The new Jim Crow: Mass incarceration in the age of colorblindness*. New York, NY: New Press.

Bamberg, M., & Andrews, M. (Eds.). (2004). *Considering counter narratives: Narrating, resisting, making sense*. Amsterdam, NL: John Benjamins Publishing Company.

Bedi, S. (2003). The constructed identities of Asian and African Americans: A story of two races and the criminal justice system. *Harvard Black Letter Law Journal, 19*, 181–199.

Berry, T., & Stovall, D. (2013). Trayvon Martin and the curriculum of tragedy: Critical race lessons for education. *Race, Ethnicity and Education, 16*(4), 587–602.

Cobb, J. (2012, April 12). What got George Zimmerman charged with second-degree murder. *The Daily Beast*. Retrieved from http://www.thedailybeast.com

Feagin, J. (2010). *The white racial frame: Centuries of racial framing and counter-framing*. New York, NY: Routledge.

Hartlep, N. (forthcoming). The model minority as a rhetorical device. In S. Thompson (Ed.), *The encyclopedia of diversity and social justice*. Lanham, MD: Rowman & Littlefield.

Hartlep, N. (2013a). *The model minority stereotype: Demystifying Asian American success*. Charlotte, NC: Information Age Publishing.

Hartlep, N. (2013b). The model minority? Stereotypes of Asian-American students may hurt more than they help. *Diverse: Issues in Higher Education, 30*(2), 14–15.

Hartlep, N. (Ed.). (2014). *The model minority stereotype reader: Critical and challenging readings for the 21st century*. San Diego, CA: Cognella Publishing.

Hayes, C., & Hartlep, N. D. (Eds.). (2013). *Unhooking from whiteness: The key to dismantling racism in the United States*. Boston, MA: Sense Publishing.

Justice Policy Institute. (2002). *Cellblocks or classrooms?: The funding of higher education and corrections and its impact on African American men*. Retrieved from http://www.prisonpolicy.org

Korean Churches for Community Development (KCCD). (2008). *Pushed to the edge: Asian American youth at risk*. Retrieved from http://www.kccd.org

Le, C. (2013, October 21). Anti-Asian racism & violence. *Asian-Nation: The landscape of Asian America*. Retrieved from http://www.asian-nation.org

Lee, C. (2003). *Murder and the reasonable man: Passion and fear in the criminal courtroom*. New York, NY: NYU Press.

Lee, C. (2013). Making race salient: Trayvon Martin and implicit bias in a not yet post-racial society. *North Carolina Law Review, 91*(5), 1555–1612.

Lee, S. (2012, June 20). By the numbers: the US's growing for-profit detention industry. *ProPublica*. Retrieved from http://www.propublica.org

Lee, S. (2009). *Unraveling the "model minority" stereotype: Listening to Asian American youth* (IInd ed.). New York, NY: Teachers College Press.

Levinson, J. (2007). Forgotten racial equality: Implicit bias, decision making, and misremembering. *Duke Law Journal, 57*(2), 345–424.

Levinson, J., & Smith, R. (Eds.). (2012). *Implicit racial bias across the law*. Cambridge, MA: Cambridge University Press.

Levinson, J., Cai, H., & Young, D. (2010). Guilty by implicit racial bias: The guilty/not guilty implicit association test. *Ohio State Journal of Criminal Law, 8*(1), 187–208.

Lyotard, J. (1984). *The postmodern condition: A report on knowledge*. Manchester, England: Manchester University Press.

NCSC, National Center for State Courts. (n.d.). Helping courts address implicit bias. Retrieved from http://www.ncsc.org

New Century Foundation. (2005). *The color of crime: Race, crime and justice in America* (IInd expanded ed.). Oakton, VA: The New Century Foundation. Retrieved from http://www.colorofcrime.com

Omi, M., & Winant, H. (1994). *Racial formation in the United States: From the 1960s to the 1990s*. New York, NY: Routledge.

Petersen, W. (1966, January 6). Success story: Japanese American style. *The New York Times Magazine*, 20–21, 33, 36, 38, 40.

Rudolf, J., & Lee, T. (2012, April 9). Trayvon Martin case spotlights Florida town's history of 'sloppy' police work. *The Huffington Post*. Retrieved from http://www.huffingtonpost.com

Smith, D. (1972). *The ideological practice of sociology*. Unpublished paper, Department of Sociology, University of British Columbia, British Columbia, Canada.

Winant, H. (1998). Racism today: Continuity and change in the post-Civil Rights era. *Ethnic and Racial Studies, 21*(4), 755–766.

DONNA VUKELICH-SELVA

29. WE ARE TRAYVON'S TEACHERS

Disrupting Racial Profiling in Schools

While the fault lines of class inform much of what plays out in schools today as the opportunity gap continues to widen, the racial realities marking children's lives are uniquely damaging and salient in the terrains both of school and society. The case of Trayvon Martin challenges educators to understand and explicate the ways in which racial profiling in schools affects students from a very young age.

Though it is both distressing and accurate to say that what happened to Martin was, on one level, not unusual, his murder provoked an unusually sustained wave of anger across the country. I was profoundly affected, mired in grief and rage like many others, as I imagined the scenario through the eyes and skin of so many young men I know, respect, and love. Working with mostly white pre-service teachers at a small midwestern college, I often encounter an attitude that is generally dismissive and fundamentally unaware about race as an ongoing and palpable reality. Much has been written about white pre-service teachers and the racially diverse students they will teach, including the indispensable work of Noguera (2007; 2008), Howard (2008; 2010), and Solorzano, Ceja and Yosso (2000; 2009). It was imperative that I spoke about Martin in my classes of pre-service teachers, and continued to spark a sense of urgency in those students who have not previously given much thought to race.

A standing challenge in my education classes is facilitating authentic and useful discussion about race with my students, most of which are white and from small towns in southwestern Wisconsin. A critical lens on race informs my classes not merely to shock my students into an awareness many of them have not learned, but more explicitly to offer a new understanding of race and racial politics in the US and, importantly, what that means for our schools. The crucial pieces are both to see and understand the racialized structures of power at work in school settings, and to begin as well to intuit how they can disrupt those structures. An understanding of Critical Race Theory (see Dixon and Rousseau, ed., 2006; and Fernández, 2002) becomes absolutely fundamental to facilitating useful discussions on the racialized reality of schools today. Thus my classes seek to interrogate the narrative of benevolent schools as safe spaces for students of color and reframe student understandings of the critical question of race, both historically as well as in today's schools.

K.J. Fasching-Varner et al. (Eds.), Trayvon Martin, Race, and American Justice, 185–189.

Martin's death sharpened this issue in many ways. While there are far too many instances where young men of color have been brutally mistreated, even killed, by law enforcement, this case touched a chord across the country. Twitter and Facebook both blew up in the days following Martin's murder, which eventually led to more sustained media coverage. The outrage was palpable, as was the fear of many like me whose sons are young men of color. One of my sons asked bitterly and sarcastically just what young men like him were allowed to do, as it seemed that a routine trip to purchase Skittles had thrust Martin into the realm of the feared and criminal, and sealed his fate. As mothers, the rage and despair was terrifying, as it was for the many young men saw themselves in Martin, along with older men who remembered those days when merely *being* put them into the category of suspect. A young Latino man I have known for years posted a particularly damning comment on his Facebook wall.

Trayvon Martin happens *every day* in America. The police kill our youth indiscriminately year after year. This case only got attention because it was a lone "neighborhood watch" gunman...Wake up people. [my emphasis]

He understood all too well the reality of what he and many other young men confront on a daily basis. His voice and others informed the way we began to think about Martin in my class. As we talked, most of the students were saddened and angry, though many of them had not heard about the case until they came to class. Yet there was also a serious disconnect, with most of the white students expressing shock, openly wondering how such a thing could happen. Thus the voice that names this as normal, as part of daily life, was particularly powerful, as we worked to make palpable the daily reality of being 'profiled' -- the systematic racial profiling that is embedded in the everyday experience of people of color across the United States. That systematic racial vision both condones and promotes the vigilantism of a George Zimmerman.

While there are always a few white students who 'get' the issue of race, the lived experience of many of our students is such that they have not given it much thought because they have not had to before coming to college. Those white students who are more aware of the way race functions in schools and society can be important allies and mentors to their fellow students.

Even the students who felt a sense of shock were emotionally distant from the reality, understanding the situation as something completely outside them and far removed from the school environment. They did not recognize that while school might be a safe space for some, it is where racial profiling may first surface for too many others. More crucially, it is hard – if not impossible – for them to see well-intentioned teachers like themselves as complicit in that profiling. Thus one aim in my classes is precisely that of disrupting the comfortable assumptions that allow students to believe they are somehow detached from the problems of race and thus absolved of any responsibility in building an authentically inclusive and just classroom and school environment.

Several former students have expressed the anger they feel now that they are teachers and are seeing how distinct school experiences are for different groups of students. One former student who works primarily with immigrant Spanish-speaking students sees the profiling unfold in several ways. Her English Language Learners (ELL) are often the victim of scant expectations by teachers who are in positions of power and able to make crucial decisions about what happens to those students. She has also heard teachers in her school referring to African American students as 'the shadow kids.' She notes as well that 'culturally relevant' curricular training too often overlooks the central component of really getting to know and understand each child, relying instead on packaged, and often stereotyped, notions of a particular racial or cultural group. She is not white, and not afraid to speak up, and because of that believes that she has taken much pushback from some of her white colleagues who are all too willing to write her off or paint her as problematic simply because she advocates for her students and their families. Another teacher notes that the African American students in her schools are derisively referenced by a combination of their class and race, with some teachers and staff grouping them by the fact that they eat the free breakfast available at the school each morning.

High school students of color have long talked about getting stopped in the halls more frequently than their white peers, not being believed when they attempt to explain themselves, or being assumed to be doing something wrong when in fact they are just in school. These attitudes lead to more punishment, from detentions to suspensions and beyond, and as students gain a reputation as troublemakers or 'bad' kids, their relationship to school is ever more tenuous and the likelihood of academic success increasingly distant. This assumption that certain kids do not *really* belong is the same vision that led to the catastrophic consequences of Zimmerman questioning Martin's very presence in his neighborhood.

Thus one of my class goals has become precisely that of unsettling the comfort zone of privilege (or, as one student put it, inaction) where many students live, and having them figure out how to disrupt those conversations in which they may be the one person who decides to be the voice taking on those teachers too quick to racially profile their students. But how do we embed the issue of privilege into our classes? At my small college, there are several groups that explicitly and regularly take up the issue of white privilege, but (and I believe that this is common across many colleges) it does not happen explicitly in so-called whiter venues--for example, our teacher education program. By the time students get to college, most have learned well that they are not supposed to talk too much about race, and that makes them more susceptible to falling into stereotypical ways of dealing with students of color once they get out into the classroom.

There are clearly some crucial gaps in how students understand the issue of race. One example is the still widely-held belief that race is a rigid, fixed category. We interrogate and trouble this vision by looking at the history of race in the United States, with particular attention to the ways in which whiteness was first defined and how it has constantly been amended and expanded. This helps students to understand themselves as part of a racialized structure, rather than understanding race as, inexplicable though it may seem, somehow outside themselves. Another crucial issue is the narrative of ongoing progress that underpins much of national identity within the United States; without a clear sense of the conflict, resistance and backlash to the progress that has been made. As one example, most of my students know a little about the 1954 *Brown v. The Board of Education of Topeka Kansas* Supreme Court decision desegregating schools, but their understanding stops there. Students have heard about this decision in high school, but it was taught without any careful examination of what happened in its wake – from Little Rock to bussing to the ongoing legal challenges. Therefore, they believe that some of the most serious structural problems revolving around how race plays out in schools were solved decades ago. This approach creates a critical problem–these students will end up in the schools and may witness complicated or serious issues, often revolving around the ways with which race is, or is not, dealt. Since they believe that key structural issues are a thing of the past, the next best explanation to which they turn is that something must be wrong with the *students*, as is common with a model framing certain students as somehow deficient. We see frequent evidence of people, especially men, of color being stopped for walking/driving/shopping because they are Black. Martin's murder touched such deep reserves of both rage and grief precisely because incidences of aggression at many levels are all too common. Are we not doing the same thing in schools, even when we might lament the most obvious or egregious cases that happen in other arenas?

None of this is new, of course, but it is a call that is increasingly urgent. Mandated diversity programs do not seem to be the answer, and neither are pre-packaged curricula that claim to be culturally relevant without directly taking on the issue of teacher attitude and dispositions, along with their knowledge. Perhaps, then, we can say that the challenges are many. We must strip bare those structures – both institutional and psychological—that impact the lives of young students of color in our schools. That involves not only looking at the external or societal elements that harm our students, an easier step to take than one imagines, but also closely examining the ways in which we, as white educators, participate in the system – even if most often, that is by doing absolutely nothing to question, challenge, or make right what is taking place around us. To truly be teachers of all students requires nothing less.

REFERENCES

Dixson, A., & Rousseau, C. (Eds.). (2006). *Critical race theory in education: All God's children got a song.* New York, NY: Routledge.

Fernández, L. (2002). Telling stories about school: Using critical race and Latino critical theories to document Latina/Latino education and resistance. *Qualitative Inquiry, 8*(1), 45–65.

Harcourt, H. M. (2010). *Why race and culture matter in schools: Closing the achievement gap in America's classrooms.* New York, NY: Teachers College Press.

Howard, T. (2008). "Who really cares?" The disenfranchisement of African American males in PreK-12 schools: A critical race theory perspective. *Teachers College Record, 110*(5), 954–985.

Noguera, P. (2007). How listening to students can help schools to improve. *Theory into Practice, 46(3)*, 205–211.

Noguera, P. (2008). *The trouble with black boys:…and other reflections on race, equity, and the future of public education.* San Francisco, CA: Jossey-Bass.

Solorzano, D., Ceja, M., & Yosso, T. (2000). Critical race theory, racial microaggressions and campus racial climate: The experiences of African American college students. *Journal of Negro Education, 69*, 60–73.

Solorzano, D., & Yosso, T. (2009). Counter-storytelling as an analytical framework for educational research. In E. Taylor, D. Gillborn, & G. Ladson-Billings (Eds.), *Foundation of critical race theory in education.* New York, NY: Routledge.

MICHAEL E. JENNINGS

30. TRAYVON MARTIN AND THE MYTH OF SUPERPREDATOR

A Note on African American Males as Problems in American Society

HOW DOES IT FEEL TO BE A PROBLEM?

"white man is somethin' that I tried to study, but I got my hands bloody"
(Ice Cube, 1992)

In 1959, Rodgers and Hammerstein produced the iconic Broadway musical, *The Sound of Music.* I remember seeing a production of this show as a young kid in elementary school some 20 years later. For some reason there was one particular song that stood out for me. The song revolved around the show's lead character, Maria, and discussed how her problematic behavior made her very presence a major problem for everyone around her. The song *How Do You Solve a Problem Like Maria?* examined the complexity and pain of dealing with someone who was different and who did not fit in. In a similar vain, the life and death of Trayvon Martin captured the attention of the American public in February 2013. He was cast by some as an outsider, as someone who did not "fit" and who didn't belong in the neighborhood he was visiting. In this sense, Martin was racially profiled and implicitly labeled as a "problem." Once labeled as a problem the question became, "How Do You Solve a Problem Like Martin?"

The view of African Americans as problematic within the context of U.S. society is nothing new. In1903, imminent scholar W.E.B. Dubois (1903, 2007) wrote passionately about the African American experience at the turn of the twentieth century and asked the question, "How does it feel to be a problem?" (p. 1). Embodied in the body of African American youth, this so-called problem reflects the U.S. legacy of racial oppression and the discursive and institutional practices that were born of this legacy. It also impacts the worldviews of both the oppressors and the oppressed. Oppressors are prone to elevating their perceptions and understandings of the world above the worldview of others (Spring, 2004). Such a viewpoint allows oppressors to justify their oppression, and support a worldview that justifies their perceived superiority. In doing so, this perceived superiority "…acts to provide blindness to the injustices that oppress others and provides oppressors, a form of privilege that

K.J. Fasching-Varner et al. (Eds.), Trayvon Martin, Race, and American Justice, 191–196.
© *2014 Sense Publishers. All rights reserved.*

benefits them in multiple ways" (Khalifa, Jennings, Briscoe, Oleszweski, & Abdi, 2013, p. 7). This privilege is also supported by centuries of officially sanctioned racial violence, intimidation, and marginalization that has contributed to the perceptions that imbue the African American community with a certain mistrust of white society (Khalifa, et al, 2013).

HERE COMES THE PREDATOR

There's no stopping what can't be stopped, no killing what can't be killed (King Willie, Predator 2, 1990)

One of the primary ways that this mistrust manifests itself is in the pervasive fear of African American crime in the U.S. (Russell-Brown, 2008). More specifically, there exists a fear of crime that is strongly associated with African American men (Rome, 2004). It is in this context that Martin was seen as part of a collective 'problem' signaled by his status as a young African American male. African American men have become associated with a range of pathologies including crime (Russel-Brown, 2008), poor educational achievement (Noguera, 2003; Thomas & Stevenson, 2009), and unemployment (Mong & Roscigno, 2010).

These negative associations have given rise to a perception of African Americans males that links a pervasive individual hypermasculinity with a violently aggressive predatory sub-culture. DiIulio (1995) conceptualized this particular vision of young African American men as the 'super-predator' thesis. This thesis hypothesized that a dangerous group of mostly African American young male criminals would wreak havoc on U.S. society as they matured into adulthood. Bennett, DiIulio, and Walters (1996) further explained that:

> Based on all that we have witnessed, researched, and heard from people who are close to the action, here is what we believe: America is now home to thickening ranks of juvenile "super-predators" - radically impulsive, brutally remorseless youngsters, including ever more teenage boys, who murder, assault, rape, rob, burglarize, deal deadly drugs, join gun toting gangs, and create serious communal disorders, They do not fear the stigma of arrest, the pains of imprisonment, or the pangs of conscience. They perceive hardly any relationship between doing right (or wrong) now and being rewarded (or punished) for it later. To these mean street youngsters, the words "right" and "wrong" have no fixed moral meaning. (p. 27)

This rise of the super predator was widely reported in the media (Muschert, 2007), and supported by both criminologists (Dilulio, 1995) and law enforcement officials (Baer & Chambliss, 1997; Elikann, 2007) across the country. This widespread support 'confirmed' long held beliefs that: a) African American males lack a sufficient moral imperative which led to a lack of understanding between 'right' and 'wrong' moral choices; and b) these super-predators, signified as African American young males, represent a serious threat to the moral and physical well being of society. Therefore, logic tells us that African American males, like all dangerous predators, need to be hunted in an effort to ensure the maintenance and safety of a 'civilized' society.

Hip-Hop artist Ice Cube emphasized this point poignantly in his 1992 album titled "Predator." Throughout the album, Ice Cube chronicled the African American experience in Los Angeles and offered an analysis of the conditions leading up to the 1992 riot that engulfed the city. Specifically, his lyrics offered a strong critique of the 'predatory culture' (McLaren, 1995) that undergirded the racial tension and nihilism that characterized the urban landscape of Los Angeles in the early 1990s. Educational theorist McLaren (1995) defined predatory culture as:

> ...a field of invisibility — of stalkers and victims — precisely because it is so obvious. Its obviousness immunizes its victims against a full disclosure of its menacing capabilities. In predatory culture identity is fashioned mainly and often violently around the excesses of marketing and consumption and the natural social relations of post-industrial capitalism. (p. 2)

Despite panicked assertions about the coming rise of urban super predators in U.S. cities, no such occurrence occurred (Hayden 1995; Muschert, 2007; Snyder & Sickmund, 2002). The animal imagery summoned by the suprepredator label, however, had strong racial overtones (Mauer, 2006) that linked African American males to a predatory culture lacking in moral character and committed to violent consumption (McLaren, 1995). It is against this backdrop of predatory culture and the moral panic induced by the predicted rise of the super-predator, that Martin was racially profiled, stalked and killed.

WHAT DO WE TELL THE HUNTED?: YOUNG AFRICAN-AMERICAN MEN AND "THE CONVERSATION"

There is no hunting like the hunting of man, and those who have hunted armed men long enough and liked it, never care for anything else thereafter (Hemingway, 1936, p. 119)

The days and weeks following the death of Martin were exhausting. Not because of the media frenzy that followed, or even because of the righteous indignation that labeled Martin's death as symptomatic of a larger problem in society. It was exhausting for me because I worried about my oldest son. What would I tell my son about Martin? How could I explain his death in the context of U.S. democracy? How did his death reflect the ideas of justice, fairness and meritocracy in our society? Would we ever feel safe again?

When I broached these subjects with my then 12 year-old son, he seemed mildly disinterested. As with other discussions that I initiated regarding race, I could not tell if he understood the true essence of what I was trying to explain. In the past, I had talked to him extensively about his role as an African American male in a racist society. I explained that his behavior would be monitored closely for the slightest infractions and that failure to "follow the rules" could result in disciplinary measures that would be harsher for those imposed on his white peers. He did not seem to deny this possibility, but did not acknowledge its existence either. I am unclear as to whether or not this meant that I was telling him something that he already knew, or if he did not believe that such unfairness happened in the public school that he attended and seemed to love. Like many pre-teens he was not always keen on talking to his parents about his feelings. Despite this, I knew that an important conversation between Black father and son needed to take place (Brewster & Beard, 2014).

The conversation to which I am referring is one that most African American families eventually have with their sons. It involves discussing the racial realities of life as an African American male in America. There are many variations of this conversation, but the one I had with my oldest son involved at least three important issues of which he needed to be aware. First is the idea that he would be treated differently because of both his race and gender. Although I believe that race would play the major role in his differential treatment, I also believe that his status as a male singled him out for a high level of surveillance and harassment within the larger societal context as well as within the specific context of schooling (Smith, Yosso, & Solorzano, 2007). This in no way negates the privilege that my son has as a male in our society (Carbado, 1998), nor does it seek to minimize the difficulties faced by African American women (Berry, 2010). It does recognize the unique issues faced by African American men as they maneuver in a society that negates their humanity (Smith, Hung, & Franklin, 2011).

The second thing that I communicated to my son is that the differential treatment that he experiences is not an isolated phenomenon (Noguera, 2003). Racial discrimination is endemic in American society and is part of a larger construct of privilege that places whites on top and people of color on a lower level. This privilege shapes the experiences that people have in society, and makes it easier for some people to succeed and harder for others (Kendall, 2012).

Third, I explained that although this system is complex and unfair, he must plan carefully how to challenge the tyranny of this system while simultaneously navigating the system. This was important to me because one of the dangers of concentrating solely on learning to navigate societal barriers related to race is that it helps to advance particular individuals within the system while leaving the system largely in tact. Overcoming this dilemma means a focus on challenging the status quo in ways that advance social justice and a part of his preparation for dealing with the world as an African American male.

CONCLUSION

I wanted my son to know that life is not solely about the advancement of individuals, but that it also involves working towards social justice in society as a way to challenge the status quo and increase equity. This ideology of critique goes against the grain of a capitalist society that emphasizes rugged individualism and self reliance as tools to be deployed in the in pursuit of the financial, social, and cultural capital most valued by our society.

Utilizing a "problem posing" (Freire, 2000) methodology, I often question my son about his ideas regarding race and its impact in his personal life. I use the same methodology, however, to interrogate broader notions of power and hegemony. Within that context I also interrogate gender and class in an effort to identify how these constructs intersect in ways that shape inequality in our society.

In many ways, this personal pedagogy of race I attempt to impart to my son is very similar to what I attempt to teach the students in my university classes. I often find myself asking the same question about by son that I ask about them: do they really get what I am trying to convey, or is this just another lecture or discussion filled with 'talk' that means little outside of the classroom door? For some of the students, the lecture or discussion is just an academic exercise. For others, it is the discussion they have always wanted to have for much of their lives. For some of my students, and for my son, these issues are not just about making society 'better' or more just, they are actually about life and death -- survival.

Only when we understand the continuing importance of what Pollock (2009) terms "race talk," will we have a chance to openly engage young African American males in meaningful dialogue. Otherwise, our discussions will too often follow tragedy and will continue to be *about* young African American men rather than discussions *with* young African American men. While we must concede that to be like Martin is to be a problem in our society, we must acknowledge that solving this problem necessitates a recognition of the larger issue of racial subjugation faced by African American males in our society.

REFERENCES

Baer, J., & Chambliss, W. (1997). Generating fear: The politics of crime reporting. *Crime, Law and Social Change, 27*(2), 87–107.

Bennett, W., Dilulio, J., & Walters, J. (1996). *Body count: Moral poverty--and how to win America's war against crime and drugs.* New York, NY: Simon & Schuster.

Berry, T. R. (2010). Engaged pedagogy and critical race feminism. *Educational Foundations, 24*(3), 19–26.

Brewster, J., Stephenson, M., & Beard, H. (2014). *Promises kept: Raising black boys to succeed in school and in life.* New York, NY: Random House.

Carbado, D. W. (1998). Black male racial victimhood. *Callaloo, 21*(2), 337–361.

Dawson, M. (2012). Racial tragedies, political hope, and the tasks of American political science. *Perspectives on Politics, 10*(3), 669–673.

Dilulio, J. (1995, December 15). Moral poverty: The coming of the super-predators should scare us into wanting to get to the root causes of crime a lot faster. *Chicago Tribune*, p. 31.

du Bois, W. E. B. (2007). *The souls of black folk.* London, England: Oxford University Press.

Elikann, P. T. (2002). *Superpredators: The demonization of our children by the law.* Cambridge, MA: Da Capo Press.

Freire, P. (1970, 2000). *Pedagogy of the oppressed* (M. B. Ramos, Trans.; XXXth anniv. ed.). New York, NY: Continuum.

Gabbidon, S. L., & Jordan, K. L. (2013). Public opinion on the killing of Trayvon Martin: A test of the racial gradient thesis. *Journal of Crime and Justice, 36*(3), 1–16.

Hayden, T. (1995). The myth of the super-predator. *Los Angeles Times*, p. B13.

Hemingway, E. (1936, April). On the blue water: A gulf stream letter. *Esquire, 31*, 184–185.

Kendall, F. (2012). *Understanding white privilege: Creating pathways to authentic relationships across race.* New York, NY: Routledge.

Khalifa, M., Jennings, M., Briscoe, F., Oleszweski, A., & Abdi, N. (2013). Racism? Administrative and community perspectives in data-driven decision-making: Systemic perspectives versus technical rational perspectives. *Urban Education.* doi: 10.1177/0042085913475635

Mauer, M. (2006). *Race to incarcerate.* New York, NY: The New Press.

McLaren, P. (1995). *Critical pedagogy and predatory culture: Oppositional politics in a postmodern era.* New York, NY: Psychology Press.

Mong, S., & Roscigno, V. (2010). African American men and the experience of employment discrimination. *Qualitative Sociology, 33*(1), 1–21.

Muschert, G. (2007). The Columbine victims and the myth of the juvenile superpredator. *Youth Violence and Juvenile Justice, 5*(4), 351–366.

Noguera, P. (2003). The trouble with Black boys: The role and influence of environmental and cultural factors on the academic performance of African American males. *Urban Education, 38*(4), 431–459.

Pollock, M. (2009). *Colormute: Race talk dilemmas in an American school.* Princeton, NJ: Princeton University Press.

Robles, F. (2012, April 2). A look at what happened the night Trayvon Martin died. *Tampabay Times.* Retrieved from http://www.tampabay.com

Rome, D. (2004). *Black demons: The media's depiction of the African American male criminal stereotype.* Westport, CT: Greenwood Publishing Group.

Silver, J., Gordon, L., Davis, J. (Producers), & Hopkins, S. (Director). (1990). *Predator 2* [Motion Picture]. United States: Silver Pictures.

Smith, W., Hung, M., & Franklin, J. D. (2011). Racial battle fatigue and the misEducation of Black men: Racial microaggressions, societal problems, and environmental stress. *Journal of Negro Education, 80*(1).

Smith, W., Yosso, T., & Solórzano, D. (2007). Racial primes and black misandry on historically white campuses: Toward critical race accountability in educational administration. *Educational Administration Quarterly, 43*(5), 559–585.

Snyder, H., & Sickmund, M. (2000). *Challenging the myths (NCJ 178993).* Washington, DC: U.S. Department of Justice, Office of Justice Programs, Office of Juvenile Justice and Delinquency Prevention.

Thomas, D., & Stevenson, H. (2009). Gender risks and education: The particular classroom challenges for urban low-income African American boys. *Review of Research in Education, 33*(1), 160–180.

KENDRA N. BRYANT

31. BUT CAN WE MUSTER COMPASSION FOR GEORGE ZIMMERMAN?

If we must die, let it not be like hogs
Hunted and penned in an inglorious spot,
While round us bark the mad and hungry dogs,
Making their mock at our accursed lot.
If we must die, O let us nobly die,
So that our precious blood may not be shed
In vain; then even the monsters we defy
Shall be constrained to honour us though dead!
O kinsmen! we must meet the common foe!
Though far outnumbered let us show us brave,
And for their thousand blows deal one death-blow!
–Claude McKay, 1919

The oppressed people of the world must not succumb to the temptation of
becoming bitter or indulging in hate campaigns. To retaliate in kind would do
nothing but intensify the existence of hate in the universe. Along the way of life,
someone must have sense enough and morality enough to cut the chain of hate.
This can only be done by projecting the ethic of love to the center of our lives.
Martin L. King, Jr., 1958

When the unjust murder Trayvon Martin made national news, many in the Black community echoed the sentiments that Claude McKay expresses in his 1919 poem, "If We Must Die." African American influences like Malik Zulu Shabazz, leader of the New Black Panther Party (NBPP), issued a $10,000 bounty for the "dead or alive" capture of Hispanic, white-identified George Zimmerman, who tracked and killed Martin. Shabazz said Zimmerman will "always be hunted and hated like the villain that he is and the demon that he is to many" (Campbell, 2013, p. 2). Shabazz and the NBPP claimed, via *Twitter*, "Were at war. Its (sic) silly and immoral to call for peace when war has been declared" [author's parenthetical inclusion] (Campbell, 2013, p 3).

The NBPP's idea of waging a war with Zimmerman and/or white America has infiltrated some members of the Black community—as evidenced in water cooler banter, social network discourses, and Million Hoodie Marches where Zimmerman

K.J. Fasching-Varner et al. (Eds.), Trayvon Martin, Race, and American Justice, 197–201.

has been the center of Black rage. Preachers like Jesse Jackson, Al Sharpton, and Jamal Bryant have made concerted efforts to encourage all people, especially Black people, to maintain integrity and peace throughout the Martin case. After Zimmerman's not guilty verdict, Zimmerman averaged 400 death threats per minute on social media sites. According to his brother Robert, the family has since been living in constant fear (*news.com.au*, 2013).

In the light of this 21st century where Black males are lynched by blue suits versus white sheets, preachers are center stage of reality television versus civil rights movements, and the government is more vested in funding wars versus housing the homeless, feeding the hungry and employing the impoverished, many Black Americans like Shabazz are—as Fannie Lou Hammer so adamantly expressed— "sick an' tired of being sick an' tired (Campbell, 2013, p. 3)." As a result of their dis-ease, while many of America's Black citizenry *have not* advocated for war, many have consciously and unconsciously cloaked themselves in a hatred that only begets hate. However, pulling us so low as to hating George Zimmerman—even if it is an expression of our love for Martin, his parents, and other Black males lynched—is depersonalizing and soul defying.

Although Black Americans may feel entitled to "meet the common foe / and for their thousand blows deal one deathblow (Campbell, 2013, p 2)," such reactionary behaviors—even when merely thought about—reinforce the inhumanity that continues to divide, dis-ease, and devastate our nation. While the "New" Black Panther Party is stuck in what Martin Luther King Jr. (1968) called "romantic illusions and empty philosophical debates about freedom" (p. 249), many Black Americans are stuck in feelings of disempowerment, rage, and inferiority, and they are in danger of being the cause of their own dispiriting. So, *where do we go from here*? It is a question that King posed in his last address as the Southern Christian Leadership Council president in 1968; it is a question that is relevant 50 years later, since George Zimmerman's acquittal.

If America, particularly her Black citizenry, hopes to remain humane under current inhumane situations—while memorializing Martin, who was killed as a result of another human being's fears, tensions, and violence—then as King (1958) suggested throughout his tenure as a preacher and civil rights activist, "We must meet the forces of hate with the power of love" (p. 17). We must muster compassion for Zimmerman. And yes, the very idea of extending kindness, empathy, and consideration to Zimmerman, who, like the unnamed antagonist in McKay's poem, hunted and penned Martin as though he were a hog seems hellacious. The love that we must muster for Zimmerman is a compassion that will maintain our own humanity so that peace on earth is always possible. This love is neither aesthetic nor personal, but it is an active love that is willing to *forgive* the oppressor in order to restore the community. This love we must muster for George Zimmerman is what the Greeks call *agape*.

King's (1957) nonviolent movement—which he claimed "is the most potent weapon available to the Negro in his struggle for justice in this country" (p. 249)—

depended on *agape* love. *Agape,* which means "understanding, redeeming good will for all men," does not refer to "some sentimental or affectionate emotion," wrote King (1958, p.19). For, "It would be nonsense to urge men to love their oppressors in an affectionate sense" (p. 19). Instead, *agape* love is an "overflowing love which is purely spontaneous, unmotivated, groundless, and creative. It is not set in motion by any quality or function of its object. It is the love of God operating in the human heart" (p. 19). In other words, *agape* love is the unconditional love that God has for humankind: For God so loved the world that He gave His only begotten son so that we might be saved (Bible, John 3:16). Mamie Till, to whose son Emmett Martin has been compared, wholeheartedly represents this idea.

In 1955, when Mamie Till's unarmed son Emmett was brutally murdered in Mississippi for allegedly acting inappropriately toward a white woman, she responded with *agape* love. Instead of "indulging in hate campaigns," Mamie Till urged the media to display the hatred, violence, and injustice of Emmett's lynching by orchestrating an open casket funeral that allowed the nation to confront America's race matters. By forcing America to *witness* the violence, of which King claimed America is the greatest purveyor, Mamie Till "shook the consciousness of the nation" (Jackson, 2003, p. xi). She then spent the remainder of her life memorializing Emmett and serving the country as a civil rights activist.

Mamie Till neither advocated an "eye for an eye" resolve, nor did she make Emmett's murderers the center of her rage. Instead, Mamie Till, as Jackson (2003) noted in the "Foreword" to Till and Christopher Benson's *Death of Innocence: The Story of the Hate Crime That Changed America*, "turned a crucifixion into a resurrection" (p. xiii). Emmett Till's murder was "an earthquake and Mamie used the aftershocks of that earthquake to awaken, to transform a people, and to redirect our course," wrote Jackson (2003, p. xii). Mamie Till's integrity, peace, and dignity inspired both Black and white Americans to transform their own rage and upset toward Emmett's killers into a love for humankind that energized the Montgomery Bus Boycott, the Little Rock Nine, and the Civil Rights Act of 1957.

Fifty-eight years after Emmett Till's murder, Martin's parents Sybrina Fulton and Tracy Martin aroused the nation when they encouraged the media to release the 911 audio tapes that allowed us to *hear* 17-year-old Martin's shrilling screams, his terror. Like Mamie Till, they, too, have avoided expending their energy on hate and violence, and instead, have committed to using Martin's death as a catalyst for social change. They have created the *Martin Foundation*, which will assist families affected by gun violence; they are organizing a Martin retreat, which aims to mentor young Black males; and they are calling to amend stand- your-ground, which George Zimmerman used to defend killing Martin (Burbank, 2013).

Indisputably, Sybrina Fulton and Tracy Martin are operating through an *agape* love intended to transform rage and restore community. If they brooded in hate, raged wars, and engaged in death threats, they would only encourage the dis-ease many of us desire to un-do. "Hate cannot drive out hate; only love can do that" (King, 1968, p. 249). Since many people in the "sick an' tired" generation are

199

tragically aroused by an open access to violence that tends to desensitize them, and therefore, make them more susceptible to inflicting pain versus inspiring peace, a radical return to love is in order. Surely, King's 1958 "An Experiment in Love" makes such transformation possible. It is necessary to the vitality of Black America and the restoration of the *United* States of America.

Much of King's love experiment rests in Christian theology and Mahatma Gandhi's nonviolent movement and requires participants to: engage in a "passive resistance" that avoids physical aggression toward the oppressor, while mentally and emotionally persuading the oppressor of his or her wrong actions; win the friendship and understanding of the oppressor versus defeating or humiliating him or her; attack evil forces versus the person who has done evil; accept suffering without retaliation; avoid internal violence of spirit, including refusing to hate the oppressor; and maintain deep faith in the future' (King, 1958, p. 17-20). While King's nonviolent strategies were intended for a 20th century population suffering through bus boycotts and sit-ins, freedom rides and jail sentences, the violence and injustice upon Black America then continue to affect this 21st century, thus making King's nonviolent approach, the way of *agape* love, apropos to the current generation suffering through Zimmerman's acquittal.

To stand at the brink of King's initiatives, human beings must muster compassion for Zimmerman, which can be achieved through a *contemplative inquiry* that inspires understanding. According to Buddhist monk Thich Nhat Hanh, understanding engenders compassion, and the act of understanding requires *agape* love. *Agape* love inspirits human beings to foster what Buber termed an "I-Thou" relationship that invites human beings to *enter* into one another via the spirit. By way of a contemplative inquiry that challenges us to interrogate George Zimmerman's personhood in relationship to the system of which he is a product, we enable ourselves to understand Zimmerman's fear and to ultimately muster compassion for him, so that we can wholeheartedly participate in movements that are transformative.

With that said, have we considered how the patriarchal system of oppression in America informed Zimmerman's perceptions of Black maleness? How a nation that has "thingified" Black people contributed to the "I-it" attitude that inspired Hispanic, white-identified George Zimmerman to hunt Black Trayvon Martin? That a media that incessantly portrays Black males as monstrous incited the danger Zimmerman felt when he saw Black, hooded Trayvon Martin? That this nation's police officers, who killed unarmed Amadou Diallo, Sean Bell, and Oscar Grant, assured Zimmerman of his right, his duty, his privilege to kill unarmed Trayvon Martin? That white America's disillusionment with post racial identity may have led to the dismissal of Black America's angst? That U.S. laws protect white males who exist within a culture that has been conditioned to fear Black men, and can, therefore, "stand their ground"?

Although these questions may remain unresolved, they helps us to understand, as King (1968) noted, "[T]he white man's personality is greatly distorted by segregation, and his soul is greatly scarred" (p. 19). We are tasked with, said King

(1957), removing white people's tensions, insecurities, and fears regarding Black people, by loving them: "Love the person who does the evil deed while hating the deed that the person does" (p. 13). In other words, be saviors. *Agape* love makes this saving possible.

REFERENCES

Burbank, J. (2013, August 3). Trayvon's parents continue call to amend 'stand your ground' laws. *Orlando Sentinel*. Retrieved from http://www.orlandosentinel.com

Campbell, J. (2013, July 18). Black Panthers $10,000 bounty to capture George Zimmerman 'dead or alive' was from 2012 [Video file]. Retrieved from http://www.christianpost.com

Jackson, J., Till-Mobley, M., & Benson, C. (2003). Foreword. In *Death of innocence: The story of the hate crime that changed America* (pp. xi–xiii). New York, NY: Random House.

King, M. L. (1958). An experiment in love. In J. M. Washington (Ed.), *A testament of hope: The essential writings and speeches of Martin Luther King Jr.* (pp. 16–20). New York, NY: HarperOne.

King, M. L. (1957). The power of nonviolence. In J. M. Washington (Ed.), *A testament of hope: The essential writings and speeches of Martin Luther King Jr.* (pp. 12–15). New York, NY: HarperOne.

King, M. L. (1968). Where do we go from here? In J. M. Washington (Ed.), *A testament of hope: The essential writings and speeches of martin Luther King Jr.* (pp. 245–252). New York, NY: HarperOne.

Zimmerman, R. (2013, August 4). Brother of acquitted killer George, says family get 400 death threats a minute. *News.Com.Au*. Retrieved from http://www.news.com.au

SOPHIA SOFTKY

32. "YOU'RE THE ONE MAKING THIS ABOUT RACE!"

American Racism and the Unconscious

> To many Americans, because our president is Black and interracial families advertise cereal, it appears as though the march of liberal progress has finally reached Dr. King's dream. Yet the statistics on racial inequity suggest that in many ways, racism remains endemic to our society. (Austin, 2013, p. 5)

As the fantasy of a post-racial utopia collides with the reality of racial inequality, many white, liberal, educated U.S. citizens cannot acknowledge the gravity of the situation because doing so entails recognizing how dominant American culture is organized to maximize white privilege. Law professor and critical race theorist Charles Lawrence (1987) described delusions of post-racial equality as a 'defense mechanism' that enables 'privileged individuals to continue practices they would otherwise condemn and in which their complicity would be painful to admit' (p. 326). Psychoanalytically speaking, defense mechanisms smooth over the discomfort of cognitive dissonance we feel when our actions and feelings do not align. A collective cognitive dissonance is evident in the polarized reactions to the Trayvon Martin tragedy, while the defensiveness is plain in Zimmerman apologia.

A psychoanalytic prism applies to racism outside of the law as well. The split consciousness and attendant defense mechanism Lawrence described are more consistently visible in American youth culture, particularly in a style of humor dubbed 'Hipster racism'. Humor, from a psychoanalytic perspective, is the bubbling-up of latent content from the unconscious (Freud, 1960). As Freud (1960) saw it, "jokes... evade restrictions and open sources of pleasure that have become inaccessible" (p. 103). Jokes represent repressed hostility, satisfying instincts that would in other forms be socially unacceptable. So-called hipster racism, the blithe assumption that having Brown friends entitles one to a "pass" for ironically offensive behavior, especially highlights the tension between inaccessible white supremacy and the moral victories of the Civil Rights movements. The belief that irony transcends "true" bigotry is at the core of how youth culture manifests an unconscious racism that operates *micrologically* through the personal, in stark opposition to the national drama of racism writ large. Though outwardly different, the unconscious racism of youth culture results from the same psychological principle that allowed the

K.J. Fasching-Varner et al. (Eds.), Trayvon Martin, Race, and American Justice, 203–207.

Zimmerman jury to deliver a technically legal verdict, which was clearly unjust. Latent, unconscious bias allows racism to operate, sometimes lethally, through the supposed neutrality of Law.

Analyses of hipster racism have circulated in the blogosphere for several years, but the issue has not received the academic scrutiny it deserves, considering its wider socio-historical context and implications. For that reason, the examples I present here will be primarily anecdotal, but I will attempt to show their connection to the larger matter of culture-wide unconscious racism.

The history of racism in the United States unfortunately needs no introduction, but a psycho-ideological analysis explains its resilience. In classical psychoanalysis, the unconscious is a repository of wishes, beliefs and images which are generated by a desiring Id and repressed by the Super-Ego, but which continue to dictate our behavior in revealing ways (Freud, 1989). Various cultural theorists have discussed the possibility of a Freudian collective unconscious, but here I have found it useful to depart from pure psychoanalysis, turning from the individual to the collective through an Althusserian (1971) understanding of ideology as the "imaginary relationship of individuals to their real conditions of existence"(p. 153). Ideology is the collection of desires, etc., stored in a public unconscious for use by a ruling class to justify and reinforce its own position, interpolating individuals into conformity. According to Althusser (1971), "there is no practice except by and in an ideology" (p. 159). This is because for any culture to reproduce it, the power relations upon which it depends must be continually reinforced by Repressive State Apparatuses (RSA) and re-circulated by Ideological State Apparatuses (ISA). The latter 'interpellates' the individual through social and institutional interactions, producing him or her as "*always-already* subjects" whose material practices are inevitably and invariably a function of that ideology (Althusser, 1971, p. 161).

In this schema, white privilege (or perhaps more insidiously, white normativity) is the ideology used by white Americans to maintain a privileged position. Unconscious racism is one component of that ideology, and the defense mechanism of denial produces the hallucination of living in a post-racial society. In Althusserian terms, the ruling ideology of white privilege and the misrecognition of post-racialism operate more or less directly through RSA's such as the Law (as exemplified in the Zimmerman case), and more subtly through ISA's (youth culture and the media).

Hipster racism can be roughly divided into three categories: appropriation, pop-minstrelsy, and "hatred immunity," a supposedly tongue-in-cheek use of slurs (Lim, 2008). The racism of appropriation, pop-minstrelsy, and hatred immunity defends the borders of privileged whiteness by reminding non-white others of their inferior status, but playfully. Irony is both cathartic, minimizing the strain of cognitive dissonance, and defensive—by construction jokes cannot be confronted directly. When charged with giving offense or hurt, the jokester merely counter-charges, "You're the one making this about race!"

Appropriation includes sporting Native American headdresses as festival-wear, 'tribal-themed' fast fashion (Urban Outfitter's infamous "Navajo panties"), the accessorization of bindis by indie-idol Grimes, and Lady Gaga's self-styled 'burqa swag.' The Othering and objectification of non-white cultures is historically rooted in white supremacy, while the typical self-justification (appreciating the exotic) implies an unconscious element. One egregious example: a (former) Facebook friend posted a picture of herself wearing a cheap 'squaw' costume and the caption, "Wild as a native American tonight!:)." This truly bizarre juxtaposition of the clearly offensive and politically correct encapsulates the self-delusion characteristic of unconscious racism.

Pop-minstrelsy entails a satirical appreciation for trappings of an otherwise disdained minority group, usually Black American culture. The hijacking of 'twerking' and "ratchet" culture, earnest acoustic covers of gansta rap by white artists, or henna tattoos reading 'Thug Lyfe' across the knuckles are readily available examples. Pop-minstrelsy is also highly appropriative—exploiting an otherwise vilified subculture for shock value, insta-sexuality and laughs, masquerading as admiration. Miley Cyrus' distancing of herself from child-star roots, by way of caricaturing certain notions of Black female sexuality during her 2013 VMA performance, is a paradigmatic example.

But the smirking entitlement to racial slurs is most telling. White twenty-something's who are highly educated and otherwise liberal throw around terms like 'gypped' and 'jewed' in ways that present as self-reflexive, and therefore excusable. In a recent interview, white comedian Lesley Arfin declared her love for the word 'nigger' precisely for its shock value, saying, "It gives me chills that a word can hold so much power" (Read, 2012, p. 2). More personally, a housemate who repeatedly referred to me as "nigger-Sophia" (I am multi-racial) was genuinely baffled when I took offense because, as she explained to me, she was allowed to use the word because she was not *really* racist.

The slurs themselves, and their painful history, are clearly inherited from white supremacist ideology, but the sense that not "feeling" racist gives an individual permission to deploy such slurs illustrates the unconscious functioning of contemporary racism. When we are not permitted to be consciously aware of aggression, we laugh instead, which functions as psychic tension-relief, but by the same token indicate real underlying hostility (Freud, 1960). The unfailingly ironic character of "hatred immunity" and hipster racism more generally, therefore reveals thinly veiled racist ideology, pushed into the unconscious. Old message, new medium.

Concealed racist ideology arguably generated the oft-repeated claim that a coterie of liberal commentators "made" the coverage of Martin's murder and Zimmerman's trial "about race." Morrissey (2013) of *The Week* bemoaned the "sensational narrative of racism" surrounding the case, and accused *The New York Times* of fueling the "racial angle." Morrissey would surely not consider himself a racist, but such uncritical rationalizations of pure legality combined with the inability (or unwillingness) to acknowledge the clear racial dimensions of the tragedy are telling. Morrissey (2013) wrote:

> Criminal trials take place in an environment of law, not justice. That allows citizens on a jury to objectively apply the explicit and specific laws when a crime is alleged against a defendant...prosecutors in criminal trials have to prove the crime and the defendant's guilt outside of any reasonable doubt. (p. 1)

The verdict is treated as unfortunate but inevitable, even desirable. This legalistic rationale sidesteps how unconscious bias shapes the *interpretation* of formally objective standards in a particular case by judge or jury, in ways that often depend on the race of defendant, victim, and witness.

As Lawrence (1987) reminded us, legal decision-makers, like everyone else, are embedded in a symbolic network of culturally received biases. Because the law is structurally unable to address unconscious motivations, these decision-makers are uniquely vulnerable to what he calls "process distortion." The effect of process distortion is such that a governmental decision-maker may be unaware that she has devalued the cost of a chosen path, because a group with which she does not identify will bear that cost (Lawrence, 1987, p. 347).

Black men are more likely to be stopped by police, cited if stopped, prosecuted if cited, convicted if prosecuted, and incarcerated if convicted. The statistical evidence of accumulated systematic bias is overwhelming (ACLU, 2011). Process distortion produces racialized "selective sympathy or indifference," which is rendered almost completely invisible by the supposedly strict neutrality of Law (Lawrence, 1987, p. 347). Unfortunately, it therefore makes little sense to look for and condemn racial bias in the courtroom, because if the purpose of the law's search for racial animus or discriminatory intent is to identify a morally culpable perpetrator...there will be no evidence of self-conscious racism where the actors have internalized the relatively new American cultural morality (Lawrence, 1987, p. 344).

The effect is that, the less aware we as a society and legal decision-makers are of tendencies towards racial bias, the more treacherous these biases, and the more grotesque the state-inflicted inequities become. For instance, Marissa Alexander and Michael Giles, both Black Floridians, are now incarcerated for non-lethal crimes similar to, but much milder than, the killing for which Zimmerman was acquitted.

Racism in the United States is alive, well and unconscious. This is why "raising awareness," a standard anti-racist tactic appealing to the moral sensitivities of those in power, has such limited transformative influence. The problem is cognitive, not moral: from a psychoanalytic perspective, confronting and dismantling the contents of the unconscious is ineffective at best, and could result in the actual deepening of pathological ideology at worst. One recent study seems to corroborate this view: a pair of researchers found that explaining the racial bias in death penalty and three-strikes convictions to white participants actually made those respondents *more* likely to support those policies. They found that subjects only responded to *implicit* but not overt race baiting, confirming both the continued existence of a repressed racist ideology and its ability to function through unconscious behavior (Hurwitz & Peffley, 2010, p. 157-165).

Appealing to the better nature of one person at a time has not worked because the totality of racist ideology lies in the public unconscious, which is not reducible to the particular people embedded within it. To have a productive discussion about racism in the United States, we must shift the terms of discussion from individual virtue to ideological systems and unconscious beliefs. And until we as a society take responsibility for the culturally conditioned ignorance, callousness, and paranoia that produced a man like Zimmerman, we must expect the tragedy of Trayvon Martin to repeat itself, over and over again.

REFERENCES

Alexander, M. (2010). *The new Jim Crow: Mass incarceration in the age of colorblindness*. New York, NY: New Press.

Althusser, L. (1971). Ideology and ideological state apparatuses. *Lenin and Philosophy and Other Essays* (pp. 121–173). London, England: NLB.

Austin, A. (2013, June 18). *The unfinished march*. Retrieved from Economic Policy Institute: http://www.epi.org

Combating Mass Incarceration. (2011, June 17). *American Civil Liberties Union*. Retrieved from https://www.aclu.org

Freud, S. (1960). *Jokes and their relation to the unconscious*. New York, NY: W.W. Norton & Company Inc.

Freud, S. (1989). *The ego and the id*. New York, NY: W. W. Norton & Company.

Lawrence, C. R. (1987). The id, the ego, and equal protection: Reckoning with Unconscious Racism. *Stanford Law Review, 39*(2), 317-388

Lim, T. (2008, July 23). The delusion of hatred immunity. *Racialicious the intersection of race and pop culture*. Retrieved from http://www.racialicious.com

Morrissey, E. (2013, July 16). The George Zimmerman trial: Justice, tragedy, and the law. *The Week*. Retrieved from http://theweek.com

Peffley, M., & Hurwitz, J. (2010). *Justice in America: The Separate Realities of Blacks and Whites*. New York, NY: Cambridge University Press.

Read, M. (2012). A 'Girls' writer's ironic racism and other 'White people problems.' *Gawker*. Retrieved from http://gawker.com

Reeve, E. (2013, April 8). Accidental racists and more: A field guide to the racists of America. *The Atlantic Wire*. Retrieved from http://www.theatlanticwire.com

The war on Marijuana in Black and White. (2013, June 3). *American Civil Liberties Union*. Retrieved from https://www.aclu.org

West, L. (2012, April 26). A complete guide to 'Hipster Racism'. *Jezebel*. Retrieved from http://jezebel.com

LAURA S. YEE & RODERICK L. CAREY

33. WRITING RACE

Children's Perspectives

As educators committed to preparing PK-12 students for their role as citizens within an increasingly diverse society, it is essential that we create space within classroom discourses for students to grapple with the role race plays within both the socio-historical and current contexts of U.S. society. The Trayvon Martin incident and the resulting verdict was a clarion call that anti-racist work is not complete in the U.S. society, a notion which further underscores our increasing responsibility as educators to help students work through how race continues to prove salient in human interactions. So, as PK-12 educators, how do we respond? How can we equip our students from an early age with the tools and understandings to interpret a racialized society, empathize with the experiences of others, and identify oppressive systems to interrupt structures and messages that legitimate them?

Through its creation as the first integrated school in a segregated city, the families who founded Georgetown Day School (GDS) were intentionally committed to disrupting widely accepted notions of racial and religious prejudice. What began as a group of seven families committed to providing both opportunities for educational excellence and developing in children an abhorrence to bigotry, this founding mission lives today as we openly address various aspects of diversity, equity, inclusion, and social justice among faculty, staff, and, especially, with children.

The material included in the following reflections provides a glimpse into the daily work – both academic and cultural – that we do at GDS to intentionally disrupt hegemonic cycles of oppression in schools and society through both our direct teaching and modeling as well as through providing safe spaces for students to explore race and their own experiences. While the Martin case serves as a troubling and painful reminder of the continuing role race plays in our post-Obama era, it simultaneously serves as a call to action for us to engage in necessary, age-appropriate conversations with our students. As tomorrow's change-makers, our hope for a more just and equitable society rests on their abilities to understand intersecting systems of oppression and feel moved to work to counteract the hegemonic norms holding oppression in place.

K.J. Fasching-Varner et al. (Eds.), Trayvon Martin, Race, and American Justice, 209–213.

LESSONS FROM KINDERGARTEN: FACING COLORS OF OUR SKIN

Nichelle Dowell, Kindergarten Teacher, with Laura S. Yee

We understand how important it is to thoughtfully discuss subjects such as multiculturalism, diversity, equity and social justice. We empower our students and equip them with skills to act, with others or alone, against prejudice and/or discriminatory actions. At the beginning of the year, we asked our kindergarten students to share what they already know about the subject of 'skin color.' In response to our prompt, "What do you know about skin colon?", our five- and six-year olds generated the following list:

Brown

white

Grayish

Light skin

Tan

Can change because of what time of year it is

Color is different on different parts of your body

Until the 60s, African Americans were treated badly because people didn't like them.

People didn't want to be nice to certain people because of their skin color

Our students responded without any context, and yet, these comments prove their early awareness of the historical relationship between skin color and discriminatory treatment. This list illuminates both what children know to be true as well as what they believe to be true about the past rather than the present. Even at five and six years old, these students recognize that different skin colors exist. They also voiced a belief that the relationship between skin color and poor treatment is a fact of the past.

What do we as social justice educators do during moments of increased racial tension like those seen during and after the Martin case? We have a responsibility to respond. While explicitly discussing Martin's case may not be appropriate with kindergarteners, we can intentionally and explicitly work to develop our students' understandings and appreciation of skin color as a source of pride, a fact of life, and an outcome of biology. These lessons set an important foundation for future conversations about race and justice in later elementary grades.

In Kindergarten one way we respond is by teaching lessons focused on our different faces and hair. We read Todd Parr's *It's OK to be Different* that focuses on all kinds of differences that deal with appearance, feelings, life style, experiences, and choices. The most salient message in the book is at the end: "It's OK to be different. You are special and important just because of being who you are." In addition, we read books about skin – some serious and some just fun: *It's a Colorful World, Shades of People, The Unexpectedly Bad Hair of Barcelona Smith and Cowlick*. The children engaged in a project drawing their faces in great detail including eyelashes and eyebrows, and

210

mixing paints to match their skin tone to paint in their skin colors on their drawings. We also read a book called *Your Skin Holds You In* to look at skin from a more scientific perspective as it talks about melanin that gives skin its pigment and changes in skin color due to cold and heat. We continue to encourage children to use multicultural markers when drawing themselves and to admire the differences of individuals. This is but one project that highlights our overall focus on the celebration of diversity within our kindergarten family. We continue to encourage children to use multicultural markers – an assortment of varying, complex hues – when drawing themselves.

While these actions may seem minor, they are examples of the ongoing, intentional ways we work against pedagogical practices that push discussions of skin color to the periphery or only talk about race when we want to contextualize a Martin Luther King Jr. Assembly. Working in classrooms and throughout our school community, we can create spaces where we engage in these conversations to empower our children to create a more just society, rather than leaving them to react to injustices as they occur.

WRITING WRONG

Claire C. & Pallavi B., Fourth Graders

Is life fair? It wasn't always as fair as it is now, but even now it *still* isn't fair. A long time ago, people of color weren't treated fairly at all. This was called 'segregation.' The schools were segregated. Restaurants were segregated, and even water fountains were segregated. Before 1964, when the civil rights law was passed, Black were treated wrongly! They were forced to be separated from the whites in a strict way. They even got sprayed by fire hoses if they if they stood up for themselves or in extreme cases, sent to jail. But it was especially unfair for women of all colors. They weren't allowed to vote and men that weren't rich weren't allowed to vote either. Women had a lot less rights than men did. The women always got low-paying jobs that required them to work really hard, and many had to quit these jobs after they got married. These women had to rely on men, so life wasn't always fair and it still isn't.

Arthur H. & Teddy S., Fourth Graders

Violence is never an option! We think that Martin should have never been followed. George Zimmerman had NO right to kill ANYONE. Zimmerman should have never been there. He should never have had the opportunity to be arrested because he chose to follow Martin when the police told him not to. Our opinion is that there should be a new rule that says you should not carry a gun unless you are authorized to.

Viki F., Fourth Grader

Everyone is different. Just because Martin was African American doesn't mean that he should have been killed - even if he looked suspicious. I think George Zimmerman should be placed under arrest. The police told George not to follow him. But he did. Actually, I don't get it. How did Martin look suspicious? I think George killed Martin because he was African American.

Aidan K.M., Fourth Grader

I think this is crazy! Why did this happen? This is not fair or equality. What happened to "all men are created equal?" I hope Martin's family is okay. Where is the love?

Eve S., Fourth Grader

Injustice is...

- When kids go to bed hungry every night
- When people are judged by color of their skin
- When people have to go to sleep on the streets
- When you want to go to school but you can't afford it
- When you have to work all day no matter how old you are
- When you aren't able to practice your religion
- When you can't get a job because of the color of your skin
- When people are not tolerant and they are mean
- When people tease people because of their race, religion, the amount of wealth you have, or even what you wear
- When wealthy people make young children walk miles for water
- When you don't have any electricity in your home (if you have a home)

What can you do to make sure things like this don't happen?

CONCLUSION

These selected writings provide a window into the daily work of preparing students to participate in a more just future as well as to create one themselves. As a school founded on principles of social justice, GDS has the obligation and commitment to continue the mission of not only bringing together a community of diverse individuals, but also to engage students and faculty in conversations about race and other social identifiers in order to develop more critical thinkers and change-making citizens.

As social justice educators we believe that education serves as a tool to empower and emancipate minds; education holds powerful potential to shape students' perspectives and transform business-as-usual, color-blind lenses into more equitable ones - ones in which race becomes a central rather than peripheral consideration (Carey & Yee, 2013). What if all schools took seriously this responsibility to educate our future citizens with not only skills to navigate their future careers, but also with habits of mind that critically analyze existing hegemonic, racialized norms?

What would our society look like if it were comprised of citizens equipped with deep understandings of the structures, policies, media, and daily interactions that perpetuate oppressive cycles for those who do not reflect to dominant cultural norms? While we cannot guarantee that future Zimmermans would not exist, we would certainly hope that fewer individuals would perceive a Black boy in a predominantly white neighborhood as 'suspicious'. In fact, we hope for change that extends beyond interpersonal interactions; if schools commit to social justice education, we can envision a nationwide cultural shift that provides truly equitable opportunities for all students and citizens alike. We are obligated to providing our children this possibility.

REFERENCE

Carey, R., & Yee, L. (2012). Equity at the fringes: The continuing peripheral enactment of equity and diversity in the preparation of k-12 teachers. In C. Clark, M. K. J. Fasching-Varner, & M. Brimhall-Vargas (Eds.), *Occupying the academy: Just how important is diversity work in higher education?* (pp. 174–182). Lanham, MD: Rowman & Littlefield.

L. KAIFA ROLAND

34. BETWEEN BELONGING AND THE F/ACT OF NIGGERISATION

As a race theorist, I seek to clarify the artificiality and arbitrariness of racial categories that nonetheless have implications so real that they can structure who lives and who dies, who is imprisoned and who goes free. In this chapter, I analyze the Trayvon Martin tragedy through the frame of "niggerization," drawing conceptually from my previous work (Roland 2006). I argue here, as I argued elsewhere (Roland, 2013), that racialization is about belonging, and I define "niggers" as social non-beings who do not belong.

PARTIAL BELONGING AND THE ORIGINS OF NIGGERIZATION

It is generally agreed that the word "nigger" derives from the Spanish *Negro*, which translates to 'Black' in English, and the term seems to have gained its derogatory connotations as slavery spread across the Western Hemisphere.

In the United States, where the term "nigger" gained particular potency, the new nation was founded amidst debates about how to evaluate slaves' liminal role as compulsory laborers who were non-citizens by birth and color. For electoral purposes, slaves were ultimately determined to be three-fifths of a person, though they had no voting rights (Franklin, 2010; Valelly, 2004). I contend that the moment when slaves were defined as "less than" fully human was the seminal act of niggerization in the United States. In being defined as partial humans, enslaved Africans became a source of power for whites while they themselves were niggerized—reified as social and political outsiders, *de jure* as well as *de facto*.

The *Plessy v. Ferguson* Supreme Court case of 1896 established the legality of "separate but equal" facilities for Blacks and whites (Baker, 1998; Woodward, 1974). The finding legalized segregation and paved the way for the South to institute Jim Crow laws that reaffirmed the supremacy of whiteness and the amended nature of Black citizenship, reinstituting it as partial and unstable (Woodward, 1974). These early legal framings constitute what I am calling the "act of niggerization"— behaviors and actions that delineate who belongs and who does not.

I distinguish the "act" of niggerization from what I call the "fact" of niggerization, which involves the actual use of the n-word. I want to be clear that I do not contend there is any such thing as a "nigger," which is why I insist on activating the term by making it a verb. The fact of niggerization is the attempt of the speaker to put the

K.J. Fasching-Varner et al. (Eds.), Trayvon Martin, Race, and American Justice, 215–219.

target of the term back in what is presumed to be his/her place as a social outsider. The inflections with which the term has been uttered may have changed over time—under slavery, after emancipation, and throughout the Jim Crow period—but the meaning remains the same: "You are not one of us and you do not belong here." I refer to invocations of the term as a "fact" because it involves making plain the sentiments behind the perhaps less legible, if more tangible "acts." I situate the murder of Martin at the intersection of such f/acts.

POST-CIVIL RIGHTS AND "ACCEPTABLE" BLACKNESS

The Civil Rights movement sought to address the niggerizing laws and practices of the Jim Crow era. After the 1954 *Brown v. Board of Education* decision that de-segregated schools, white America had to contend with its longstanding niggerizing acts toward their fellow citizens while the courts had ruled against them (Baker, 1998). Through the lens of televised media, the world watched as restaurant patrons, police dogs, and fire hoses tried to force African Americans into outsider status as they protested in a quest for their rights as full citizens. The passage of the Civil Rights Act of 1964 and the Voting Rights Act of 1965 are generally accepted as the moment when the act of niggerizing became illegal as Blacks again were legally granted full and equal citizenship status with whites (Franklin, 2009; Valley, 2004). Like the amended citizenship granted in the late nineteenth century, African American membership in the national and social body continues to require white permission—it is not a given.

Because the Civil Rights Movement, and subsequent Black Power Movement, facilitated a degree of African American mobility into the white worlds of education, work, and residence, whites came to know a pioneering class of Blacks who could gain entry into white spaces, often due to their high social status in segregated Black America based on their color, material wealth, and/or education. Then, as is also the case now, those who most closely enacted white norms and values might be deemed "acceptable" Blacks. This acceptance is presumably in contrast to the rest of those unacceptable, non-conforming Blacks.

Because Blacks and whites are often in the same spaces in this new era—as friends, neighbors, classmates, and colleagues—niggerization must be practiced more subtly. The fact of niggerization had to go underground; whites can no longer toss about that offensive term to express the sentiment that they find *most* Blacks unacceptable intruders into white spaces. There remain, however, innumerable acts of niggerization—from following them while shopping, to stopping and frisking young Black and Brown man while walking down the street, to killing them with impunity. A frequent excuse for the niggerizer's actions is "Well s/he should not have been there (i.e., wherever they were) in the first place." Certainly, the most common means of enforcing that Blacks (and Latinos) do not belong in broader American society today is through their mass imprisonment.

Bill Cosby, Don Lemon and Well-meaning Niggerisers

Because the post-Civil Rights era has seen significant social mobility among African Americans, many people—African Americans included—argue that those Blacks who remain in the country's massive underclass after the removal of legal structures must somehow be at fault: they are not smart enough, they are not working hard enough, they are bad parents, they do not dress or wear their hair the right way, etc. (D'Souza, 1995; O'Reilly, 2006). Some of the most cited propagators in recent years are African Americans (Mosbergen, 2013; Obama, 2013; Trice, 2008). Philanthropist and entertainer Bill Cosby regularly uses his privilege and position to address the Black underclass about its perceived inadequacies (Mosbergen, 2013; Trice, 2008). President Barack Obama, the first Black elected to the nation's highest office, also publically cajoles Blacks into participating more fully in "the land of opportunity" without himself attending to the niggerizing structures that remain in place that prevent them from getting a decent job, getting out of debt, or getting the same quality of education as their suburban peers (Obama, 2013). Following the verdict in the trial exonerating George Zimmerman of the murder of Martin, CNN news anchor Don Lemon joined Dr. Cosby and President Obama in condemning those Blacks who emulate hip-hop or 'street' culture for behaving unacceptably, with the subtext being that if they do not change their ways and begin to act acceptably, they may find themselves in the same position as young Martin (Lemon, 2013).

What none of these well-meaning niggerizers recognizes is the insightful, counter-hegemonic message underclass members who enact aspects of hip-hop culture may be trying to communicate to the broader society about acceptability and belonging through their rejection of white middle class norms: that Blacks can only ever contingently be accepted in a nation in which the standard for belonging is a white ideal they will never achieve. Why try to fit into a society that will never wholly accept you? From the perspective of the middle and upper classes, such a position may be interpreted as a self-fulfilling prophecy. From the perspective of families that have seen generations struggle through public housing and other forms of public assistance while working multiple shifts to take care of basic necessities, it may be involve a new definition of progress and how to "live the good life" (Thomas, 2006).

Paula Deen, George Zimmerman, and the F/Act of Niggerizing

Before proceeding, I should remind readers what was going on in U.S. race relations in the weeks preceding the Zimmerman verdict. Early in July 2013, during a court case to resolve a discrimination suit by a former employee, Southern-style chef Paula Deen admitted to having used the n-word in the past. The story was reported on all news outlets amidst public outrage and disgust. However, as an African American who grew up in the South, I found it difficult to imagine a white person of her generation who could honestly answer the same question in the negative—hence

Deen's nonchalant, "Yes, of course." Did the Food Network, from which Deen was promptly fired, think they had hired the one authentic white Southern cook who had not niggerized at some point in her life? Should Deen have lied about the fact of niggerization? Despite a tearful video apology, Deen lost much of her business empire in the aftermath of her admission.

Two weeks after Deen was pilloried in the press for using the n-word, attorneys concluded Zimmerman's trial for killing young Martin as he walked from the neighborhood store to his parents' home wearing a hoodie on a drizzly evening. Neighborhood watchman Zimmerman followed Martin first in his car and then on foot, finding him to be a suspicious outsider who did not belong in that neighborhood. While there was a great deal of discussion at the time—in court and in the press—on whether Zimmerman had uttered the n-word himself on the 911 call, I suggest that the mere fact of niggerization on February 26, 2012, would have proved far less dangerous than the act of niggerization that I have argued was actually at issue. Deen lost everything for uttering the word, while Zimmerman walked free for killing an unarmed youth who was deemed to be out of place.

CLOSING THOUGHTS: ON SELF-NIGGERISATION

Countering well-meaning niggerizers who identify hip-hop culture as the source of Blacks' continuing outsider status, I have great respect for hip-hop's counter-hegemonic style. While I have apparently aged out of understanding rap lyrics and video culture in the 21st century, I do not care if Black males pull their pants up or not. Indeed, you never know what manner of genius—or idiot—may be disguised in any exterior presentation. However, this chapter has been about the practice of niggerization, whether in act or fact, and I would be negligent to suggest Blacks are not also perpetrators of these f/acts.

The most prevalent form of self-niggerization is Black-on-Black gun violence; however, we must attend to the societal contexts in which violence occurs. Urban districts throughout the United States have been sorely neglected for decades, in terms of investment in family-sustaining jobs, quality education, and community-relevant infrastructure development. Generations of youth grow up trapped in this hopeless cycle and take their frustrations out on whoever is closest to them. Black youth have taken ownership of the few things at their disposal, like the re-worked word "nigga" which is distinguished from the slur 'nigger' (see Neal, 2013). They also take ownership of street corners, neighborhoods, and symbols associated with group membership. In-group members are part of the brotherhood of niggas, while outsiders must be made to know they do not belong and are niggerised. Black life remains devalued, just as it has been at so many points in U.S. history.

Can anything be done to curb niggerisation? A start would be to invalidate the "nigger" category because there is no such being. If all humans are equal, and all Americans belong fully to the nation, then we as a society need to stop treating some people as though they belong more than others. Another suggestion is to stop paying so much attention to the *fact* of niggerisation and attend more to *acts* of niggerisation. If racists are freed to utter the n-word once again, there might be some hint that s/he may perpetrate an act that mobilizes beliefs about belonging before it becomes a fact.

REFERENCES

Baker, L. (1998). *From savage to Negro: Anthropology and the construction of race, 1896-1954.* Berkeley, CA: University of California Press.

D'Souza, D. (1995). *The end of racism: Principles for a multi-racial society.* New York, NY: Free Press.

Franklin, J., & Higginbotham, E. (2010). *From slavery to freedom: A history of African Americans* (IXth ed.). New York, NY: McGraw-Hill Higher Education.

Hartigan, J. (2005). *Odd tribes: Toward a cultural analysis of white people.* Durham, NC: Duke University Press.

Hartigan, J. (1999). *Racial situations: Class predicaments of whiteness in Detroit.* Princeton, NJ: Princeton University Press.

Hurston, Z. (1943, May). The pet Negro system. *The American Mercury*, 593–600.

Lemon, D. (2013, July 27). CNN's Don Lemon: Bill O'Reilly's criticism of Black community 'doesn't go far enough'. *Real Clear Politics.* Retrieved from http://www.realclearpolitics.com

Mosbergen, D. (2013, September 16). Bill Cosby talks 'No-groes,' black leadership with CNN's Don Lemon. *Huffington Post.* Retrieved from http://www.huffingtonpost.com

Neal, M. (2006). NIGGA: The 21st-century theoretical superhero. *Transforming Anthropology, 14*(2), 556–563.

Obama, B. (2013, May 20). Transcript: Obama's commencement speech at Morehouse College. *The Wall Street Journal: Washington Wire.* Retrieved from http://blogs.wsj.com

O'Reilly, B. (2006). *Culture warrior.* New York, NY: Broadway Books.

Roland, L. (2013). T/Racing belonging through Cuban tourism. *Cultural Anthropology, 28*(3), 395–418.

Roland, L. (2006). Tourism and the negrificación of Cuban identity. *Transforming Anthropology, 14*(2), 151–162.

Thomas, D. (2006). Modern blackness: progress, "America," and the politics of popular culture. In D. Thomas & M. Clarke (Eds.), *Globalization and race: Transformations in the production of Blackness.* Durham, NC: Duke University Press.

Trice, D. (2008, June 2). Cosby to Blacks: Come on people, it's time for change. *Chicago Tribune.* Retrieved from http://newsblogs.chicagotribune.com/

Valelly, R. (2004). *The two reconstructions: The struggle for black enfranchisement.* Chicago, IL: University of Chicago Press.

Woodward, C. (1974). *The strange career of Jim Crow* (IIIrd ed.). New York, NY: Oxford University Press.

ABOUT THE EDITORS

Kenneth James Fasching-Varner, PhD, is Shirley B. Barton Endowed Assistant Professor of educational foundations and elementary education at Louisiana State University. Dr. Fasching-Varner is the author of *Working Through Whiteness: Examining White Racial Identity and Professor Among White Pre-Service Teachers* (Lexington Press) and editor of Occupying the Academy: Just How Important is Diversity Work in Higher Education? (Rowman & Littlefield) as well as *Student Teaching: A Journey in Narratives* (Sense). Fasching-Varner holds a doctorate in language, literacy, and culture with a focus in Critical Race Theory from The Ohio State University.

Rema Reynolds, PhD, is Assistant Professor in the Education Policy, Organization and Leadership Department at the University of Illinois at Urbana – Champaign. Dr. Reynolds' examines issues of parent participation as they relate to Black families and student achievement, instructional strategies educators employ to honor and incorporate literacies students bring to the classroom, cultural competencies counselors and school counselors acquire through their respective preparatory programs, and the roles of school administrators in community and civic development. Her forthcoming books focus on engaging underrepresented parents in schools and provide practical guides and strategies for parents and school officials. Reynolds holds a doctorate in education from the University of California, Los Angeles.

Katrice A. Albert, PhD, is Vice President for Equity and Diversity at the University of Minnesota. Dr. Albert is charged wit leveraging the transformative power of equity and diversity to advance excellence in teaching, research and community engagement at the University of Minnesota. Dr. Albert is responsible for a significant portfolio as it relates to equity, diversity, and outreach. Dr. Albert holds a doctorate in counseling from Auburn University.

Lori Latrice Martin, PhD, is Associate Professor of sociology and African and African American studies at Louisiana State University. Dr. Martin is the author of Black Asset Poverty and the Enduring Racial Divide (First Forum Press) and Out of Bounds: Racism and the Black Athlete (Praeger). Her forthcoming published works include *White Sports/Black Sports: Racial Socialization and Athletic Destinations and Lost in the Storm: America's Black Working Class in the Age of Obama (Lynne Rienner Publishers) with Hayward Derrick Horton.* Martin holds a doctorate in sociology from University at Albany, State University of New York.

ABOUT THE FOREWORD AUTHOR

Tyrone Howard, PhD, is Professor in the Graduate School of Education & Information Studies at UCLA. He is the Director of Center X and the UCLA Black Male Institute. His work is concerned with race, culture, gender, and equity in urban schools.

CPSIA information can be obtained at www.ICGtesting.com
Printed in the USA
LVOW01s1759250115

424266LV00025B/725/P

9 789462 098404